AFTER **AQUARIUS** DAWNED

HOW THE REVOLUTIONS
OF THE SIXTIES BECAME
THE POPULAR CULTURE OF

AFTER
THE SEVENTIES

AQUARIUS
DAWNED

JUDY KUTULAS

THE UNIVERSITY OF NORTH CAROLINA PRESS   Chapel Hill

Manufactured in the United States of America

Designed by Richard Hendel

Set in Arnhem, Serif Gothic, and Owen types
by Tseng Information Systems, Inc.

The University of North Carolina Press has been a
member of the Green Press Initiative since 2003.

Cover photograph courtesy of Photofest

Library of Congress Cataloging-in-Publication Data

Names: Kutulas, Judy, 1953– author.

Title: After Aquarius dawned : how the revolutions of the sixties became
the popular culture of the seventies / Judy Kutulas.

Description: Chapel Hill : University of North Carolina Press, [2017] |
Includes bibliographical references and index.

Identifiers: LCCN 2016045889 | ISBN 9781469632902 (cloth : alk. paper) |
ISBN 9781469632919 (pbk : alk. paper) | ISBN 9781469632926 (ebook)

Subjects: LCSH: Social change—United States—History—20th century. |
Social values—United States—History—20th century. | Popular culture—
United States—History—20th century. | Radicalism in mass media—
History—20th century. | Nineteen sixties. | Nineteen seventies.

Classification: LCC E839 .K88 2017 | DDC 306.0973/0904—dc23

LC record available at https://lccn.loc.gov/2016045889

To my sisters,

Janet Kutulas, Nikki Kutulas,

and Sandra Kutulas Perez.

We are family, I got all my sisters

with me.

Contents

Acknowledgments ix

Introduction 1

1 I FEEL THE EARTH MOVE:
Redefining Love and Sex 14

2 THE LOOK I WANT TO KNOW BETTER:
Style and the New Man 44

3 YOU'RE GONNA MAKE IT AFTER ALL:
The Mary Tyler Moore Show Helps Redefine Family 75

4 DIFFERENT STROKES FOR DIFFERENT FOLKS:
Roots, Family, and History 106

5 OBVIOUSLY QUEER:
Gay-Themed Television, the Remaking of Sexual Identity,
and the Family-Values Backlash 137

6 DON'T DRINK THE KOOL-AID:
The Jonestown Tragedy, the Press, and the
New American Sensibility 167

CONCLUSIONS: Free to Be, You and Me 199

Notes 205

Bibliography 237

Index 249

Illustrations

Carole King and Gerry Goffin on their wedding day 16

Carly Simon's *Playing Possum* album cover 29

James Taylor 35

John Travolta in *Saturday Night Fever* 45

Earth Shoes advertisement 61

Earth Shoes cartoon 62

Running cartoon 65

The Mary Tyler Moore Show opening credits 76

Mary Richards and Lou Grant from *The Mary Tyler Moore Show* 92

LeVar Burton in *Roots* 116

Alex Haley on *Roots* set 122

Cicely Tyson and Maya Angelou in *Roots* 125

Carroll O'Connor in *All in the Family* 141

Hal Holbrook and Scott Jacoby in *That Certain Summer* 144

Congressman Leo Ryan in Jonestown 170

Plane on the airstrip at Port Kaituma 175

Jonestown bodies 178

Acknowledgments

More than most works, this was a very personal project, for I am a child of the seventies. For much of my youth, I fought that admission, preferring to think of myself as a sixties person. But while my early adolescence might have been shaped by love beads and Jefferson Airplane, I graduated from high school and college in the seventies and first lived on my own in the midst of what the country now stereotypes as the cultural vacuum and economic black hole of the "me decade." I do not. At first I was a closet seventies-ist, because the academy gives you little enough respect when you teach recent U.S. history and even less when it involves watching television and listening to music. So for a while I dabbled in other, more traditional projects, but I ultimately ended up writing about an era and set of experiences for which I am both scholar and witness.

Overall, my colleagues have been fairly tolerant of my seventies fixation. At first I thought it was my steely professionalism that transformed the topic for them, but I have come to realize that it's because so many of them also have complicated relationships with that decade. Colleagues have been willing—often enthusiastic—readers of chapters and listeners to ideas and people willing to let me talk to their classes about my obsessions. I would especially like to thank Dolores Peters, Robert Entenmann, Eric Fure-Slocum, Carol Holly, Mark Allister (an eighties child), Colin Wells (ditto), Matt Rohn, DeAne Lagerquist, and Steve Hahn for their contributions. Mary Titus, who let her American Studies senior seminar read an early draft of one chapter and who always keeps her eye out at garage sales for seventies objects, has been a particular help. I can't tell you how inspiring it was when she read a chapter draft and declared, "*This* is my life." My role model for interdisciplinary work, the late Jim Farrell, read versions of a good chunk of the manuscript and offered, as always, excellent advice about analytic focus.

For years, I have offered seminars on the seventies as part of my teaching rotation, as well as regular classes for first-year students on America since 1945. Many student guinea pigs have thus heard, seen, or read my interpretation of the era. Their curiosities and questions and occasionally their comments have helped me distinguish between larger themes and interesting-but-less-important details. I appreciate their enthusiasm for my stories, which, one student said, "made the course."

St. Olaf librarians have long since adjusted to my interlibrary loan requests for *TV Guide* and episodes of *Policewoman*. They have found new databases for me, safeguarded my access to the Alternative Press Index, and maintained microfilm readers that few other scholars use anymore. Kris MacPherson, History librarian, has consulted with me on many occasions, as have Dawn Moder, Kim Fragley, Molly Westerman, and Ken Johnson. The libraries at Carleton College across town and at the University of Minnesota have expanded my range of searchable newspaper runs, and I thank those in charge at both institutions for enabling my use of them. While I sometimes feel stuck in the seventies, this project could not have been completed by someone like me with a heavy teaching load and too many interdisciplinary commitments without the tools of the twenty-first-century library.

Old friends from graduate school, some of whom weathered the end of the seventies with me, have helped a lot. Michael Furmanovsky continues to share my scholarly interests in popular music and fashion, and we have had numerous electronic consultations. Monte Kugel understands and commiserates about the personal/professional divide women of our generation faced and continue to experience. Jill Watts brought both a fabulous command of American media and an impish eye to bear on the project. What else can you say about someone who once left a phone message referencing "Muskrat Love"? I would be remiss if I did not thank my friend and graduate school adviser, Richard Weiss, for helping me discover my affinity for cultural history long before I knew what cultural history was.

When a version of one chapter of this appeared in the *Journal of American History*, I gained a whole new batch of supporters and informants, who recalled their youth or expressed their regret at being too young to remember the seventies. The opportunity to put forth part of my research before I was done with the project enabled the work to grow by leaps and bounds. Thanks very much to the anonymous readers for the *Journal* and the editors, who taught me a lot about the process of writing efficiently. I've been privileged to work out other bits and pieces of thoughts in several anthologies, and I would like to thank the editors of those works, the late Sherri Inness, Avital Bloch, Lauri Umansky, Laura Linder, and Mary Dalton, for letting me plunge headlong when I should have, perhaps, been a bit more hesitant.

St. Olaf College has helped to fund this project via both specific grants and the more general annual scholarly allotment. A Marshall Fishwick Travel Grant to Research Collections from the Popular Culture Association funded a trip to the UCLA Film and Television Archives. St. Olaf Associate Dean for the Humanities Corliss Swain has provided me with extra funds on several occasions to make this project a reality.

At University of North Carolina Press, editor Chuck Grench has been both sympathetic and helpful. I really appreciate his faith in this project. A number of readers, anonymous and otherwise, have made many very useful and practical suggestions about shaping this work. Many thanks to my copyeditor, Dorothea Anderson, and my indexer (and friend), Sarah Entenmann, for their contributions to the project.

My extended family has always supported my scholarship in the abstract, but this time family members have been able to be more concrete. My three sisters, Janet and Nikki Kutulas and Sandra Kutulas Perez, have become informal resources for obscure information, having their own long histories with seventies culture, parts of which were shared. Janet served as my research assistant at the Bancroft Library, locating the pictures of Jonestown that grace the text. Neither of my parents lived to see this work come to fruition. Both, however, watched me discover history as a vocation in the seventies and offered encouragement and support thereafter. Their work ethic and commitment to family really inspired me. I want to apologize to my extended family in advance for revealing the kind of information that generally doesn't find its way into scholarly histories in the chapter on Jonestown and to recognize my cousins, Danny and Edith Kutulas, who perished there. I have lost track of most of the people who lived through the era with me, so rather than embarrass them without first getting their permission, I will just note that I think of my seventies friends with great fondness and admiration. There are, however, two I would like to single out. I first met Linda Brown when we were "freshmen" (as they used to say) at Berkeley. She died at the very end of the 1970s, but reliving the decade has reminded me how much she modeled scholarly discipline for me. Lin Cheney Spangler, with whom I shared one of those 1970s Berkeley houses with a constantly changing number of people and a dog, was an instant kindred spirit and lover of the culturally absurd. She deconstructed commercials and fads as they happened and stands ready even today to remember offbeat details.

My husband and colleague, Michael Fitzgerald, specializes in the era of Reconstruction and political culture, where history is an oh-so-serious undertaking. Perhaps initially skeptical of my project, he has been a generally enthusiastic participant in the parts of my research that involved listening or watching. My sons, Alex and Nate, probably suffered more than they benefited from this project, having watched their mother dance in public at a Bruce Springsteen concert. All three members of my family have lived with the difficult parts of this project more than the fun aspects—my physical as well as mental absences; the books, papers, DVDs, and CDs scattered all over the house; and my domination of the car radio, inattention when the writing was going well, and battles with technology—and loved me when I got grumpy or frustrated and were kind when I was insufferably jubilant. It is not easy being related to a "me decade" scholar, so I'd like to say publicly what I hope they already know: they inspire me to do my very best.

AFTER **AQUARIUS** DAWNED

Introduction

"This is the dawning of the Age of Aquarius," announced the famous song of 1960s possibilities from the popular rock musical *Hair* (1967). Pundits, commentators, promoters, and advertisers, knowing a marketable concept when they heard it, promptly appropriated the word "Aquarius" to associate themselves with the future it represented. "Aquarius" symbolized a new way of life facilitated by the rapid unseating of norms and traditions wrought by the civil rights movement, the antiwar movement, the sexual revolution, the counterculture, and the beginnings of the women's and gay liberation movements. These challenges to the status quo began on the edges of American society, finally reaching the public consciousness around 1967 or 1968, until they were undeniably present and frequently puzzling in their significance. Photographers filmed the most startling expressions of change and journalists described them, while sociologists tried to quantify their dimensions. The public response to the newness chronicled in public forums was mixed. Some welcomed Aquarian values. Others feared the nation hovered on the brink of revolution. Most were ambivalent about the prospect of radical sixties causes, ideas, and new institutions becoming the norm.

A decade later, America was a different nation. Not everybody changed, and few fully embraced the sixties ethos shorthanded in the song from *Hair*. Still, across the country, values like sexual freedom, gender equality, more complex notions of identity, work, family, and new attention to leisure, pleasure, and informality found their ways into the everyday lives of ordinary people. Americans worried less about fitting in and following rules. They did not trust the leaders or institutions that had governed previous generations. Instead they were, as a Joni Mitchell song said, "busy being free."[1] Freedom took them to many new places. Whatever "Aquarius" actually meant, and it meant different things to different people, versions of it became the new normal for millions of Americans.

This book explores that cultural process, the ways that Americans incorporated—or sometimes didn't—ideas and lifestyle choices represented by sixties movements into their lived experiences. Its focus is a decade, the 1970s, often popularly stereotyped as tacky, tasteless, or just plain boring. Its narrative is a sort of classic from-the-margins-to-the-mainstream story, but with some significant twists and turns along the way. It borrows from the ideas of a prescient 1970s pollster, Daniel Yankelovich, who set out to do something relatively new then, to "measure . . . changes in the national psychology." He tried to chronicle what interests me here, the rapid assimilation of seemingly radical ideas into the mainstream, although I have the luxury of time, distance, and more sources than did he. His understanding of the normalizing process in this particular instance helps to frame my work. His process begins with what we today would call "early adopters," middle-class, often white, college youth. "Cultural diffusion" followed, rarely evenly or smoothly. Sometimes change's earliest adopters weren't even those privileged college students. And, although Yankelovich barely mentions it, there was also a 1970s backlash against change. Indeed, historians of American conservatism would rightly remind us that social or "family values" conservatism emerged in response to creeping liberation movements, women's, blacks', and gays'.[2] Thus, while the main thrust of my work considers the spread and assimilation of new ideas and values growing out of the 1960s, so too does it explore the countercurrents and advocates for tradition and against change.

Eyewitnesses, journalists, and now historians have documented the confluence of forces that significantly remade American society in such a short time. Coming off of depression and war, members of the so-called Greatest Generation of Americans and of the Silent Generation that followed them reveled in the comfort and security of the postwar era. They plotted secure, cautious, and often materially comfortable lives. So confident were they of the future that they had a lot of children. That generation of children, of course, was the baby boom, an age cohort large enough to command centrality whatever its life stage. The first of that generation reached what Yankelovich called the "most change-sensitive" moment of their lives,[3] young adulthood, just as the civil rights movement raised significant and troubling moral questions about justice and equality in the United States. A cascade of questioning followed, about economic inequalities, America's place in the world, the worthiness of leaders to lead, social, racial, and gender hierarchies, sexual and institutional norms, even Americans' treatment of the natural environment. The impact of all these forces converging could lead to a simultaneously scary and exciting personal epiphany: rules, traditions, and norms were not set in stone. Each person could—should—determine how to live his or her own life.

Contemporaries often misunderstood the results. Even those who welcomed the revolutions of the 1960s as political, social, and economic correctives regarded the focus on personal values espoused by advocates for change as potentially antisocial. In 1976, journalist Tom Wolfe famously dubbed the era the "me decade," the moment when self-absorption overtook sixties' activism. Historian Christopher Lasch lamented the era's emerging "culture of narcissism." Even Joni Mitchell's "busy being free" lyric suggests too much attention to the self to the detriment of others. The most positive spin most contemporary commentators seemed to put on the 1970s was to suggest that national decline rather than innate selfishness motivated Americans to turn inward. Movements lost momentum as people tended their own gardens. Watergate finished off any remaining illusions people might have had about making change; the deck seemed stacked against protesters and dissidents. Instead of changing society, Americans decided to change themselves, becoming obsessed with their personalities and their lifestyles.[4]

Reality, of course, was far more complicated. The baby boom's numerical dominance and its members' particular stage of life in the 1970s practically guaranteed that the nation's attention would be focused on questions of personal identity. Activists did not disappear; the big-ticket protest causes did. The draft ended in 1971, and the last U.S. combat troops left Vietnam in 1973. Still, as Michael Stewart Foley's "on-the-ground history" of the era shows, civic engagement and community activism persisted.[5] The most dynamic phases of the gay liberation and women's movements occurred in the 1970s. The model of activism introduced by the freedom struggle in the early 1960s served liberals and conservatives alike. Americans continued to press for change or defend continuities and to relate to their governments, their communities, their families, and one another. Interested though millions of Americans might have been in themselves in the seventies, they remained engaged by the larger world and its seemingly endless need to be made better.

Even though it "seemed like nothing happened," as the title of the first big history of the 1970s (published only a few years after the decade ended) asserted, there is a pretty clear historical consensus that plenty did. Most scholars focus on the seventies as an important political "turning point," the transitional moment between New Deal liberalism and Reaganesque conservatism.[6] The war in Vietnam cost money Lyndon Johnson finessed so as not to compromise his expensive Great Society domestic programs. Inflation followed. Rustbelt economies and unions weakened as populations and political power shifted to the Sunbelt and the Southern white conservatives, whose loyalty Richard Nixon cultivated with his "Southern Strategy." The New Deal coalition came apart because the working class faced new competition from the beneficiaries of 1960s movements, women and members of minority groups. The middle class began to lose ground. Jimmy Carter's outsider persona initially satisfied an electorate outraged by Richard Nixon's manipulative pursuit of power, but Carter was unable to reverse either the declining economy or the more general malaise engendered by popular feelings of losing control. In 1980, Ronald Reagan finally halted the perceived decline by promising Americans that while there were not easy answers to the nation's general funk, there were simple ones embedded in a nostalgic American past.

Although there is historical consensus about the overall American trajectory from the 1960s to the 1980s, different historians emphasize different details of the progression. Jefferson Cowie's *Stayin' Alive* suggests that the decline of New Deal liberalism was, first and foremost, a consequence of a weakening working class. American workers ran out of options, so they accepted the "New Right's retooled discourse of what it meant to be born in the USA: populist nationalism, protection of family, and traditional morality." Journalist Rick Perlstein regards the working class as a more passive entity, at first naive enough to allow Richard Nixon to use "angers, anxieties, and resentments in the face of the 1960s chaos" to his political advantage (*Nixonland*) and, finally, easily convinced by Ronald Reagan's "cult of official optimism" that "foreclosed" certain aspects of the 1960s (*The Invisible Bridge*). Dominic Sandbrook sees anger and resentment too, but not a people rendered passive by politicians. Rather, he imagines a populace "mad as hell," as his title—and the catchphrase from the 1976 film *Network*—declares, and, consequently, far less politically tractable. Philip Jenkins stresses that the late-1970s angst was a visceral reaction to change that manifested as fear and paranoia. "The post-1975 public," he writes, "[envisioned] a strict moralistic division; problems were a matter of evil, not dysfunction." Randall Balmer's biography of Jimmy Carter, *Redeemer*, captures the crystallization of evangelicals as a conservative force that, as in Jenkins's narrative, saw politics through a moral lens. Taken together, these histories outline a sometimes-contested political trajectory that was complicated, not inevitable, and, above all else, relatively unmoored from what came before.[7]

The fact that so many scholars can find so many different themes in the 1970s suggests just how complicated the era was. Plenty happened, good and not-so-good. Even as the economy declined, virtually all historical narratives acknowledge countercurrents, the energies unleashed by feminism, justice movements, identity politics, and the sexual revolution, that also remade the political landscape and the social milieu. It is these countercurrents and their cultural expressions that most interest me, those ongoing parts of the sixties coexisting with rising political conservatism—what they signify about the era, what their impact was, and precisely what they tell us about individual lives and values that changed in the 1970s. The earthquakes of the 1960s rattled our social and cultural assumptions at least as much as our political ones, but often more effectively. We lost any consensus about how people ought to live their lives somewhere in the late 1960s, and, ever since, most of us do not seem to want to get it back. In the 1990s, we fought "culture wars" in the hope of recapturing a postwar "normalcy" almost no one had actually lived. What critics perceive as the defeatist-inspired meness of the 1970s was actually the next logical step in a longer process of assimilating 1960s values, as millions of individuals liberated from social expectations reconstructed their relationships to institutions and their personal values. The array of life choices that alarmed conservatives in the 1970s have become standard practices today, buttressed now by legal precedents, laws, and commercial practices.

My path through the 1970s emphasizes traits lurking as secondary characters in most historical interpretations of the era, themes of agency, diversity, and tolerance, along with the senses of malaise, passivity, or populist anger scholars sometimes note. In the 1970s, Americans might have felt impotent against authority but typically did not act that way. Rather, the idea of liberation reverberated throughout the culture, endorsed by new role models Americans trusted. People gravitated, as they always do, to others who shared their points of view, but, minus the organizing strength of a single set of authorities, those clusters of the like-minded built their own communities and cultures. The result, sociologists tell us, was cultural pluralism. Others reacted by creating anti-subcultures, ironically dedicated to getting America back to a hierarchical monoculture. Whatever the specifics, the result was greater individual agency, whether to reshape the self, the family, institutions, or the society. My work focuses on the smaller individual explorations and the inevitable backlashes that followed in the wake of the many more-visible, distinctly national movements of the 1960s, the joys, fears, and tentative first steps ordinary Americans took toward liberation and the fights over liberation's consequences.

The seventies populace was not, as Rick Perlstein suggests, "think[ing] like children, waiting for a man on horseback [Ronald Reagan] to rescue them."[8] I find much more persuasive the historical accounts of active, angry, vocal, engaged citizens, like Cowie's or Sandbrook's, who saw that as traditional authority waned they had more individual freedom and power. Jenkins's notion that the nation shifted from a more to a less rational mode of thinking over the course of the 1970s also suits my portrait of a citizenry beginning to imagine new ways of being. My goal here is to build off of these and other histories of the 1970s but then to focus on more subtle and individual aspects of the 1970s using very specific cultural lenses like songs, television programs, journalism, and clothing to explore themes of individual agency, taste, value systems, and choices. It is in the realm of personal choices that ordinary Americans embraced aspects of once-radical sixties values. As one journalist writing in 1970 put it, the choices people made about seemingly superficial things "became symbols of more than just a life *style*; they became symbols of another *life*."[9] Whether Americans greeted the promises seemingly contained within Aquarius's symbolic dawning with excitement or with dread, they greeted them not just in their political candidates or opinions about corporations or the arms race, but in the day-to-day arenas of their own lives.

Mediating the inchoate promises implicit in the sixties for ordinary citizens were cultural experts of various kinds. Writers, musicians, and actors offered interpretive frames that helped people understand the era. Culture generally provides context and structure for individuals' encounters with authority. It helps shape our understandings of concepts like "normal," "attractive," or "desirable." In the 1970s, with so many new ideas out there and so many traditional sources of authority seemingly spent, cultural producers had even more influence than usual.

This was particularly true for youth. Young people's heroes in the 1970s were far more likely to include performers, journalists, or writers than politicians. To satisfy those "mad as hell" feelings inspired by the wrong turns of Vietnam and the Watergate scandal, culture needed to be critical of authority and tradition. Cultural leaders had to embody or "represent values of the Sixties," an informal youth poll, the *Woodstock Census*, tells us, and, thereby, function as cultural ambassadors to those values.[10]

Culture, however, is not neutral, especially in a capitalist society. It sells things. It manipulated "Aquarius" to suit its purposes. Americans tend to believe that they are wise to such huckstering. That attitude might not have been born in the 1970s, but skepticism with authority—including cultural authority—grew significantly as sixties activists unmasked various corporate and governmental lies. Many traditional cultural authorities lost their influence, especially censors. Younger, more irreverent cultural leaders remade media to reflect the anti-Establishment feelings arising out of sixties clashes with authorities. Having grown up in a very sheltered, kid-centered, family-friendly environment, Yankelovich's early adopters found truth-telling, however ugly or shocking, exhilarating. The public culture became the crucible in which more-mainstream versions of once-radical values had their extreme edges smoothed. Television shows, movies, music, newspapers, and magazines packaged change in positive ways, emphasizing individuality, diversity, pleasure, and freedom.

As the 1960s ended, many Americans, or at least their cultural authorities, rushed to assess the meaning and portent of those cataclysmic years. The photo-magazine *Life* saw the 1970s as a tipping point, the moment when "an unconscious alliance for change," consisting of youth, African Americans, and the college educated, would shift the nation away "from the old ethic of continued hard work and success." Business-oriented *Fortune* magazine, by contrast, predicted that youth would finally realize that rebelling against authority was not "a reasonable way to spend one's adult life," returning the nation to the status quo antebellum. The pollster *Fortune* hired to survey youth's opinions, Daniel Yankelovich, thought otherwise. He sketched out for the magazine's readers a dispersal pattern for new ideas and values, from "forerunners" on college campuses, to their more "practical-minded" classmates, to all young people, and, eventually, to everybody else. Whether

Americans feared, welcomed, or merely took as inevitable the changes that loomed in 1970, virtually everyone believed that the younger generation was an important factor in their acquisition.[11]

Scholars, including myself, share this conviction that the baby boom generation (Americans born between 1946 and 1963) played a pivotal role in spreading once-radical 1960s ideals. Boomers' felt need to establish independent identities emanated in part from their large numbers, 76 million by most estimates, a demographic reality that meant that teenagers were nearly 40 percent of the American population during the 1960s.[12] Having matured during a time of general prosperity rather than depression and war, they were not as interested in security and stability as were their parents. Their power as consumers made them culturally significant long before they had direct political power. A shared culture and consumerism bound them together and separated them from their elders — songs and movies and fads their parents did not understand. What contemporaries called the generation gap ensured that their primary identities and loyalties often remained generational. Their affinity for their shared culture helped to transcend their differences. Boomers quickly established their distinction from their parents by gaining more education, having more sexual partners, making fewer earlier marriages, and having fewer children, demographic realities that also contributed to a unique generational identity. As sociologist Robert Bellah noted in his famous assessment of their inner lives, *Habits of the Heart* (1985), the generation coming of age in the late 1960s and 1970s rejected the stereotypical conformity of their childhoods, seeking "freedom *from*," in Bellah's words. Yankelovich's "forerunners" sought the freedom to be who they wanted to be rather than falling into roles defined by their gender, race, or class. Peer groups tended to shape their values rather than the more-eternal veracities their parents, teachers, or churches might have taught them. "At college I got to be more knowledgeable and generally became more sophisticated and more cynical," revealed a boomer to a consumer research information researcher in 1973.[13] That generation's expectation that society would conform to it rather than vice versa significantly shaped the American 1970s.

Life magazine's beginning-of-the-decade story depicted these forerunners poised on the brink of changes about which the rest of the country felt less sure. In 1970, majorities still opposed premarital sex and "new styles in hair and dress." They disliked the way "traditional values are being torn down." Nevertheless, what Tom Wolfe might think of as me-ness and what *Life*'s survey called "personal goals" topped their lists of aspirations, significantly eclipsing "hard work and saving money." Americans were already intrigued by what it would mean to have "an open lifestyle," peace of mind, and "honest relationships."[14] The assimilation of 1960s values had begun, in short, and while *Life* did not comment upon it, several broader themes were already present. First was the way that making judgments about the counterculture, protest, or anything else that seemed 1960s-inspired looked different when it happened in your own front yard. Americans might criticize their friends' children for joining communes, moving in with partners, or wearing beards or miniskirts but were far less critical when it was their own children. And once their own children did it, well, reinvention often looked pretty seductive to the elders too. Second, freedom meant less emphasis on money, work, family, or competition. People wanted happiness, contentment, and peace, intangibles rather than tangible assets. They were more likely to live in the moment and less inclined toward the qualities that prevailed when security was the end result, especially long-range planning. Finally, having freedom but still living with others meant that individuals also needed to redefine relationships between friends and romantic partners, within families, within their communities, and with authority. Finding "freedom from" was communal as well as individual. Indeed, until the very end of the decade, a majority of entering college students deemed it "essential" that they "develop a meaningful philosophy of life" and "help others who are in difficulty."[15]

Sixties activism made Americans more cognizant of the need to reconcile values and lifestyle. It did not make them narcissistic. The New Deal promoted greater economic equality; World War II accelerated those trends, linking, as Lizabeth Cohen has argued, "democratic values" with "the expansion of mass consumption." The economy became postindustrial, affecting work and play. Sociologist Herbert Gans assured *New York Times* readers that as more Americans achieved the rudiments of the first two-thirds of the promise "life, liberty, and the pursuit of happiness," they were free to concentrate on the last third. Happiness, however, required more than just "personal and material improvement." It required congruence between values and everyday decisions. It required tolerance and equity for others pursuing their own happiness.[16]

The power to choose what one wanted from life and the freedom to pursue it rested on an often unrealized revolutionary concept in 1970, that there was no one right way to live your life. If the economy was post-industrial, the society was becoming postmodern. Before the 1960s, America was hierarchical, divided by age, class, race, gender, and sexuality. A "Divine Architect of the human race," as conservative activist Phyllis Schlafly put it, bestowed upon the populace a place for everyone.[17] Secularism and science were well on their way to undermining the notion of a great master plan when sixties social justice movements toppled wobbly hierarchies. Equality and diversity were supposed to follow. But once your color, gender, class background, or sexual identity did not determine your future, you had more ability to do so for yourself. Finding, creating, maintaining, justifying, and protecting a unique and expressive way of life became a central, individual part of mainstreaming in the 1970s.

Lifestyle choices existed not just because they could be imagined but because verities and their traditional advocates lost their legitimacy. By 1970, even fairly conservative individuals used the word "Establishment" pejoratively to describe practices that seemed undemocratic or unhealthy and decidedly antithetical to individuality. The "credibility gap" that existed between the Johnson administration and the American people, Nixon's secret wars in Cambodia and Laos, and the abuses of power collectively known as Watergate undermined citizens' trust and faith in their political authorities. Similarly, inflation made consumers skeptical of corporations, the treatment of protesters made citizens wary of police, and the war in Vietnam seriously weakened confidence in the military. Consequently, an amorphous Establishment often seemed to loom between an individual and his or her desires.

A cultural apparatus supported the Establishment. It used censorship, marketing practices, and sponsorship to promote a particularly American way of life. "Normative America," historian Andrew Hartman notes, "was more omnipresent, and more coercive," in the 1950s "than it had been before." Cultural rebellions by youth or other forerunners caused that apparatus to shrivel or transform. Its venues broadened, as street performers gained currency, new record labels emerged, and magazines like *People* and *New York* offered hip commentary. As Lizabeth Cohen has demonstrated, the idea of a niche market rose to prominence, finally ending the conceit of the undifferentiated audience. Cultural producers expressed themselves in new genres. Baby boomers were more likely to make this new anti-Establishment culture to ensure its authenticity, its rebellious essence, and its exclusivity. As Bruce J. Schulman has so aptly put it, 1970s culture often allowed individuals to feel as though they possessed "a certain kind of knowingness—an ability to see things for what they were, without romantic illusions."[18] While 1950s popular culture reassured Americans that they shared similar desires and values, the culture of the 1970s positioned individuals to feel unique and maybe even superior.

Yet the "hip capitalism" that scholar Thomas Frank deconstructs does not automatically signify consumer co-optation,[19] just as liberation could not be achieved merely through shopping. Attitude shifts were also necessary. Accompanying liberation was a new frame of reference. This book looks at a series of pivotal attitude shifts expressed culturally that, together, speak to a changed understanding of the place of the individual within a larger community. The emerging *mentalité*, overall, emphasized the artificiality of social constructs, undermining traditional beliefs about race, gender, and sexuality and stressing the importance of pleasure over duty, the present over the past or the future. Lifestyle rests on a very postmodern idea, that reality is self-consciously constructed and self-consciously read; and it was both the constructing and the reading that grew out of sixties movements, with their undermining of established truths and conventional wisdoms. Still, constructing the self also reflected America's most cherished ideals, including freedom, democracy, independence, and resourcefulness.

While capitalism's inevitable co-optation of radical themes and Americans' own limited tolerance for truly revolutionary ideals mainstreamed the more extreme parts of the sixties, the forces of social conservatism represented the most powerful challenges to change. Novelist John Steinbeck decried the "cop-out insurgency of our children and young people, . . . the rise of narrow, ugly, and vengeful cults of all kinds, the mistrust and revolt against all authority," mourning a time when "the rules were understood and accepted by everyone." By the 1970s, though, many versions of "normal" coexisted. Social conservatives and evangelical Christians responded to the mainstreaming of the sixties with panic. Matthew D. Lassiter has argued that they feared they could not hold back the ugly tide on their own but required the intervention of the federal government, as the Reverend Jerry Falwell said, "to keep others from jamming their amoral philosophies down our throats."[20] Social conservatives could not stop the assimilation of the sixties into

American lives; however, they certainly reshaped the decade's impact. This work looks at both the spread of Aquarian ideals and the backlashes against them.

The book looks at three overlapping areas where social revolution played out in the 1970s. The first is the remaking of individual gender identities, modeled and reflected in popular music and clothing. The second is more elastic notions of family identity reflected particularly through television sitcoms and dramas. The third is changing ideas about the relationship between subgroups—here an emerging gay and lesbian community and a cult—and everyone else, presented by television and print journalists. Contained within each section are similar themes: individual agency, freedom and its scarier aspects, and the ways 1960s values of tolerance, diversities of various kinds (gender, sexual, racial, ethnic), and beliefs about equality and justice interact with more traditional American institutions, including the family and the economy. No one of these categories is discrete; they overlap and echo one another. Change is messy, incomplete, and complicated.

In each chapter, I have chosen a cultural representation that both informed and expressed new values. The values chose themselves; one cannot talk about 1970s culture without considering changing understandings of race, gender, or sexual identity, for instance. To trace the particular path of assimilation these changing values followed, I look to the culture and cultural expressions of change. This is not a full-blown cultural history of the seventies, however. Any scholar who naively aims to write something so complex will end up describing rather than interpreting. My scholarly models in my endeavor are Susan Douglas and Natasha Zaretsky,[21] whose works slice into different cultural specifics in illustration of larger themes.

I should also add a couple of caveats to all that I am about to say. The first has to do with terms. Defining a generation is a complicated business. "Baby boom" covers a lot of territory, age-wise, and most people make distinctions between early and late boomers; some even add middle boomer as a separate category. Scholarly historians generally do not gravitate to generational explanations as much as do popular historians, rightly skeptical of their invisible privileging of certain categories of people. While baby boomers, far more than the generations that preceded them, grew up with a well-established popular culture framing their issues for them, other factors and institutions also powerfully shaped their lives, particularly race, gender, and class. Not all boomers thought alike, and not all shared politics or values. However, as an age cohort, they did share certain predilections and experiences. That does not mean every baby boomer lived in a commune or tuned in, turned on, and dropped out after Timothy Leary advised them to. This book is about trends; it cannot devote as much time to exceptions to trends.

Similarly, "seventies" is a state of mind more than a decade. The election of Reagan in the fall of 1980 marks a fairly discrete end point for the decade, but there is no such easy bookend for the beginning. Activism certainly did not stop, and several of the movements I discuss, especially the push for gay rights, were more 1970s phenomena than 1960s ones. The decade does not exist on a flat historical plain, either. Important economic and political realities separate the earlier years of the era from the later ones. Most scholars of the 1970s subdivide it into two periods. I share their sense that the mood in 1978 or 1979 was very different from 1971 or 1972, and I have tried, whenever possible, to make that distinction in my text.

What I offer here is a new lens, another way to look at the 1970s. While we see that era as the birthplace of a familiar brand of contemporary political conservatism, so too should we see the 1970s as the place where some other familiar modes of thought and expression began. That modern sensibility was not quite fully formed by decade's end, but its outlines were emerging. It was more individual, more tolerant, more pleasure-seeking, and somewhat less engaged in civic activities, but more public, skeptical, and even ironic. Today's America is often branded as solipsistic and narcissistic, with Americans obsessed with curating their lives. It is beyond the scope of this work to comment on the present. However, the parts of contemporary life that I see growing out of the 1970s are not marked by self-absorption but by the valuing of freedom, diversity, and tolerance.

1 : I Feel the Earth Move

Redefining Love and Sex

Like many other Americans her age, singer-songwriter Carole King grew up expecting one kind of life and living another. Born in Brooklyn in 1941, she was groomed for marriage and motherhood, milestones she reached in a less than socially desirable fashion. She got pregnant, married, and dropped out of Queens College, all before the age of twenty. The more unexpected part of her early biography was that, despite being a wife and mother, King, along with husband Gerry Goffin, wrote songs at Aldon Music, part of the famous Brill Building salon of pop music composers, which enabled a comfortable suburban life. But then the sixties intervened. Beatles-inspired musicians wrote their own songs, dispensing with the Brill Building's services. Goffin, meanwhile, "wanted to be a hippie." His interest in drugs and sex with other women undermined their marriage. King initially lacked Goffin's enthusiasm for sixties currents but, like many of her female peers, came to appreciate the opportunities opened up by social change. She moved her young daughters to Los Angeles. She joined a folk-rock trio. Urged by friend James Taylor to go solo, she recorded an album almost no one heard, and then a second one, *Tapestry*, which won the Grammy Awards' "grand slam" of awards in 1971.[1] Thanks to the 1960s, Carole King's life possibilities opened up in surprising ways.

King's biography demonstrates the changing nature of American music and the changing experience of musicians, but especially the emergence of new romantic and sexual patterns. She became an unexpected role model for young women, who, like her, found themselves in a transformed social landscape. Musicians represented one of the leading edges of sexual and romantic change in American society. They helped to introduce young adults to a broader range of sexual possibilities and values. King and her ilk, singer-songwriters like Joni Mitchell, Paul Simon, James Taylor, Carly Simon, and Jackson Browne, wrote autobiographical songs and lived very publicly. They provided middle-class youth, Daniel Yankelovich's forerunners, with some compelling examples of modern gender, romance, and sexual practices. "Joni Mitchell taught your cold English wife how to feel," Emma Thompson's character tells her husband in the 2003 film *Love Actually*. Like Thompson's character, a lot of Americans, especially women, in the 1970s learned to think differently about love from the singer-songwriters.

Nowhere was the much-discussed generation gap larger in the 1970s than when it came to understandings of love and romance. Traditionally, the date began the well-worn path to marriage and sexual intimacy. Everything from romantic comedies to college courses laid out a progression that started there, proceeded to the exclusivity of going steady, culminated in a proposal, marriage, and then intercourse. After World War II, the sequence sped up because marriage marked the entrance into glorious adulthood.[2] In the late 1940s and the 1950s, millions of young people settled into marriages and adult responsibilities when they were barely out of their teens, dazzled by their ability to obtain so quickly what their parents had struggled to achieve. Yet only a few years later, young people were already beginning to question the date-marriage-sex sequence. For King, saving sex for after marriage was not compelling, and, ultimately, neither was the conventional practice of dating.

The traditional date ceased to fit with youth's realities. Its primary function was to introduce males and females to one another as potential partners, unnecessary in the less-gender-divided world of the seventies, with its coed dormitories and nontraditional jobs. "Boys and girls," a *Village Voice* reporter noted, were "becoming friends," a trend King would highlight with her song "You've Got a Friend."[3] Dating's gendered etiquette felt artificial or sexist to a generation that believed in equality. Its obstacles to sex made no sense when birth control was easily accessible. The women's movement inspired many young women, especially those with college educations, to emphasize careers rather than husband-hunting. Baby boomers mustered little enthusiasm for their parents' dating rituals or the settling down for which their parents waited.

This was particularly true for people like King and Goffin, Yankelovich's collegiate forerunners. "The old certitudes were crumbling," social observer Vance Packard noted in 1968, and to study what that meant, he went straight to what he perceived as ground zero, the college campus.[4] Packard was right to look there first for evidence of a changing set of moral and sexual values; college campuses were hotbeds of

Carole King and Gerry Goffin on their wedding day in 1959.
She was seventeen and already pregnant. Photo courtesy of Photofest.

social change. College prolonged the process of adolescence, providing young adults with the freedom to experiment and immersion in a peer culture. Those opportunities diminished the allures of young marriage. Marriage became something you did after you established your career, sowed your wild oats, or backpacked through Europe, if you married at all. Defining and then executing a new romantic progression fell to middle-class youth because they had the luxury of freedom and time of prolonged adolescences.

Traditionally, middle-class, college-educated boomers followed sexual rules because those rules privileged them. Dating conventions paired like with like in ways that helped them maintain or exceed their parents' status. When someone white and middle class like King transgressed norms, moreover, as Rickie Solinger has demonstrated, she was insulated from the sorts of consequences that derailed many poor or African American girls' lives. Traditionally, social outliers tended to be sexual rule-breakers. The sexual revolution, however, went "beyond the usual suspects," as historian Beth Bailey has noted. It reflected a set of "major transformations in the structure of American society."[5] The same commitments to equality, justice, and individual conscience that drove the civil rights movement and the women's movement also reshaped sexual norms.

The earliest version of the sexual revolution, though, was not boomers' sexual revolution. *Playboy* magazine, launched in 1953, promoted a hedonistic bachelor subculture of seduction that challenged social definitions of "good" men, exactly what *Cosmopolitan* magazine under the stewardship of Helen Gurley Brown did for "good" women about a decade later. Neither presumed that the ideal encounter between the sexes was an equal one. Both new archetypes presupposed gender difference and were consumer driven. Those were problematic concepts for late-sixties youth. Hugh Hefner's stereotypical playboy deployed sports cars, stereos, and liquor to lure "playthings" into his bachelor pad, while Brown's single girl, derived from the title of her 1962 book, *Sex and the Single Girl*, plucked, dieted, and wore high heels to attract and fascinate men. In the gendered world of the so-called swinging single, as Nora Ephron once noted, men dominated effortlessly, confident they would get what they wanted from life, while *Cosmo* girls struggled with problems and insecurities: "menstrual cramps, pimples, budget squeeze, hateful roommates." The confidence gap reflected the realities of the status quo and engrained male privilege.[6] Goffin and King both had sex before marriage, but only he had affairs once they tied the knot. She was too busy trying to meet social expectations about women's roles.

Typically, societies pass along sexual norms "in a thousand unseen and unspoken ways." Yet no less a social observer than famed anthropologist Margaret Mead noticed that, in 1970, disjuncture ruled: "The experience of the young generation is radically different from that of their parents." That same observation took Vance Packard into "the sexual wilderness" of the college campus to explore new sexual etiquettes. In the ten-year span between 1965 and 1975, the percentage of male college students who had had premarital sex rose from 65 percent to nearly 74 percent. More significant, the percentages of female college students who did the same climbed from just under 29 percent to 57 percent. Thanks to the birth control pill, fewer young women found themselves in King's situation, pregnant and having to marry. Social norms mattered less to teens and young adults; the peer group influenced young people's sexual choices and, in particular, their attitudes toward female sexuality. Youth less frequently used words like "immoral" to assess sexual behavior, and notions of individual preference rather than customs or familial obligation guided their decisions about sex.[7]

As young people rejected their parents' mores, Mead noted, they had to "develop new styles based on their own experience and provide models for their own peers." And that's precisely what they did. Yankelovich observed that new sexual attitudes began on college campuses in the late 1960s, reaching youth not in college by the mid-1970s. He described a shift "from universally held prescriptions of what is not appropriate behavior . . . toward looser, freer codes," from early marriages to more casual sexual encounters.[8] Eventually many Americans embraced these behaviors, but the new sexual attitudes did not immediately transform society. Rather, they slowly percolated down. In the meantime, those college youth in the pivotal (and privileged) position of going first often had to improvise their sexual values.

At a time when sex manuals still distinguished between vaginal and clitoral orgasms, the sexual establishment held no more credibility for many younger Americans than did any other source of authority. Young people, in fact, often resisted the idea that sexual choices should be judged. One counterculture slogan urged that "if it feels good, do it." Notions of liberation situated sexuality within a larger discourse of individuality and freedom. Sex surveys, nearly fifty of which examined college students' sexual behaviors between 1970 and 1975, already suggested the power of this subgroup to reshape sexual attitudes, while their more neutral language and a "nonjudgmental tone" confirmed that a belief in sexual freedom more commonly prevailed. Alex Comfort's 1972 best seller, *The Joy of Sex*, used, its publisher said, "humor, honesty and directness" to emphasize pleasure over clinical explanations. Its famous pictorial section, "The Art of Making Love," visually equated sexual liberation with countercultural style with its drawings of a couple "wearing blue jeans and long hair, smoking pot, listening to rock music . . . engaging in premarital sexual behavior."[9] *Joy*'s models looked as different from *Playboy* or *Cosmo*'s swinging singles as they did from boomers' parents.

Joy was popular because young people seeking information about changing romantic and sexual ideas and values turned not to their parents or ministers or teachers, but to their peer culture to validate their choices. While hip sex manuals or surveys provided some frameworks for defining those norms, it was music that, in particular, conveyed the mystique of newer romantic modes. Music was the most fully realized part of boomer culture, "the prime medium of communication," according to music critic Ralph J. Gleason, a language and common set of references for young people. "Everybody listened to the same music on the radio," recalled another critic, providing "a shared experience." Music told stories, especially romantic ones. Rock and roll undermined authority, loosened inhibitions, and dramatized peer experiences, contemporary commentators noted, providing "anthems to their freedom." Writing in *Life* magazine, journalist Richard Goldstein explained that sixties rock allowed listeners "to make their own judgments about societal taboos." One musician pointed out music's cultural advantage as "the first reflection of social change": "You can record an album today and have it on the shelves in a week or two, which gives you immediacy and flexibility." Popular music had unique cultural power to influence youth.[10]

Rock's associations with cultural rebellion likewise reinforced youth's generational identities. The music encouraged youth to "resist the authority of parents, be more sexually adventurous, and learn from their peers about what to wear, watch, and listen to," scholar Glenn Altschuler observed. The sort of music King and Goffin wrote offered compellingly emotional highs and lows and the vicarious rebelliousness of challenging norms, with its frequent allusions to class differences and bad boys. By the early 1960s, rock was such a big business that it almost seemed co-opted; folk was the hipper genre for activist youth. The Beatles, however, revived its authenticity as a youth genre with revolutionary overtones. The group was a crucial center to baby boomer popular culture, providing "privileged wisdom," one fan suggested.[11]

As a generational peer rite, listening to the Beatles required a shared foundation of knowledge and a changed interaction between producers and consumer. Unlike most previous artists, the Beatles wrote their own songs, a fact that meant the beginning of the end for King's and Goffin's Brill Building careers. The Beatles took control over the rest of the creative process as well, by imagining orchestrations and album cover art. The group's refusal to tour after 1966 pushed the definition of a rock band. Fans learned to "expect meaning and significance" from their music and lives, according to Goldstein. By 1967's *Sergeant Pepper's Lonely Hearts Club Band*, thoughtful listeners interrogated lyrics, discerned musical influences, formed aesthetic opinions, and identified with performers' intentions and values. To discuss music knowledgeably and make informed musical choices required familiarity with performers' backstories, a rock music vocabulary, and awareness of the critical reception of songs. As *Life* magazine observed about a year after *Pepper* was released, the stereotypical categories left over from television's *American Bandstand*: "It's got a nice beat. Y'can dance to it," had been replaced by new criteria: "It has truth. I empathize with it."[12] Complexity made rock music personal.

Thanks in part to youth's insatiable appetite for all things Beatles, musical performers were public figures and role models, the people, critic Jon Landau explained, who "stand for all our fantasies." By the 1970s, musicians had become celebrities young people followed. Many could recite not only their discographies, but also the names of their lovers or children. Carly Simon's 1972 hit, "You're So Vain," for instance, prompted a massive public debate about its subject that still rages today. Magazines and newspapers eager to gain baby boomers as readers showcased musicians' lifestyles, and professional critics served up authoritative opinions about the relative value of different singers and songs. *Rolling Stone*, founded in 1967, intended to become, its editor promised, a forum for music and "the things and attitudes that the music embraces." Indeed, its readers saw it as "a compact with our generation" forged over "serious, trenchant coverage of rock 'n' roll." Purchasing a copy, one recalled, was a college "rite of passage." Beyond musical reviews and political coverage, its pages included interviews and performer biographies, and its gossip column, "Random Notes," reported on their marriages, breakups, and public appearances. It functioned, ultimately, as "a glossy life-style publication" full of celebrity news. Similarly, the *Village Voice* employed writers who spoke with the same generational voices as their readership. *People* magazine, launched in 1974, broadened the audience for rock gossip, granting musicians the sort of public attention once given to movie stars. Musicians' lifestyles became accessible to young people in the process of defining their own ways of being.[13]

The growing complexity of discourse about music and musicians also revealed something unforeseen in 1960: "Rock and roll had lasted," wrote Ellen Willis in her *New Yorker* column on rock, "and we had not grown out of it." Carole King might have become a wife and mother, but she still loved her generation's music. Market segmentation, a key component of Lizabeth Cohen's "consumer republic," divided music fans into "better" and "best" categories. Those like King who were college-age or twenty-something were "advertisers' most desired demographic segment"—musically assumed to have "deeper" tastes, Jon Landau said, because they had longer histories with music, bought albums rather than 45's, and listened to FM radio. Buying music, going to concerts, and following artists well into their twenties signified youth's anti-Establishment and countercultural values, just as their ongoing cash flow suggested their freedom from the financial burdens of marriage. For this generation, the Beatles' 1969 breakup marked a profound turning point, a musical fragmentation that mirrored their often-confusing paths to maturity. Once the Beatles ceased to be, the "middle-class, college-educated, elitist brigade," one reporter noted, "seemed to crash all at once."[14]

The rush to fill the Beatles' void started immediately. Tempted by the "loads of disposable income" middle-class boomers generated, record companies searched for lucrative Beatles-replacements. Discovered by Paul McCartney and initially promoted by the Beatles' Apple Corporation, James Taylor was, a *New York Times* reporter proclaimed, the "first superstar of the seventies." Executives at Warner Brothers Records dismissed his 1970 album, *Sweet Baby James*, as unlikely to sell, but the sound found its niche with the college set. Taylor "launched a new era in rock," a reporter said, providing a "reassuring, almost therapeutic tonic for the somewhat frayed nerves of a generation in this country that had just gone through the sociopolitical turmoil and upheaval of the late

1960s."[15] With his hippie looks, publicly acknowledged drug habit, and eagerness to throw over the prestige of his background for an alternative rock lifestyle, Taylor also embodied the counterculture. What he lacked, however, like the singer-songwriters who followed him to stardom, was traditional rock authenticity.

Male rebellion defined rock authenticity. Male consumers mattered more than females when it came to rock as they had more money and were assumed to have better taste. Tastemakers, including record company executives and rock critics, were generally young, white, and male, who conflated their subjective opinions with objective quality. Girls, the record industry assumed, chose their music based on the cuteness of the performers and not the quality of the songs. Money-generating heartthrobs who appealed primarily to girls were the rock establishment's pariahs, like the so-called Pre-Fab Four, the Monkees. The gendered realities that still prevailed during this generation's adolescences meant that while guys might fantasize about being guitar heroes, girls could only imagine themselves as romantic partners to performers. To be truly resonant with the genre's connoisseurs, rock music could not be too popular. Singer-songwriter music's audience was disproportionately female, and performers often worked a college circuit. From a commercial standpoint, these were valuable audience segments.[16] They were not, however, socially understood by the rock mainstream to be very authentic.

In fact, critics complained that the rise of the folksy singer-songwriters signaled rock's decline. Their music lacked social commentary; it was far too focused on performers' autobiographical details. The rock establishment used words like "'wimpy,' 'navel-gazing,' 'narcissistic,' and worse" to describe performers like Taylor, as one critic later noted. Even a feminist critic like Ellen Willis called them "upper-class brats," performers lacking street cred. But they spoke to middle-class youth "creeping out of post-adolescence toward some kind of proto-adulthood" and, as a *Saturday Review* writer opined, hungry for "artists who personify themselves." Rebellion had been a powerful motivating force for young people drawn to the outlaw qualities of the sixties, but as they confronted their twenties, the "prosaic details" of making their lives modern (and different from their parents') consumed more of their energy. Paul Simon has suggested that his music generates serotonin, causing listeners to "feel safe and comfortable." "[I'm] just trying . . . to write what's around me, inside of me," Jackson Browne once said. Essayist Chuck Klosterman suggests that the "Carly Simon Principle" defined the bond forged between certain performers and their audiences, a shared recognition of singers' low-keyed versions of a resonant "espoused reality" listeners could use to "construct . . . meaning" themselves. Singer-songwriters helped middle-class baby boomers coming of age reconcile their lived experiences with the sixties.[17]

The Carly Simon Principle was most apt with respect to the romantic narrative. Singer-songwriters rewrote the formulaic pop cultural love story that ended in the happily-ever-after of marriage. The "marriage plot," as literary and cultural scholars call it, reinforced what social experts advocated, particularly the idea that sex came after "I do's." For the first two-thirds of the twentieth century, censorship limited the public articulation of other possibilities. Hollywood's Production Code of 1930 held that "pure love," defined as "the love of a man for a woman permitted by the law of God and man," was a fit subject for movie plots but that "passion" was not. Well into the 1960s, commercially viable American music emphasized these cinematic conventions. One mid-1950s study of romantic songs found that 83 percent focused on love and "courtship." "We could be married; then we'd be happy," sang the Beach Boys in "Wouldn't It Be Nice." When Brian Wilson wrote those lyrics in 1966, the sentiment was already out-of-date. By 1969, the lyrical emphasis in popular music shifted from pairing up to autonomy. A similar shift in social conventions occurred. "In barely two decades," notes historian Stephanie Coontz, "marriage lost its role as the 'master event' that governed young people's sexual lives. . . . Premarital sex became the norm."[18]

So when Carly Simon included what one reviewer called "a haunting, ambivalent song about marriage" on her second solo album in 1970, "That's the Way I Always Heard It Should Be," it struck a nerve, capturing youth's conflicted feelings about their parents' institution. Simon acknowledged her generation's fear that marriage was not the beginning of adulthood but the end of personal growth: "Soon you'll cage me on your shelf, I'll never learn to be just me first, by myself." Her normally robust voice wavered as she sang about her parents' marriage, conveying their loneliness. At song's end, she succumbed to convention, even though she could not reconcile what she saw around her with "the way I always heard it should be." Simon's song addressed, she later explained, "the pressure to get married" that society traditionally imposed on women. Critic Robert Christgau remembered that he "almost . . . cheer[ed]" when he heard "a woman questioning marriage." The lyrics triggered an epiphany for him, the realization that, contrary to cultural stereotypes, young women shared men's fear that marriage "ties you down."[19] Simon's song was thought provoking, challenging listeners to think about what they had always heard and believed about marriage.

Explicit in Simon's song was the waning attraction of marriage; implicit was the alternative: sex outside of marriage. Heretofore, virginity culturally defined relationships between single men and women. It was something men hoped to claim and women were supposed to protect until their wedding nights. "Will You Still Love Me Tomorrow?," wondered the Goffin-King song (for which Goffin wrote the lyrics), a fear that loomed over many a young woman's sexual decisions. But by the 1970s, obtaining the Pill from college dispensaries was almost de rigueur among entering female students, a symbolic transition into womanhood for teenagers who had learned via the counterculture to imagine intercourse as a satisfying-but-transitory physical pleasure. Twelve separate 1960s studies replicated in the 1970s demonstrated rising rates of premarital intercourse for high school and college students. Early marriage in the 1950s had given that generation license "to try it out," as one young man said of sex; but as the average age at first marriage grew, a lot of teens simply "tr[ied] it out" before marriage.[20]

The sixties loosened Americans' sexual inhibitions overall, but not traditional authorities' attempts to control youth's sexuality. Ministers and teachers emphasized the importance of waiting until marriage to try out sex. Mainstream media actively discouraged teens and young adults from sexual experimentation. Television movies-of-the-week and afterschool specials pitched at young people depicted the harm that could befall those who indulged in the new sexual freedom, including unplanned pregnancies and sexual exploitation. The popular culture was particularly explicit about females' place in the universe of expanding sexual possibilities. Good girls, like Carole King, got married. The Establishment's version of the sexual revolution denied young women the freedom to express their sexuality in ways consistent with their perceptions of personal liberation.[21]

Sixties rock music was neither respectful of parental fears nor consumed by elders, so it often referenced sex; however, its vision of modern sexuality did not quite mesh with young Americans' lived realities either. In the late 1960s, traditional cultural arbiters lost control over rock music, which enhanced artists' authenticity and rebellion. However, the end of censorship also ensured that rock would become crude and male defined: "Why don't we do it in the road?," asked Paul McCartney on the Beatles' *White Album*. "By 1969," one music critic recalled, "the rule book of decorum was basically out the window." Stories about musicians' wild nights and the female fans who sexually serviced them—groupies—provided, *Rolling Stone* editor Jann Wenner thought, "an index of emerging contemporary values in the United States." Groupies, though, like musicians' drug-filled excesses and trashed hotels rooms, existed apart from ordinary teens' real lives. Fans of rock music understood that, as James Taylor put it, there was a difference between the "dating" that was part of the social contract imposed upon them and the easy "fucking" musicians enjoyed.[22] Finding a middle ground more realistic than the fantasy realm of rock's gods but less retrograde than traditional social expectations engaged middle-class teens as they went off to college and jobs.

Finding a middle ground, though, was especially problematic for young women. "It was 1969," King recalled. "It was okay to love lots of people. Indeed, it was mandatory." The ideal of free love was hardly free, as feminists pointed out, in a world where men had disproportionate power and nothing better demonstrated that point than the ubiquitous image of the so-called hippie chick. This stereotype appeared across sixties popular culture, "more sexually playful and less inhibited," Vance Packard noted, gyrating uninhibitedly to psychedelic rock. She transgressed her parents' morality and pleased young men but had no other expectations. In rock, she was all too often the groupie, who confirmed the outrageous sexual behaviors of male rock stars. Although enticingly rebellious, the promise of free love as it was culturally constructed by a male-dominated society actually offered women little control over their own sexuality. The implicit social contract of the date gave females the power to set the level of sexual intimacy. As the Pill and the overall ethos of the sexual revolution made "no" or "stop" less justifiable, young women discovered they had either to comply with male sexual expectations or gain a reputation as sexually repressed. "Could sex be casual?," Carly Simon remembers wondering. Even when transferred from the pages of *Playboy* to the corner of Haight-Ashbury, the sexual revolution made men the sexual initiators, the more experienced partners, and the ones whose desires got the most attention.[23]

Singer-songwriters' romantic template helped to bridge the gap be-

tween the sexual revolution and the feminist one. Their songs represented, as critic Loraine Alterman said of Gordon Lightfoot, not "the
loves of boys and girls but [of] men and women," an important distinction for sexually maturing females. Performers looked relatable in
their jeans and denim work shirts. The stripped-down musical sound
emphasized lyrics, traditionally more the purview of female fans, with
the words provided on album covers. This was not dance music or background noise at a party; these were songs to be savored, alone. Actor
Rita Wilson remembers listening to Joni Mitchell "on the floor or on my
bed" while "read[ing] the lyrics, obsessed." Singer-songwriters felt like
people you could be friends with, people who understood your experiences, slightly more sophisticated versions of you, at least if you were
white, middle-class, and coming of age. "I'm just one or two years and
a couple of changes behind you," sang Jackson Browne in "Fountain of
Sorrow."[24] That lyric summed up the perceived relationship between
singer-songwriters and their audiences, positioning them to be near-
peer guides to life, romance, sex, and love, especially for females, who
for so long had been relegated to fandom, with all that it entailed.

Although James Taylor was a big seller on the college circuit and
Carly Simon's song about marriage reached number ten on the *Billboard* charts, for many young women, singer-songwriters' appeal boiled
down to one event, the 1971 release of Carole King's album *Tapestry*. The
opening track was "something different," expressing a mature, female-
centered celebration of sex rarely heard in the mainstream popular culture. Heretofore, one critic noted, "straightforward, assertive sexuality
was not a legitimate style for women." King undermined that convention in short order, starting with a forceful piano melody and a "raunchy"
first line,[25] "I feel the earth move," a euphemism for orgasm. The song
was about "los[ing] control, down to [the] . . . very soul." Its rhythm
mimicked an orgasm too, building to a climax and then slowing. With
her ex-husband, King wrote the music while he wrote the lyrics; however
"I Feel the Earth Move" was hers alone, words and music, expressing a
women's sexuality.

Tapestry rocketed King to the top of the charts, and the album especially connected with young women, who memorized the songs and
pored over its cover. King did not fit the stereotypes rock seemed to
impose on women, "the virgin, the sexpot, and her close relative, the
sufferer." She was, instead, a sort of earth mother. Articles described

the homey circumstances that prevailed when she recorded, how her young daughters ran around the studio during practice sessions, how she labored over the tapestry featured on the back album cover between takes. The front cover, photographed in King's own home, suggested a life not that far removed from her fans', with its "hatch-cover bench and Indian-print curtains" and fat family cat, Telemachus. King gathered her musical friends around her as backup singers, including James Taylor and Joni Mitchell. Her personal story illustrated the way women's lives suddenly opened up. King looked like the "natural woman" about whom she sang, as the carefully straightened hair and shift dresses of early promo pictures gave way to the woman on the *Tapestry* cover, with her wild, curly hair and jeans. More than forty years after its initial release, women still approach her with their personal stories about how it inspired them. It was a cultural phenomenon, coming just as the women's movement was beginning to have its impact on American culture. It changed the way the music industry looked at female consumers.[26]

Tapestry was an unexpected success, selling more copies than any album preceding it and garnering critical acclaim and four Grammy awards. Women loved it and bought it, forcing the industry to reassess their second-class status as music consumers. *Time* magazine noted the impact King had on her female listeners, with her "way of living" that was "worlds apart" from their mothers'. She seemed "genuine," individual, outside the "male-dominated culture," full of "emotional honesty and authenticity," reviewers noted. The album "touch[ed] the elusive common nerve . . . and really affect[ed] people on a personal level."[27] *Tapestry*'s critical and financial success encouraged other female singer-songwriters and gave them cultural space to express a distinctive and modern female point of view through music.

After *Tapestry*, the "sexual politics of consumer marketing" enhanced women's status as performers and audience. Their unconventional choices—later marriage and pursuit of jobs and independence—made them an attractive market segment, even in an industry that still valued males over females. "*Billboard* magazine recently reported the most significant upsurge in female record sales since the popularity of hard rock groups," the *Los Angeles Times* noted in 1973. "Women's music sells," *Time* concluded a year later. The percentage of top-selling albums recorded by females jumped from single to double digits in the early 1970s and accounted for more than a quarter of all top-fifty singles recorded in 1971.[28] Female listeners found a truly resonant voice mapping out an attractively countercultural way of life and romance.

Record companies scrambled to create fresh marketing campaigns aimed at women. An ad for Joni Mitchell's 1970 release, *Ladies of the Canyon*, recounted the story of fictional Amy Foster, twenty-three and "incredibly down" over a recent breakup. Listening to the album, she is consoled and reassured because "there was someone else, even another canyon lady, who really knew." Foster's story identified a familiar experience and modeled a consumer response. Partly by word of mouth and partly through marketing, albums by Mitchell, Simon, and King became touchstones for young women. Simon's producer distributed copies of "That's the Way I Always Heard It Should Be" to receptionists and secretaries at radio stations, figuring that "once women heard it, we had a shot." The first beneficiaries of the women's movement, young, well-educated, and well-off white women, purchased female singer-songwriter music because it offered them an authentic woman's voice and "an alternative to the romance 'script.'"[29]

That alternative accessibly fused contrary elements of the 1960s, free love, the counterculture, and second-wave feminism. Female listeners could hear pleasure, independence, and rebelliousness when Simon declared, "Daddy, I'm no virgin" ("Waited So Long"), and sensuality when she told of a lover who "used to make me moan in bed" ("Carter Family"). Her music legitimated the release from sexual convention that *The Joy of Sex* promised. She moaned the tagline of "I've Got to Have You," written by then-lover Kris Kristofferson, communicating something "so primal and so private that it takes your breath away," the *Rolling Stone* reviewer opined. In each of these songs, the woman was the subject, not the object, modeling her own sexuality, especially her satisfaction. The *New York Times* called Simon "the prototypical, high-achieving urban baby boomer—liberal, 'liberated' and determined to have it all." Her songs were the "pop music equivalent of the diaries of Anaïs Nin or Erica Jong's autobiographical novels," meaningful snippets of sexual expression for young women who had few other compelling female perspectives on modern love.[30]

Female performers' much-publicized biographies and the ways the music establishment talked about them, meanwhile, spoke to the contradictions between sexual freedom and feminism, providing an informal course in feminist consciousness-raising. The common experi-

Carly Simon's Playing Possum *album cover contributed to her sexy and sexual image. Later she would wonder, "What was I thinking?" Photo courtesy of Norman Seeff Productions.*

ence of objectification often bonded female listeners to female per-formers. The music business was almost exclusively male at the top. *Rolling Stone* was a "male oligarchy" that employed women as secre-taries, not record reviewers or reporters. When a female voice sang, record companies and journalists felt no qualms about commenting on the performer's looks and love life. *Rolling Stone* "tortured" (her word) Mitchell by designating her its "Old Lady of the Year" for 1971 and charting her sexual relationships with male singers, even though "I just don't find these things very interesting." One *Rolling Stone* inter-viewer opened an article about Simon by envying her nursing son's ac-cess to her breasts. When she tried to divert the conversation toward her music, another journalist told her that her string of lovers was "what the public wants to know about." Like Mitchell, Simon was "offended" when reporters "ask[ed] about my various affairs" and wished her record com-pany would have chosen a "more ordinary, mundane shot" for her *Play-ing Possum* album cover than the celebrated one of her in a black teddy and boots. "There was no free love," Mitchell recalled. "It came with great strings attached. It was free for men, but not for women, same as it ever was."[31] One did not have to be as famous as Mitchell was to concur with her assessment.

Female listeners connected with the vulnerability female singer-songwriters represented. Polls from the era demonstrate that women were more cautious about their sexuality than were their male peers. In 1975, only half as many female as male first-year college students agreed with the statement, "Sex is OK if people like each other." Young women doubted that men accepted feminism's messages. *Ms.* magazine described "love between equals," but television reporter Betty Rollins wondered, "Where are the men worthy of us?" A 1971 Harris Poll identified a lot of "annoyed women," as the *New York Times* put it, unhappy with the way men treated them. Half agreed that "most men are more interested in their own rather than a woman's sexual satisfaction," and a plurality believed that "men find it necessary for their egos to keep women down." "Ordinary women" reshaped the sexual revolution in the 1970s by expecting mutuality and pleasure from their partners. As Graham Nash, one of Mitchell's lovers, noted, "Women of Joan's generation raised the bar of how men should treat women and how women should treat themselves."[32] No longer pining for marriage or preoccupied with their virginity, a lot of young women sought autonomous sexual and romantic arrangements that still offered them some security, that is, relationships.

The term "relationships" was just beginning to refer to specifically sexual situations in the 1970s. Words like "dating" and "going steady" failed to describe modern youth's behavior. "Dating" was too formal for a generation that moved fluidly from friendship to sex, while "going steady" was for TV teens. "Relationship" better conveyed the sexual and romantic habits of adults, people of marrying age who did not marry. A "relationship," as a *Rolling Stone* article noted, covered "anything from living together to . . . just messing around," nicely noncommittal. A 1973 book on youth sexuality explained that young people "frequently" used the term to describe their encounters with the opposite sex. It implied, the author continued, "sexual activities and other modes of communication" without "formality or ritual." *Mademoiselle* magazine argued that the relationship served as an alternative to the "swinging singles" stereotype of the earlier sexual revolution, a "meaningful, on-going, serial, monogamous" arrangement "between equals." Although Americans struggled to find an appropriate term for it, cohabitation achieved "recognition . . . as a phenomenon in American life" in 1980, a representative from the Census Bureau reported, when that agency began tracking it. By 1977, roughly a quarter of U.S. college students had cohabitated, and about half saw nothing wrong with couples living together without being married.[33] Middle-class youth, who traditionally had a longer period of freedom before fully assuming adult responsibilities, were best positioned to experience relationships.

Joni Mitchell, Carly Simon, and Carole King presented feminist-inspired, countercultural portraits of modern relationships in both their songs and their lives. Simon thought of herself as "a new kind of woman, very strong, very, very liberated, independent," yet conceded that she had been "educated in a way that did not have much space for women's opportunities, except marriage," true of most of her female fans as well. Mitchell's songs, reviewer Timothy Crouse observed, implicitly assumed that "her lover will not give her all she wants." Female singer-songwriters articulated the limits to free love, feminist-style, realism not always present in the earnest pages of *Ms.* magazine, which many young women did not read. Mitchell was "no longer the innocent" but an adult who "had her share of downs as well as ups," one reviewer thought. "Men as well as women can relate to Mitchell's songs," Loraine Alterman suggested, but her work had "a special meaning to all women who are caught in the basic dilemma of knowing they must realize their own potential at the same time they still want to find . . . love."[34] Hearing female singer-songwriters' songs, examining album covers, and reading stories about their favorite singers' personal lives, middle-class young women saw peers "one or two years and a couple of changes" ahead of them constructing satisfying and attainable versions of modern romance.

To the attentive reader of cultural symbols, this new woman was discernibly distinct from the feminist, which enhanced her status for women who wanted more freedom but were leery of being too closely associated with feminism's contentious public face. "Women's lib," Alterman conceded, "put people off" with its "excessive pedantry and zeal." It was "trying to turn women into men," in the words of one poll. King, Simon, and Mitchell liked men, but they challenged norms. They embodied the most socially attractive feminist traits—independence, self-reliance, and sexual confidence. Simon in particular represented a merger between the expressiveness of the women's movement and the license of the sexual revolution. While some feminists found her lyrics too focused on "that old, demeaning dance of courtly love," many young women could relate to her struggles to balance independence and romance. In the popular culture, the feminist quickly assumed unpleasant characteristics, but liberated singer-songwriters pleased men and still asserted their own desires.[35]

Autonomy facilitated the new woman's liberation, and Mitchell's, King's, and Simon's songs and personal stories recognized modern women's changing lifestyle aspirations. In a world before equal pay acts, affirmative action, or feminism, economic inequality pushed women into marriage. A husband, as Beth Bailey has written, served as "the base of the pyramid" on which women could construct their comfortable domestic lives. For increasing numbers of college-educated women, however, husbands were no longer so crucial to their economic futures. By 1980, women surpassed men in the number of bachelor's degrees awarded at American colleges, and more than half of all adult women worked. Two-thirds of unmarried twenty-five-year-old females lived on their own, with roommates, or with a partner.[36] As they moved out of their parents' homes, they relished the freedom of material self-expression, choosing cars, furnishings, clothes, and haircuts that signaled their individuality. Singer-songwriter women provided a set of visual and aural lifestyle clues, whether one chose to project an arty and sexual vibe (Simon) or bohemianism (Mitchell) or wanted to be a natural woman like Carole King.

Mitchell's, Simon's, and King's songs and biographies were part of a growing woman-centered culture shaped by a mainstreamed version of feminism and demographic realities. Single, college-educated working women represented an emerging market segment, one whose members were both unprepared for independent living and, like Simon, culturally conditioned to insecurity. Lifestyle and sexual liberation offered them realizable visions of freedom. The struggling-to-be-liberated woman was the star of Erika Jong's *Fear of Flying* and sitcoms like *The Mary Tyler Moore Show*. She could be seen on Simon's *No Secrets* album cover ("project[ing]," *Rolling Stone* journalist Stephen Davis recalled, "'New Liberated Woman'—in your face") or heard on Mitchell's *Blue*. Although the *New York Times* male reviewer predicted that *Blue* would be "the most disliked of Miss Mitchell's recordings," its theme of relationships and Mitchell's willingness to expose her joys and sorrows made it go-to music for women like Emma Thompson's *Love Actually* character who were still figuring out their own paths between convention and sexual exploitation. "I hear her music in my head," noted actor Edie Falco; "[it is] the soundtrack for my life." Ellen Willis saw *Blue* as a breakthrough for the singer, revealing her to be something more than "the compleat hippie chick": "a woman pursuing her female identity" with "a blend of romanticism and stoicism."[37] Simon's, Mitchell's, and King's autobiographical songs suggested how the modern woman might straddle the line between feminism and the sexual revolution, blending romance, independence, and desire.

Compelling though this culture was for participants, female singer-songwriters did not play on rock music's main stage. If Simon offered young, white, middle-class women a public model of new-style sexuality, she was also, one commentator said, the object of men's "dirty thoughts." Like the *Rolling Stone* interviewer who fixated on her breasts, many men regarded her as "'foxy'—sensual, with-it, blessed with legs that go on forever," a woman who radiated not personal liberation, but sexuality, "a somewhat hard, aggressive, sexy broad." As novelist Angela Carter observed in 1980, "It took about three seconds flat for *liberated* to acquire the sub-meaning of 'promiscuous,'" at least within the more mainstream popular culture.[38] Middle-class women incorporated versions of feminism into their worldviews because they opened up their personal and professional possibilities. Middle-class men, by contrast, might pay lip service to feminism, but it often made them nervous, threatening their heretofore invisible privilege. At the same time that women moved from object to subject on the periphery of rock culture, men solidified their hold on its center, achieving a different version of modernity, one stereotyped as "sex, drugs and rock 'n' roll" and presided over by the hedonistic "cock-rocker." This was more fantasy than attainable reality, a seductive and reassuring promise to men disconcerted by the new attainments of their female peers that they still mattered. Lyrical styles changed once again, so that the reduction of love "simply to physical desire" occurred more commonly. While that was true of "I Feel the Earth Move," when the singer was male, the meaning changed. Female singers made inroads in the early 1970s music business, but most of the time cock rockers dominated the charts, and no one better epitomized the style than did the Rolling Stones. When the Stones' lead singer, Mick Jagger, agreed to sing backup on "You're So Vain," Simon recalled that he was more familiar with her sexy album covers than her music.[39]

Female singer-songwriters could coexist with cock rockers and function as models for women and objects for men, but male singer-songwriters enjoyed no such freedom. James Taylor's female fans saw him as the embodiment of a new man, gentle, sensitive, eager to please them, the kind of man, the popular 1970s stereotype held, not afraid to cry. While the singer had a reputation as a "lady-killer," what made him seductive to women was not his strength but his fragility. Like "no doubt millions of other women across the country," Carly Simon "saw the . . . sensitive side of James." One college student noted that women "all feel sorry for him." Certainly men listened to his music; however, "girls generally outnumber the boys by 2 to 1" at a James Taylor concert, *Time* magazine reported. Taylor lacked "the brazen flash of a Jagger" and, thereby, "incurred the wrath of the hard rockers." In an infamous 1971 piece, rock critic Lester Bangs fantasized about eviscerating him with a broken wine bottle. Bangs thought Taylor "a spoiled rich kid" who "sang like a wimp." Ex-Beatle John Lennon mocked him publicly. Critic Robert Christgau conceded that while Taylor was "intelligent and liberal and good," he seemed to be "leading a retreat" away from rock as well as masculinity.[40] Taylor's self-presentation resonated with modern women and, thereby, undermined men's more hedonistic rock fantasies.

Taylor's male fans tended to be educated and middle class, willing to be some version of the new man he personified, "a Harvard boy in spirit and style," Simon recalled, despite his best efforts to appear otherwise. *National Lampoon's Lemmings*, a 1973 off-Broadway show that spoofed Woodstock, included Christopher Guest's impersonation of Taylor, singing "Farewell to New York City, with your streets that flash like strobes; Farewell to Carolina, where I left my frontal lobes." Guest remembers Simon laughing at the performance but not Taylor, who continually struggled to rise above the stereotype of too-sensitive. While Taylor was the most picked on of the male singer-songwriters, reviewers also went after "pinin' [Paul] Simon," with his "merit badge of sensitivity" and too-enthusiastic embrace of the "poetic status of victim," as one *Rolling Stone* reviewer complained. At the height of the singer-songwriter movement, 1973, Taylor, Simon, Jim Croce, and Jackson Browne were all settled into the most traditional kind of relationship of all, marriage. They wrote songs to their children, shunned the more circus-like elements of the concert arena, and, as one critic said of Taylor, lived "quiet—even middle class" lives.[41] Their public personae

James Taylor represented a new type of seventies man, sensitive and a bit fragile. It was an image that annoyed male rock critics, who thought him a "wimp." Photo courtesy of Photofest.

seemed, thereby, to undermine or threaten the fantasy of the cock rocker that a lot of forerunner males still found seductive.

In truth, Taylor and the other male singer-songwriters hardly modeled much romantic equality. Like male singers of other musical genres in the era, they expressed their uneasiness at the new woman's sexual assertiveness and its impact on them. Although few put it as crudely as Mick Jagger's claim that a woman has "got me by the balls" ("Short and Curlies"), sexual victimization of men by women was a common musical theme of male performers. In "Ready or Not," Browne refashioned the story of meeting his real-life wife into a cautionary tale about a woman's connivance at a man's expense. It began at a bar, where he was "trying to get into her jeans." She followed him home, cooked him dinner, and "the next thing I remember she was all moved in and I was buying her a washing machine." She was pregnant, and Browne's sense that he'd been tricked is palpable. The temptress was a recurring image in male singer-songwriter music, a prostitute or woman at a bar who was so sexually enticing that she took away a man's agency, whether she lured him into "a room where you do what you don't confess" ("Sundown"—Gordon Lightfoot) or "make[s] it easy for a man to fall" ("You Make It Easy"—James Taylor). Assertive womanhood threatened male singer-songwriters' fantasies of free love.

Male singer-songwriters existed in a genre dominated by women, in a space critics regarded as feminized. Consequently, they struggled to redeem their public status as real men. They laced their interviews with symbols of rebellion, expletives, and stories of their sexual exploits and drug habits. This was particularly true of Taylor, who put his ongoing heroin addiction and his two stints in a mental institution at the center of his public biography while downplaying the private schools he attended or the summers he spent on Cape Cod. When a *Rolling Stone* reporter interviewed newlyweds Simon and Taylor, Simon talked about feminism and Taylor called her "a piece of ass," adding that "if she looks at another man, I'll kill her."[42] Still, the public was more likely to be able to list Simon's expansive string of lovers than Taylor's, and her reputation as a sexual woman undercut his macho credibility. The only real power a new man had, as Jim Croce noted in "One Less Set of Footsteps," was the power to take his jeans and go.

Most critics failed to notice male singer-songwriters' attempts to redeem their manhood, focusing instead on what their songs had in common with female singer-songwriters'—their self-absorption. Taylor's famous "Fire and Rain" chronicled the moment when he first learned of the death of a fellow patient in a sanitarium. Its lyrics were almost stream-of-conscious: "I walked out this morning, and I wrote down this song, just can't remember who to send it to." The usually political Joan Baez devoted space on her biggest-selling album, *Diamonds and Rust*, to songs about her son and her relationship with Bob Dylan. Carly Simon wrote about her parents, her siblings, and her childhood friends. Singer-songwriter music was "gentle, melodic, and direct," one commentator has observed, but devoid of "even a millisecond of political consciousness."[43] It reflected on experiences, encounters, and the past in ways that spoke to the luxury of time and selfishness, "tracing our steps from the beginning, until they vanish into the air, trying to understand how our lives had led us there," as Jackson Browne said in "Late for the Sky."

Singer-songwriters' me-ness expressed their privileged status as people with the time and money to partake of that ultimate counter-cultural luxury, finding themselves. It was precisely what made them forerunners. But their self-obsessions also suggested that me-ness rather than we-ness distinguished relationships from the traditional partnerships of marriage. The relationships imagined by these songs enhanced the individual, met his or her physical and emotional needs, and provided a nurturing environment in which to grow—all qualities that discouraged permanence. "We all want to be . . . the one and only in every relationship," Joni Mitchell noted.[44] Unlike the happily-ever-after of marriage, the relationships singer-songwriters—both male and female—sang about were transient. "Love emerges and it disappears," Paul Simon explained in "I Do It for Your Love." Later in the decade, mainstream movies with broader audiences like *Annie Hall* and *The Way We Were* embellished the notion that love did not have to last forever to be meaningful, but singer-songwriters were the first to justify mature love's impermanence. In Carole King's 1970 classic "It's Too Late," the relationship simply ceased to be meaningful to either partner: "Something's wrong here, there can be no denying, one of us is changing or maybe we just stopped trying." "What came between us," Jim Croce wondered in "These Dreams." "Maybe we were just too young to know." Gordon Lightfoot observed in "If You Could Read My Mind": "I don't know where we went wrong but the feeling's gone and I just can't get it back." Earlier teen music was riddled with breakup songs but clearly distinguished bad dating situations from those that culminated in "the chapel of love." In singer-songwriter music, there were no perfect matches or soul mates, and even a song with the title "Forever My Love" (written by Simon and Taylor) acknowledged the sheer unpredictability of romance: "Time alone will tell us, lovers born in May, may grow bitter and jealous, faded and gray."

Critics smirked at the "ruinous self-pity" of these songs but conceded that "there finally aren't any reasons when two people decide to call it quits," a view of failed romance at odds with decades of popular cultural portrayals. Along with another 1970s phenomenon, no-fault divorce, singer-songwriter breakup songs presupposed that perfectly nice people might not stay together forever, erasing the cultural stigma of failing at romance and, thereby, justifying the relationship as marriage's more realistic alternative. Breakup songs soothed and reassured nervous boomers. Like the fictional Amy Foster, who felt better about her breakup after listening to *Ladies of the Canyon*, those who put "It's Too Late" or "If You Could Read My Mind" on the turntable sought the affirmation of their choices that they were unlikely to get from parents or priests. The version of modern romance such songs modeled down-played blame and judgment, instead emphasizing the individual's capacity for rebirth. Joni Mitchell was "able to face her disappointments in love," noted Robert Hilburn, "and deal with them in an instructive way in song,"[45] with sadness and then renewal. Singer-songwriters' breakup songs encouraged young people to learn from their mistakes, make the most of their time alone, and then try again at love. It was a romantic arc both modern and traditional, focused on the self but maintaining distinctive gendered roles. It was the counterculture's version of love projected into a real world where men and women still were not equal.

Singer-songwriter relationship songs confirmed a fairly traditional view of men and women, even in a feminist era that downplayed gender difference. The relationship was culturally understood to be women's domain, a feminist-inspired version of commitment that gave women more romantic control. But their new agency circumscribed what men perceived as the essence of sexual liberation, the freedom to sleep around and the ability to request, as did British rocker Rod Stewart, "Just don't be here in the morning when I wake up" (ironically, from a song called "Stay with Me"). Newer experts supported this vision. "The footloose, fancy free man is an ideal in our society," psychologist Jerome L. Fine noted, whereas women desired "more personal relationships." Pop psychology books, including two with the same title, *The Love Crisis*, emphasized the differences between women's expectations and what men were prepared to deliver, simply assuming men's unwillingness to commit, their desire for multiple partners, and their need "to find themselves." One anthropologist described twenty-two different "types" of men, including those who enjoyed the chase more than the relationship or were afraid of emotion, commitment, adulthood, or women their own ages. Women, of course, were supposed to work around these limits. Modern women scared men, who saw themselves as victims, "the common enemy" of the newly liberated woman, one said at a National Organization for Women forum, entitled to some compensation in return. Singer-songwriter music confirmed what other modern experts believed, that women still had more to gain and lose in relationships than did men.[46]

Thus, even without a legal commitment, women were still culturally defined as the nurturers of men and relationships. In "You Turn Me On, I'm a Radio," Joni Mitchell demonstrated that she knew exactly what her lover did not like: "Weak women [because] you get bored so quick . . .

[and] strong women, 'cause they're hip to your tricks." Her "All I Want" veered from her desires to what she could do for a lover, ending with "I want to make you feel better, I want to make you feel free." "Are you . . . holding some honey who came on to you?," she wondered of a musician who sounded suspiciously like onetime lover Taylor in "See You Some-time." Indeed, by the time the song was released, Taylor was with Carly Simon, who was able to recite the details of his past, in "No Secrets." Male singer-songwriters, by contrast, seemed to fall into relationships by accident and fell out of them just as easily when the open road called or a temptress showed up. "Some child came, you never asked for her to come," Simon justified in "No Secrets," legitimating her spouse's in-fidelity. "That's what you get for loving me," sang Gordon Lightfoot in the song of the same name. Men retained their privilege, power, and fantasies even in the face of a perceived feminist assault. The relation-ship afforded women more freedom and autonomy than did traditional marriage, but it remained an unequal compromise.

Still, the liberated woman represented by singer-songwriter women rebounded from a bad relationship stronger and without guilt. Tradi-tional pop music taught women they were men's helpless victims. "Why don't you be a man about it, and set me free?," begged Diana Ross and the Supremes in "You Keep Me Hanging On." Female singer-songwriters provided another model, a forceful and angry one. The refrain of Simon's "You're So Vain" created a momentary sisterhood as it invited women to sing along, taunting a man with his ego: "You probably think this song is about you, don't you, don't you?" It was not a song of wistful long-ing or passivity. It made clear that the singer had redeemed her self-esteem. Its sassy attitude and what Ellen Willis, no fan of Simon's, called the "good-humored nastiness" in her voice helped make it so popular. Simon's response echoed the message of a 1970s self-help branch par-ticularly aimed at women, assertiveness training, which taught them to articulate their needs and feelings.[47] The assertive woman could take care of herself, negotiating a gendered reality that did not intrinsically benefit her. Of course, in the process, she learned to accommodate to a stalled feminist revolution that left her responsible for her own eman-cipation. Mainstreamed feminism laid the basis for legal equality in the classroom and on the job, but not in the bedroom or the relationship.

The feisty female voice of the liberated singer-songwriter woman soared in the early 1970s but muted rather quickly, just as the women's movement hit its first rough patch. Female performers held the top of the charts for only a few years. King was unable to replicate *Tapestry*'s success; she remarried and followed her husband to Idaho. Mitchell "just couldn't stay in that lonely *Blue* place" any longer. Already an uncomfortable public performer, Simon felt increasingly constrained by her image. Critics pronounced her 1975 release, *Playing Possum*, "rawly and elegantly all about sex," including a cover Sears Roebuck banned, one that prompted a lecture from her mother and rebukes from women on the street. More than either King or Mitchell, both of whom drew boundaries around their personal lives, Simon's willingness to live publicly and, especially, to display her sexuality made her popular with men as well as women, but it objectified her. Singer-songwriter women discovered that surviving in a male-defined musical world was professionally difficult and personally exhausting.[48]

Meanwhile, men artistically reclaimed the right to their fantasies, fantasies that simultaneously applauded and condemned too much female assertiveness and carnality. Relationships that came undone were the musical stock-in-trade of early 1970s singer-songwriters, but older female stereotypes prevailed in two influential 1975 albums, Bob Dylan's *Blood on the Tracks* and Paul Simon's *Still Crazy after All These Years*, both written following divorces. Simon dallied with an assertive hippie chick in "Fifty Ways to Leave Your Lover," while Dylan represented himself as the victim of an aggressive woman on several album tracks. He sounded what columnist Anna Quindlen called the "self-pitying cry of a wounded male chauvinist," which grew louder as the decade progressed. One *Ms.* writer likened it to a popular movie, the phenomenon of "the unmarried man" to be pitied for bearing the personal cost of modern feminism.[49]

The once-expansive horizons of liberation for younger women contracted a bit as the 1970s progressed. Personal growth was more commonly measured by what one woman called the "liberated libido." But when the libido in question belonged to a woman, sexologists noted, more and more men experienced sexual problems. In the 1970s, feminist sexual treatises undermined what Anne Koedt described in a famous piece, "The Myth of the Vaginal Orgasm." Sex researcher Shere Hite also emphasized the importance of the clitoris as the center of female pleasure, which could be just as easily—or more easily—achieved through masturbation as traditional intercourse. As women gained sexual experience and expected pleasure, some men felt threatened or inadequate. Despite a feminist discourse about mutuality and women's pleasure, men still had the cultural dominance to shape the marketplace for music. By the late 1970s, excess rather than sensitivity prevailed in the singles marketplace, and the female singer-songwriters were eclipsed by disco women like Andrea True, a former porn actress who wondered in a 1976 single written by a man, "More, More, More:" "How do you like it?"[50]

Too-assertive female sexuality disturbed not only those men suffering from performance anxiety, but conservatives as well, who thought it threatening to the family. Marriage enhancement movements, mostly faith based, prescribed submissive roles to women, promising they would protect their marriages. Male violence, the news media warned, was on the rise, including within a controversial new category, date or acquaintance rape. The new press for women's shelters, historian Philip Jenkins has noted, suggested "the need for sanctuaries in which women could be protected." As both a novel and a film, *Looking for Mr. Goodbar* featured a main character who was a sweet schoolteacher by day and persistent trawler of singles bars by night and died at the hands of a man she picked up, a cultural warning for women. A police profile of as-yet-uncaptured "Son-of-Sam" killer David Berkowitz suggested he was "shy and odd, a loner inept at establishing relationships, especially with young women," someone so desperate to reclaim his masculinity that he was willing to kill. Experts condemned predatory male sexual behavior, yet laws and customs changed very slowly or not at all. Women too often found themselves blamed for disturbing sexual and gender dynamics, a change that, some insisted, hurt them most of all. The 1982 tongue-in-cheek best seller, *Real Men Don't Eat Quiche*, skewered the sensitive new age man that James Taylor represented as wimpy, weepy, and unattractive.[51]

As a male-defined version of liberation eclipsed its more feminist varieties, women embraced the less-contentious parts of feminism, the legal equality of education and careers, minus the interpersonal possibilities of coequal relationships. Romantic equality, like the other things that happened in the home, shared second-shift work and child care, seemed more fantasy than attainable. Male singer-songwriters helped support the beginnings of a male stereotype familiar to us today, the pleasure-seeking man-child who never quite grows up. Jackson Browne sang about cocaine, and Paul Simon proclaimed himself "Still Crazy, after All These Years," conceding in "Have a Good Time" that "I should be depressed, my life's a mess, but, ah, what the hell."

Singer-songwriters lost popularity with the privileged young middle-class demographic in the second half of the decade. New styles of music emerged—disco, punk, arena rock, and heavy metal—to better capture the public mood.

No single musical genre predominated in the late 1970. Performers like the Stones, David Bowie, and Elton John made the leap to larger venues to capitalize on boomer cash. Such arenas did not suit singer-songwriters unless they amped up their music, consigning them to a never-ending circuit of college towns. Disco was commercially success-ful, much as singer-songwriter music had been, but the style appealed to more marginalized audiences of the working class, African Ameri-cans, Latinos, and gays. It too failed to gain the respect of the music establishment. Middle-class youth dabbled in disco, partly for the erotic pleasures it provided, but working-class males revolted against it with the "disco sucks" movement. Male critics continued to define authen-ticity according to their own class, racial, and gender biases. They pre-ferred—and promoted—rebellious punk rockers and Bruce Spring-steen, whom Jon Landau called "the future of rock and roll." Springsteen fused singer-songwriter tropes with traditionally masculine themes he characterized as "cars and girls." His songs addressed men's declining privilege and the many ways modern society trapped men and limited their options. In "The River," his main character did not enjoy the new-found pleasures of a relationship but experienced only the class-bound consequences after "I got Mary pregnant": "a union card and a wed-ding coat." Women were, one scholar noted, "signifiers of domesticity" to Springsteen, individuals to be "captured and then placed in the home," where the grind of daily life would wear them down.[52] Singer-songwriters represented the broader possibilities of middle-class lives in 1970; Springsteen showed how the bleaker late 1970s economy con-strained the working class.

As 1960s gender and sexual revolutions spread throughout the cul-ture more broadly, the musical tastes of a particular segment of baby boomers mattered less. Although their record sales remained decent, singer-songwriters could not compete with newer artists, and their minimalist style did not speak to people for whom liberation was a flamboyant lifestyle identity. Yet it was equally true that at least some of the interpersonal and sexual values that singer-songwriters modeled for forerunners achieved enough mainstream status that they were in-visibly folded into the culture. The dispersion of the new views Daniel

Yankelovich predicted had come to pass. By the late 1970s, "the rage for self-fulfillment . . . had now spread to virtually the entire US population." Psychologist Eleanor Macklin observed that by 1979, older people asked, "If it's OK for the kids to do it, why not us?"[53] By the end of the 1980s, cohabitation, divorce, and sex outside of marriage were widely accepted norms with clear social etiquettes. A large cross section of Americans experienced relationships.

The norms modeled by singer-songwriters in the 1970s predominate today. Two-thirds of Americans find premarital sex "morally acceptable," and 35 percent do not deem it "important" that a couple planning to spend their lives together marry. According to feminist author Peggy Orenstein, popular culture continues to help younger Americans define their sexual norms, although the medium has changed from music to pornography, where, all too commonly, "women's sexuality . . . [is] a performance for men." Orenstein's argument confirms a shift that happened in the 1960s and, especially, the 1970s, the decline of the ability of traditional authorities to police young adults' sexual mores, replaced by what she calls the "super-peer" of the media.[54] Yet what has happened, she explains, is the illusion of liberation far more than the reality. Seventies singer-songwriters' implicit promises to women of sexual liberation and romantic equality still have not been realized, although today we have the whole Internet with which to comment about—or, indeed, watch—the looks and sexual behaviors of women.

2 : The Look I Want to Know Better

Style and the New Man

Before we see Tony Manero's (John Travolta's) face in the 1977 film *Saturday Night Fever*, we see his shoes. As the sound track starts up ("Stayin' Alive" by the Bee Gees), the camera zooms from the elevated subway tracks to the sidewalk. On the sidewalk, we see two disembodied, well-shod feet moving in time to the beat. The feet stop and one shoe is held up for comparison to another in a shop window. From there, the camera fixes back onto the feet strutting in time to the music. Only then does the shot pan upward to disclose Tony's body and face. As the credits continue to roll, we watch him react to a couple of pretty girls, buy and eat a slice of pizza, and place a shirt on layaway. Finally the music fades and the story begins, revealing that all this happened while Tony was at work. That he dawdled to indulge his private interests suggests a new relationship between him and his job. Tony was not one of Daniel Yankelovich's forerunners. He had a dead-end job he barely performed to support a leisure passion, disco dancing. To convey this side of his identity, he needed not just shoes, but the other accoutrements of a personal style, a look that told others, and especially women, who he really was.

Clothing is but one public expression of "how, where and why cultural standards change," historian Deirdre Clemente has asserted, one that is "profoundly visual and utterly inescapable." So too is it profoundly gendered. For much of the twentieth century, women consumed fashion and "put on style," as Kathy Peiss said of working girls in 1900. Until the 1960s, women used style to attract suitors and, finally, husbands to support them. The pursuit of fashion and beauty branded them as consumers, and frivolous consumers at that, dressed in outrageous hats and heels that hobbled them. Fashion made them selfish as they wielded their husbands' credit cards to gratify their vanity. Too much attention to their looks tended to denigrate women as self-absorbed and superficial.[1]

Their opposites, at least as popularly constructed, were men, whose

John Travolta in the opening credits for Saturday Night Fever, *on the job but still expressing himself through his stylish clothing. Photo courtesy of Photofest.*

wardrobe disinterest signaled their discipline, sacrifice, and maturity. The American male was defined historically by producing, not consuming, and by his job. But the 1960s assaults on traditional gender roles, the sexual revolution, and the difficult 1970s economy together forced the emergence of a new type of man typified by Travolta's Tony Manero and his theatrical look. This new man was not the feminist-defined sensitive one James Taylor struggled not to be. This new man was a consumer. Demarcated not by his income, his profession, or his class status, instead Tony's clothes expressed his lifestyle, his sexuality, *and* his shopping habits. As historian Alice Echols has argued, what made Tony modern was that he was "consumed with consuming."[2] The post-1960s *novus homo* had to become comfortable with fashion in order to hold onto his status in a world substantively changed by the sixties. Like a woman, he needed to learn to express himself through style.

Tony could have let his dead-end job, his contentious family, his Italian roots, or Brooklyn define him. Instead he used dance to convey his inner man. Tony's love of a good time and the skill he demonstrated on the disco floor were partly communicated through what novelist Alison Lurie called "the language of clothes."[3] His white disco suit was iconic, and the pose he struck in that suit remains emblematic of an entire cultural movement. Tony's choices showed off his body and facilitated his dance moves. His attitude was unfathomable to his father, who believed such frivolity was not the purview of real men. What his father failed to understand was that the traditional measures of masculinity, career and the provider-role career facilitated, did not—could not—interest Tony. His path forward in life was separate from his class background, connected, instead, to his leisure time. While previous generations of American men dressed to fit in, donning various sorts of uniforms appropriate for their jobs and roles, in the 1970s men started dressing to stand out. Yet whether resplendent in a white disco suit or clad in some other style, this newly liberated man had to learn to be a consumer of style in order to prove his masculinity.

Until the 1960s, paying attention to looks and clothing were stereotyped as feminine concerns, and shopping was a female activity. Clothing and beauty products shaped a woman's public facade, that necessary first step to catching a husband. Women understood that, as Beth Bailey has written, "the right appearance . . . [was] a matter of skillful consumption," a set of skills mastered and then aimed at men. "The art and science of dress was once a standard part of a girl's education," according to Linda Przybyszewski. Jobs, earnings, and other outward signs of ambition, stability, and maturity, by contrast, marked men. For the first half of the twentieth century, few questioned these gender complements; most Americans regarded them as normal and desirable, biblically ordained, or at least hardwired into men's and women's biological makeups. Courtship, thus, required the display of the skills and qualities that made a good husband or good wife, producing and consuming. Costume reinforced the impression, "associate[ing] a man's occupation and his class," one consumer motivational report commissioned by E.I. Du Pont noted, "with the way he is dressed."[4] Too-flashy male dressing was a red flag, suggesting instability, lower-class status, or, worse yet, a deviant sexuality.

Fashion was an important part of the post–World War II consumer economy. After prolonged economic depression in the 1930s, followed by rationing and uniforms during the war, there was pent-up demand and considerable female enthusiasm for clothes. Christian Dior's 1947 New Look remade Rosie the Riveter into a youthful and feminine creature. The male adjunct to the New Look was the gray flannel suit, as nondescript as the New Look was colorful. No designer created the style. While tweaked a little for the modern era, it was what generations of successful middle- and upper-class American men wore to work. In the 1950s, it was the uniform of more men than ever before, as the ranks of the middle class swelled. These were the corporate armies, men who rode commuter trains from the suburbs and worked in offices. Their cookie-cutter suits signaled making-it in postwar America. But the look's most famous cultural evocation, the title of Sloan Wilson's 1955 novel, *The Man in the Gray Flannel Suit*, suggested its complicated baggage. Wilson's hero, a World War II veteran, was in advertising, a 1950s glamour career. Although he seemed like he had it made, he struggled with his identity. His gray flannel suit repressed those masculine qualities his wartime khakis emphasized.

The gray flannel suit quietly commented on the emasculation of postwar men. Historically, American men who worked with their hands wore clothes that reflected their physicality. Suits symbolized a shift away from the production process itself, away from the factory floor or the farm and toward less physical endeavors. A man in a suit could make a good living, but one that came at the expense of some of his manliness. Gray flannel was what well-behaved, respectable men bought after first consulting their wives. They spent their days pushing papers and their evenings helping with the children. But after World War II, American men felt like they had lost status and authority. Controversial pundit Philip Wylie argued that the "womanization" of the nation had produced a "general male emasculation." Indeed, many cultural representations of the 1950s man suggested he was the prize rather than the hunter. His clothing represented the final step in his emasculation. A wife, a 1959 report commissioned by the Du Pont Chemical Company noted, was a man's "costume consultant who will most likely help to mold, manage, and maintain his wardrobe with ever-increasing fervor."[5]

In contrast to this middle-class corporate man in suit and tie stood the working-class male. Fewer men made their livings using their hands in the 1950s than ever before, although many a unionized working-class male made enough money to partake of the same postwar economy as that of his middle-class peers.[6] Yet in the popular culture, this working-class Joe was a rube, a schemer, or an idiot, personified by TV's Ralph Cramden and Ed Norton (*The Honeymooners*). Cramden, a bus driver who wore a uniform to work, and Norton, a sewer worker whose off-hours attire featured a vest over a T-shirt, generally failed to bring home enough bacon to satisfy their much-lovelier wives. Their wacky clothing, including coonskin lodge caps, conveyed to the audience that these were not really fully matured men but perpetual children.

A new working-class type emerged in the 1950s, the rebel, more dangerous and, thereby, more exciting. Music, movies, and television represented him as alluring because he was crudely male, like *A Streetcar Named Desire*'s Stanley Kowalski (Marlon Brando). "Are you really going out with him," asked a backup singer in the Shangri-Las' 1964 ode to a biker, "The Leader of the Pack," who was undoubtedly dressed like Brando in *The Wild One*: leather jacket, white T-shirt, and blue jeans, the uniform of juvenile delinquents and other troublemakers. T-shirts showed off the rebel's muscles and jeans, and leather suggested that no nine-to-five job tied him down. Rebels dressed for leisure. The few suits they wore owed much stylistically to the wartime zoot suit favored by racial minorities and other rebels. Rock 'n' rollers, Beats, and other expressers of youthful alienation in the 1950s drew their fashion inspirations from the lower class and its more-masculine oeuvre, signaling their unwillingness to become part of that suburban army of men in gray flannel.

If hypermasculine working-class rebels existed on one extreme of the male sartorial spectrum, on the other end were men who dressed up a little too much. Closeted gay men actually dressed to fit in, even as popular culture suggested they overdressed in brocade or velvet. Costume played an important role in cultural definitions of sexuality. At a time when "invert" was still an acceptable term to describe a gay person, many people assumed gay men dressed effeminately or in drag. Consequently, paying too much attention to what one wore just was not masculine in the 1950s. A different kind of fifties sexual outlier, however, challenged that notion, Hugh Hefner's *Playboy* magazine. *Playboy*'s bachelors used fashion in pursuit of heterosexual sex. They dressed not like "sissies," as the magazine's first fashion editor, Jack Kessie, noted, but as "Ivy Leaguers," in well-tailored suits, which highlighted their earning power and made the most of their looks to attract women. The *Playboy* lifestyle required "dazzling consumption," including not just suits, but also well-crafted leisure wear, shined shoes, trimmed hair, and a masculine scent. It emphasized traditional male qualities of formality and respectability. One 1958 survey found that 63 percent of men believed they should wear ties most places outside of their homes.[7]

That was about to change. While the postwar fashion industry devoted most of its attention to dressing growing baby boomers and housewives, designers began to eye the adult male market. *Playboy's* version of male "commodity consumption," including fashion, alongside cars, furnishings, and gadgets, caught on with younger men by the mid-1950s. *Gentlemen's Quarterly*, a "fashion magazine for men," began publishing in 1957, another small sign of the changes to come. Three years later, French designer Pierre Cardin introduced a new silhouette for the suit, a fitted jacket and narrow trousers.[8] Most American men probably did not notice these fashion developments, or if they did, they deemed them effete or impractical. By the mid-1960s, though, it was harder to ignore the new culture brewing across the Atlantic.

Like so many 1960s trends, the new style of male dressing began with the Beatles. Once brought to American shores by the "British invasion" of well-dressed British rock bands, it was hard to miss. The style predated the emergence of the counterculture and so retained much of the formality of earlier public dressing. It was known as "mod," or by the part of London from which it emanated, Carnaby Street, and American magazines and newspapers initially found it amusing but unlikely to cross the Atlantic. Typified by long hair, stylish suits, short boots, fancy shirts, turtlenecks, and vivid colors, its essence was hip, aimed at the male fashion economy's then most desirable consumer, middle-aged men with money and status. In 1965, *Gentlemen's Quarterly* declared the gray flannel suit dead, literally drawing a big X through a photo of a respectable man. The ordinary suit, or as the magazine called it, "conventional garb," was simply too boring for the typical "GQ reader."[9] A year later, a mod-inspired "peacock revolution" for American men was in full bloom.

The peacock revolution brought change to middle-aged, middle-class men's closets. Nudging them toward what might have seemed improbable a decade before was a different group of forerunners than the college students who would soon carry so much clout: rich and public middle-aged men. Once television host Johnny Carson appeared in a high-necked, lapel-free Nehru jacket on the *Tonight Show* in 1968, department stores experienced high demand for the item. High-profile athletes embraced peacock style because its fitted contours showed off their "in-shape bodies," explained the *New York Times*. Soon, even team uniforms changed, as players wanted "custom tailoring and tight pants." Marketing experts credited "our mass media, especially TV," with spreading the word. By 1969, the "peacock revolt arrive[d] on Capitol Hill," prompting public servants to sprout longer sideburns and "rainbow hues." That same year, for the first time, a best-dressed men's list appeared in American newspapers alongside the best-dressed women's one.[10] The first peacocks were traditional male trendsetters. The men who followed them, however, desperately wanted to fit in.

The times made American men "more receptive to new ideas and new trends." For the millions of them whose wives bought their clothes, an estimated 80 percent, wide ties and colorful striped business shirts might not have been their first choice but embellishments supplied them by their wives. Columnist Erma Bombeck updated her "devout slob" of a husband and was surprised to discover she unleashed the clotheshorse within. Like her spouse, most men went willingly to closets full of pastel shirts and wild ties. What took them there was, often, "the aggressive quest for youthfulness that obsessed so many adults," the flowering of the counterculture, the example of masculine heroes like New York Jets quarterback Joe Namath, a desire to seem hip, or a suspicion that such attire made a man attractive to women. Peacocking represented a mainstream version of rebellion that introduced middle-class, middle-aged men to the idea of fashion and the language of clothes. "Men can now look forward to changing fashions as a way of expressing personal individuality that is otherwise lost in the mammoth corporate structure of business hours," explained one commentator.[11]

Supporting middle-aged, middle-classed men's mid-1960s ventures into the world of fashion were social messages that privileged their status as the earners of money. The menswear business nurtured men's new attention to sartorial detail because it meant bigger profits. Economists talked about the positive impact of this fashion revolution on "the marketplace" instead of mocking "male vanity." The *New York Times* interpreted men's willingness to spend on themselves as a sign of a vital economy. As more families entered the middle class, one business journalist noted that "there was more discretionary spending on apparel for men, who traditionally have been the last in the family" to buy clothing. Department stores began to expand their men's departments, and new boutiques emerged catering exclusively to men. Prices rose as well, and ancillary industries developed, all the signs, business experts noted, of a robust domestic marketplace. "The American men's wear retailer . . . [concluded that] maybe fashion was the answer," observed GQ writer Jason McCloskey.[12]

The peacock style offered a form of liberation, in this case from gray flannel, workplace conformity, and the tyranny and emasculation of being dressed by one's wife. In truth, though, it was mainly insecurity that prompted many middle-aged American men to add peacock elements to their wardrobes. The marketplace was starting to change in ways that were beyond their control. The newer emphasis on hedonism and pleasure was foreign to their experiences. Situated on the wrong side of the generation gap, many wanted to feel young, and clothing helped with that. Cashing in on the sexual revolution, or at least the vibrant urban culture encouraged by the 1960s, required a hipper wardrobe. Pundits warned that the women's movement altered the gender dynamic in ways that meant that men looking to impress women could no longer rely on their incomes. As one newspaper columnist explained, women's "equal status in the job market has forced men to compete as equals in the sex market." "We observe with exquisite irony," one fashion expert noted, "that in our era of shifting roles, it is the male who has become the object of sexual delight."[13] For peacocks and would-be peacocks, colorful and stylish clothing was part of an urbane and sexual identity.

Middle-aged men looking to buy a sartorial piece of the 1960s had to learn to adjust to a set of fashion realities their wives had long since mastered. Peacocking required consumer skills and an unfamiliar mind-set. Men had to accept obsolescence, to understand that one did not judge fashion by its longevity or its practicality, but within a particular moment in time. "Men won't wait for a suit to wear out before they discard it for a new fashion," opined *Menswear* magazine's Jack Hyde, a hard idea to accept, especially if one earned the money that paid for the trend. About the time some ordinary men were beginning to consider the Nehru jacket, it was already out of fashion, fashion's Ford Edsel, according to humorist Art Buchwald. Exclusivity, though, only partially defined the new menswear model. Far more important was the "Youthquake" in culture and style and the increasing importance of 1960s-inspired "cool" as a personal trait. According to Thomas Frank, the peacock revolution "successfully and permanently accelerated industry cycles." Fitting in or keeping up with the Joneses was not enough; standing out and being ahead of the trend enhanced a middle-aged, middle-class man's stature in the later 1960s.[14]

What prompted that change was the realization that middle-aged, middle-class men lost status as the sixties unfolded. The size of the baby boom challenged their privilege. Boomers were "the first generation to ever be marketed to" in a serious way. By the early 1960s, their needs, interests, and tastes increasingly drove the consumer economy. Their elders lost the power to set trends, leaving them to play catch-up as their children cycled through everything from hula hoops to the Beatles. Far more than ideological revolutions, a spending revolution left its impact on American society, one much broader than any liberation movement. Youth marched to a different drummer than did their parents. Making sense of the consumer ethos that drove so many younger Americans required that retailers, as one advertiser noted, "begin to deal realistically with this historical shift which is changing the whole social-sexual-political nature of life."[15]

"The impact of youth on America is everywhere," a business reporter observed, "in hair styles, clothes, music, advertising, business," inverting the traditional generational hierarchy. Young people might earn less money than did their parents, but they had a great deal of disposable income, $17 billion by 1970, and more willingness to spend it on themselves. The kinds of practical purchases that tied up their parents' income at their ages—mortgages and car payments and new appliances—were irrelevant to them since they, on average, waited longer to pass the traditional milestones of middle-class adulthood. Youth were harbingers of a new 1960s-inspired consumerism. They wanted experiences rather than things, which allocated their resources differently. One pollster assessed them as concerned with the "functional aspect" of possessions rather than the "status of owning them." An advertising executive noted that his colleagues needed to adjust their pitch to sell things, stressing novelty, pleasure, and "immediate, short-term gratification."[16] Young people's money was a constantly moving target, spent on travel, entertainment, and adventures. Big chain stores and places where parents shopped, the Establishment's economy, were, to borrow youth's word, uncool. And to many younger men, peacock fashion was a faux rebellion.

Younger men assimilated mod fashion before their elders did but quickly modified it in response to the counterculture. To many American youths, the "Carnabetian army" of mods marched in lockstep rather than with individuality, "pursuing all the latest fads and trends," as the Kinks sang in their 1966 hit, "Dedicated Follower of Fashion." As Deirdre Clemente has argued, the informality of the American wardrobe already owed much to college students, who helped to popularize soft collars, sweaters, shorts, and pajamas. In the late 1960s, those earliest forerunners resisted Carnaby Street's formality and artificiality while incorporating versions of its expressiveness. Writer Tom Wolfe noted that "funky chic," the look of "well-to-do college students," prevailed on college campuses, or even "radical chic" when the rebels were bolder. What distinguished these looks from the mod one was their emphasis on individuality. Hippie clothing was eclectic, scrounged, created, or acquired at secondhand stores. In *The Greening of America*, sociologist Charles A. Reich argued that youth, practitioners of a new way of thinking he called Consciousness III, chose clothing that was "functional, . . . earthy and sensual," expressing freedom and "a wholeness of self." In Reich's conceptualization, these new pioneers rejected consumerism and status hierarchies, donning clothes that reflected those values. "The Now People," as one ad man titled a report on American youth, lived for the moment, bringing "excitement, energy and hopefulness" to the marketplace. When they shopped at all, younger trendsetters got their clothes at unisex boutiques with names like Emotional Outlet or The Conspiracy—as one Establishment advertising man called it, "their own exclusive buying environment."[17]

Crucial to the young male's stylistic identity was a pair of jeans. Jeans conjured working-class rebels. Growing up, high school students heard their parents' and principals' complaints about them, that they were sloppy and associated with bums and hooligans. Those qualities, of course, made jeans attractive to youth. Reich, for instance, waxed eloquent over the meaning of the bell-bottom jeans that marked the first of many denim trends to come: "They express the body, as jeans do, but say much more. They give the ankles a special freedom as if to inviting dancing right on the street. . . . No one can take himself entirely seriously in bell bottoms." Young men quickly assimilated the consumer nuances of jeans' expression. While playground denim could be purchased at the kind of practical places where mothers bought their boys pants (Sears and Roebuck or J.C. Penney), the most authentic jeans came from Levi Strauss. The company's history symbolized adventure—it was founded in San Francisco after the California gold rush. Known by a number, 501 jeans were straight-legged with a button fly, sized not in conventional ways, but by waist and length, measurements displayed on the back waistband. A bright orange tag sewn into the back pocket seam made Levi's quickly identifiable. The brand was headquartered in the center of the hippie subculture, San Francisco, and was explicitly marketed to youth, including via a set of radio advertisements by another San Francisco product, the psychedelic rock group Jefferson Airplane. Beginning in 1969, they sold at a store whose name reflected its target audience, the (generation) Gap.[18]

Jeans, however, were a less controversial expression of individuality for younger men in the late 1960s than another part of their public style, long hair. The Beatles made long hair popular before mid-decade, which is to say before the hippie look existed. Their "moptops" challenged fathers' notions of manliness and proper grooming, and older men's reactions only got stronger as the hair grew longer in the late 1960s. The fashion establishment liked the look, and mothers asked barbers to give their young sons "John-John" cuts, named for John F. Kennedy Jr. But to many traditional male authority figures, the look said hippie or worse. "It is often impossible to tell the difference between the sexes," one commentator complained. Hair length became the "surface symptom" of a generational battle between fathers and sons because fathers associated trim hair "with the middle-class tradition of the good guy," while their sons often connected it to the corporate world, the military, and other Establishment institutions they despised. Even warnings that "in the adult world . . . the clean-cutter always gets the job" failed to impress most young longhairs. A lot of young men enjoyed the reaction longer hair triggered from their elders and knew that the look gave them generational credibility. Younger women, it was said, liked the look, which to them stood for "understanding, honesty, masculinity, warmth."[19]

In the second half of the 1960s, clothes and hair were sites of the most common generation-gap battles between authority and youth. As the hippie look trickled down from college campuses to high schools and even middle schools, boys joined girls in challenging school dress codes for the right to wear forbidden looks. While girls wanted to be able to wear pants, boys pressed to grow out their hair and wear beards, mustaches, jeans, and that other counterculture symbol, the sandal. By 1969, one-third of all American high schools had weathered dress-code battles. In response to student protests, authorities generally caved. The idea of self-expression through style received Supreme Court validation with the *Tinker v. the Des Moines Independent School District* case in 1969, which affirmed the right of students to wear armbands to protest the war in Vietnam.[20] Costume rebellion became the lowest common denominator of protest, the gateway drug of rebellion that provided a blueprint for other kinds of fights against authority. The seemingly simple act of asserting the right to wear what one pleased shaped a generational identity around sixties values as much as music or antiwar protest did.

The appeal of dress rebellion was its ease and its safety. It was the simplest piece of the sixties to incorporate into one's life. It united young men of different political perspectives, classes, and races. It conveyed both individuality and a generational identity. Members of the American Indian Movement wore denim jackets and headbands when they took over Alcatraz in 1969. Black Panthers covered their Afros with black berets when they marched. Young evangelical Christians looked like Sunday school portraits of Jesus in their beards, long hair, and sandals. Assembly-line workers in "shoulder-length hair, beards, Afros and mod clothing" dressed, *Newsweek* thought, like they worked in "an industrial Woodstock." The new casualness suited young people, and the vigor with which they pursued sartorial freedom expressed their confidence that they would prevail in a society that would accommodate to their tastes and preferences rather than vice versa. As they began looking for jobs, what they wanted were workplaces, as Yankelovich put it, where "conformity in dress/politics [was] not required." Not only did younger men reject gray flannel; they rejected its pedigree, "clothing [that] has been instantly processed and homogenized by the Corporate machine," as the editor of the alternative fashion newspaper *Rags* explained.[21]

Yet anti-Establishment costuming was complicated. The allure of hipness converted heretofore ordinary products, like furniture and kitchen equipment, into "fashion items," bringing a playful new aesthetic to America. Soon, stylish houses boasted shag carpeting, avocado green bathroom fixtures, foil wallpaper, and orange plush beanbag chairs. Informality ruled, as more and more Americans concluded that "it is not sinful to be comfortable." Suburban lifestyles, youth rebellions, and the counterculture took the starch out of styles, rendering them casual, functional, and expressive. Sportswear was "it," explained one New York retailer, "a way of life . . . and the fastest growing merchandise in the store." The Nehru jacket was old news by 1970, but the qualities it signified were not. It was not a workplace look but one geared for nightlife and fun. Its wearer sought to be, as the 1960s song declared, "in with the in crowd." "Casual style," Deirdre Clemente has asserted, "fundamentally changed the relationship between our clothes and our bodies."[22] When the New York Radical Women set up a "freedom trashcan" on the boardwalk in Atlantic City, feminists tossed in their bras and girdles. Soon the absence of a bra equated with liberation. In much the same way, men embraced softer, freer, and more comfortable alternatives to the suits they were supposed to wear. The highly stylized peacock look of the middle-aged, fashion-conscious male out on the town collided with the comfort and convenience of the counterculture look.

Watergate further undermined corporate-inspired formality. The parade of neatly dressed, short-haired Nixon White House aides summoned to testify before the Senate Watergate Committee in the summer of 1973 proved that a respectable package did not guarantee that the man inside was honorable. Nixon adviser H. R. Haldeman epitomized a look many fathers had extolled as clean-cut. But by the 1970s, his signature crew cut looked, as *The Mary Tyler Moore Show*'s Rhoda (Valerie Harper) noted, like what a TV criminal wore "on his way to the electric chair." "Nixon's stupefying conventional suits" conveyed too much ambition laced with a corrupt and outdated belief system. When Nixon resigned, his "full-dress confession . . . suit" also disappeared, replaced by Ford's "more cheerful" wardrobe of "suits in big plaids, . . . white dinner jacket with winglike lapels and . . . a Western-style cocktail suit," which was so "corny," the *New York Times* reported, as to make "serious tailors blush."[23]

Ford's ascension to the U.S. presidency in the summer of 1974 represented the triumph of 1960s style. Unlike Nixon, who clung to fashion anonymity, the new president expressed himself with mainstream versions of modern peacock-inspired suits, colorful shirts, and wide ties. The overall impression was of approachable middle-American solidity. "No airs for good old Jerry," noted the *New York Times*. Ford also displayed the "chief point of [tonsorial] change," the longer sideburn. The new president seemed so approachable and ordinary that his advisers recommended a more "presidential" style during the 1976 election.[24] Whether decked out in suits or casual wear, however, the electorate could easily distinguish between the disgraced president and his successor, for they were increasingly skilled at reading the language of clothes.

Hanging in the new president's closet was a garment that found its way into ordinary men's closets as well, the leisure suit. Ford was, *Rolling Stone* judged, "probably the first president of the United States ever to wear a leisure suit," which reporter Joe Klein snidely asserted was the perfect attire for courting faux-hipsters, "who strain to appear informal in their expensive sports clothes." The leisure suit's origins are unclear. Some traced it to British sporting attire, others to Los Angeles designers, and still others to Yves Saint Laurent. The style consisted of a jacket and pants, often made of a softer manufactured knit. The jacket was unconstructed, without darts or vents or padding, shaped more like a safari jacket than a suit jacket, its cuffs capable of being rolled back like a shirt. The leisure suit's color palate was bold, bright greens, dark oranges, and light blues. Leisure suits were not worn with ties but with casual shirts or turtlenecks. The look caught on quickly and spread like wildfire. Even John T. Molloy, author of the 1975 book *Dress for Success*, found the style "perfectly acceptable attire . . . if it is worn only for leisure."[25]

But the leisure suit's ubiquity suggests that its informality was not just suited to one's off-hours. A 1976 study found that 65 percent of offices no longer required that employees wear ties. "The traditional business suit—matching coat and pants—is an endangered species in the office," warned one observer. Leisure suits were comfortable, cheaper, and easier to maintain. They came in a variety of colors and fabrics and price points, "everything from those plastic-looking polyester knits to denim to the finest wool gabardines," promised one fashion writer. The leisure suit and all it represented spoke to older American men for a variety of reasons. It had nothing to do with "bizarre hippie clothes," one industry spokesman promised, but was a look "traditionalists, mostly over 35," donned without feeling foolish. The outfit's wearer "[did not] have to be a hairy-chested Sonny Bono or work at a rock FM station" to find a leisure suit useful, another commentator promised. It liberated ordinary middle-aged men from "the shackles of uniformity." It was an easy, nonthreatening way a middle-aged man could present himself as someone with a "varied lifestyle" who wanted to be "practical and comfortable."[26] The leisure suit was perfect for the man beginning to define himself by his hobbies and interests rather than his job. It had no class associations, existing in the many new public leisure spaces where Americans might gather.

The leisure suit could only exist because Middle America already coveted a sixties value that feminists, hippies, and activists alike embraced, freedom. Its very name revealed what an increasingly central aspect of life leisure time and its individualized choices had become. Daniel Yankelovich noted that by the 1970s, the "mainstream majority" craved "excitement and sensation" in their personal lives, just like his forerunners of a decade before. They wanted to travel and "pursue personal interests." "Play hard" became the rest of the phrase that followed "work hard." Facilitating this assimilation were empty nests freeing up baby boomer parents financially and giving them time to follow their adult children into a tantalizing new world filled with trips to Europe, tickets to plays, fondue parties, movies at revival theaters, and weekend getaways. The REI (Recreational Equipment Inc.) cooperative posted an eightfold sales increase between 1969 and 1970 as more Americans tried camping, backpacking, and hiking. The average American spent more time at movies, dancing, and visiting friends in 1974 than in 1966. The leisure suit was at the center of "an increasingly important, emerging new category" of men's clothing, the apparel men wore when they were not on the job.[27]

The leisure suit had notoriety as well as popularity. Many people, especially younger people, scorned its polyester variants, its loud colors, and what it represented. In the popular culture, it became the uniform of middle-aged men who fancied themselves sexy or cool, especially when accessorized with white shoes and a matching belt. Trend-setting younger Americans mocked the leisure suit, but manufacturers recognized its popularity. Wide availability, particularly at the cheaper stores in suburban malls, rendered the style tacky, even as a broad segment of American males incorporated versions of leisure suits into their wardrobes. At some point, the item became both a joke and a stylistic influence because, as one young entrepreneur noted in 1970, there was money to be made "exploit[ing] middle-class people who affect the idea of hip."[28]

Younger men might mock their elders' leisure-wear choices, but the informality at its foundation so drove the fashion economy that in 1973 Levi's had to start rationing the wider-legged flared jeans youth craved. In 1975, there was an international denim shortage. As "repudiating the establishment" by wearing jeans became a commonplace act, stylish youth struggled to express themselves uniquely. Patches, embroidery, and careful fading might personalize jeans, but whether "bleached, recycled, embroidered, painted, [or] elevated to high fashion," they remained "uniform attire" for teens and young adults. Levi's sales increased 80 percent between 1973 and 1975, reflecting the baby boom's critical mass, making the company's name as generic as Kleenex or Coke. The biggest seller for the company remained its 501 men's jeans, but Levi's also made bell-bottoms and sportswear, including denim jackets, and it was not clear how many 501 purchasers were female.

Denim had entered the American mainstream, not as work clothes or rebel wear, but as a fabric for skirts, pants, purses, hats, even suits.[29]

The ever-expanding demand for jeans tempted other manufacturers to pursue the youth market. The challenge for them was that except for the occasional brand that successfully presented itself as hip (like Levi's), youth remained skittish about big corporations and other Establishment symbols. Some rejected consumerism for environmental reasons. "I have moved away from name brands," one Houstonite told marketers—Levi's excepted—because he was "rebellious" when it came to participating in a "dehumanize[d]" system. *Cheap Chic*, a popular 1975 book, spurned "corporate marketing and designer labels. It was about the product of the adventure, the romance and the mystery and the shape and the textures: the silk-road dream of an entire generation." Young people joined co-ops or swapped goods; housemates borrowed one another's clothing. Boutiques sprang up "like McDonald's and Dairy Queen food franchises," but they could just as easily alienate as please picky young shoppers. Small-scale "hip capitalists" acquainted with the craftspeople who manufactured their goods best profited from 1960s revolutions without appearing to capitalize on them. The style was "small, comfortable, turned-on, tribal centers where everything was groovy and nobody got hassled." At that center of 1960s protest, Berkeley's Telegraph Avenue, street vendors were required to make their own merchandise, symbols of an alternative economy the Establishment could not crack. Recycled jeans piled in cardboard boxes sold like hotcakes at Cosmic Jeans, a few blocks away. "Classic symbols of success" alienated youth, according to the creative director of one top New York advertising agency, who believed that young people would not buy products pitched as symbols of "affluence and snobbism." Anyone trying to sell to youth, he advised, needed to respect the unspoken language of clothes, because "if you're selling last year's values, you're not going to go far in this business."[30]

This was hip capitalism. Thomas Frank explains that "no longer would Americans buy to fit in or impress the Joneses, but to demonstrate that they were wise to the game, to express their revulsion with the artifice and conformity of consumerism." Hip consumers imagined themselves as rebels. Comfort, convenience, pleasure, and expressiveness governed purchases—or so young people believed. Generational identity was a central feature of hip capitalism, conveying difference, trendiness, and rebellion. Yet, as Frank and others have noted, the "hip" in hip capitalism was generally less important than the capitalism part. While Yankelovich's forerunners might be able to afford the time, travel, and money necessary to stay ahead of any fashion curve, the larger number of consumers, including the younger half of the baby boom, could not. They were more interested in the end result. They were just as easily taken in by marketing ploys as were their leisure-suited elders. Moreover, as the *New Haven Register* noted, there were dozens of "Aquarian Robber Barons" out there to separate young people from their money.[31]

Whatever their conceits, even forerunners were not immune to fashion trendiness. On the very first Earth Day (April 1970), a store in New York City opened to sell the negative-heeled shoes created by a Danish woman named Anne Kalsø. Christened Earth Shoes in honor of the occasion, the shoes were supposed to mimic a foot walking in sand, realigning the spine, while the wide toe box was comfortable and freeing. The shoes were "squarish, unadorned, [and] unisex," an "antifashion fad," the very antithesis of an Establishment shoe. The company initially did no advertising but relied on word of mouth. Like Levi's, their popularity spread through peer networks, acquiring must-have significance. By 1974, Earth Shoes had become a full-blown craze, despite the brand's high price tag and podiatrists' repudiation of its health claims. Celebrities like Olympic swimmer Mark Spitz and actor Peter Fonda snapped them up in specialty stories devoted to them, mainly in college towns. In some stores, there was a monthlong wait to purchase a pair of Earth Shoes. By 1976, they were the most popular shoe in the country, imitated by perhaps a hundred different shoe companies.[32]

The Earth Shoe proved that younger men were as vulnerable to fashion trends as their elders, seduced by the idea of expressing their values through their footwear. More recent footwear designer Manolo Blahnik called the Earth Shoe "the first shoe to make a social statement." Some consumers thought them worth the money, generally less for their comfort than their statement. Earth Shoes tacitly signaled a person's familiarity with trends and the ability to negotiate an alternative marketplace. They equated with hip capitalism. "Most of our shop owners," explained the owner of the original New York Earth Shoe outlet, "as well as customers, are into things like yoga and vegetarian eating." There was an element of rebelliousness to Earth Shoes. Some couples took delight in getting married in them; while the basic ugliness of the shoe demon-

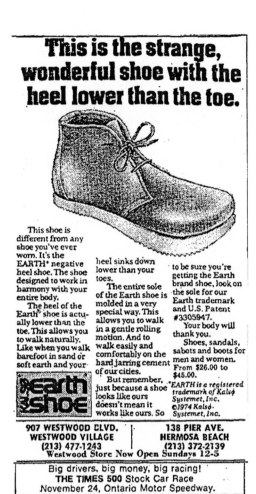

Earth Shoes emphasized a comfortable, natural, and exclusive walking experience rather than just selling shoes. Ad courtesy of Earth Inc.

strated one's contempt for traditional fashion. The product was also one of the first shoes to market the exact same product to both genders.[33]

Earth Shoes' immense popularity signaled a fundamental transformation of the men's shoe industry. Heretofore, most men found a brand of shoes that suited their needs and stuck with it. The average man owned three pairs of shoes, one-third as many as the average woman. The crucial difference between the men's and the women's shoe industries was style—women's changed seasonally and men's changed little. But with casual wear overtaking business wear for men, consumers needed a wider range of shoes. The market for men's shoes began to mimic women's.[34] Since Earth Shoes purported to be about comfort and

"New 'Earth Shoes'?"

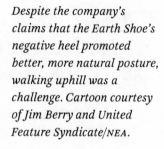

Despite the company's claims that the Earth Shoe's negative heel promoted better, more natural posture, walking uphill was a challenge. Cartoon courtesy of Jim Berry and United Feature Syndicate/NEA.

lifestyle rather than fashion and status, male fashion resisters avoiding conformity and capitalist exploitation willingly purchased them.

In the end, though, youth's Earth Shoes craze was very much like the rapid rise and fall of the peacocks' Nehru jacket nearly a decade before. While a forerunner in Ann Arbor or Princeton might have easy access to Earth Shoes and the cash to pay for them, a teen in a small town in Iowa likely had neither and so opted for easy-to-come-by knockoffs. Trend followers were less interested in the pedigree of their shoes; so long as the end result looked like Earth Shoes, they felt cool. American companies quickly exploited the style. Forced by copycat competition to expand and begin advertising, the Earth Shoe company had to "go after the non-user" with new styles and colors, touted on television ads. A new distributer of the footwear formalized relationships with independent dealers, requiring more businesslike practices. While "the stores may not have been the hippie communes that other shoe dealers considered them," the *Washington Post* noted, "they weren't Thom McAn [a mall shoe-store chain] either." The company grossed $14 million in 1975, but once the imitations emerged, that was the "end of [the] marketing exclusive." In the fall of 1977, the Earth Shoes company filed for bankruptcy.[35]

Earth Shoes' demise failed to end youth's alternative footwear obsession. Many new brands emerged: Birkenstocks, Shakti shoes, Interplanetary Soles, and Mobe's, to name a few. Birkenstocks came from Germany; Shaktis were marketed by American Sikhs and promoted as "good for the sole." Both featured foot beds that molded to a wearer's feet, a quality that quickly spread to copycats, although Birkenstocks' cork sole was patented. What set these brands apart were their countercultural reputations, unisex styling, and alternative marketing plans. Like Earth Shoe dealers before the company attempted to go mainstream, franchise arrangements were loose and stores small, reassuring purchasers that they got something both relatively unique and funky. The vice president of the Shakti Shoe Corporation, for example, was Gurusher Singh Khaisa, aka Morris Finer, a turbaned twenty-five-year-old Sikh convert. Each pair of shoes he sold came with a brochure promising that the footwear drew on the wisdom of ancient yogis. Birkenstocks could not be obtained at the mall, only in specialty stores near college campuses. The shoes, like the other brands, offered "an intelligent alternative for those who care more about how their feet (and bodies) feel than how they look."[36] Half a century later, the name "Birkenstock" still informally symbolizes a counterculture it postdated by almost a decade.

The appeal of Birkenstocks was that they conveyed to those in the know a statement about who the wearer was. They were what novelist Herbert Gold called "California pop artifacts," a must-have item for those younger men seeking to project an alternative vibe. Early adopters spread the word, but the price maintained exclusivity; and, unlike Earth Shoes, the Birkenstock Company was successful at fending off imitators. Once it became clear that men would buy shoes to be trendy or cool, mainstream companies introduced new lines of fashion-forward men's shoes pitched as rebellious or modern. "A whole new way of walking," promised an advertisement for Padrino platform shoes, whereas Dexter urged buyers to "join the Dexter movement for the abolishment of drab, dreary, old fashioned, discombobulated, depressing, outdated footwear."[37] Yet, ultimately, no shoe would carry as much status as a corporate product, the running shoe.

Running was one of the biggest self-enhancement crazes of the 1970s, surprising commentators overwhelmed by both the number of runners and their "fervor," which *Time* magazine assessed as more

overzealous than that of "adherents . . . [of] encounter-group therapy."
Running was a logical outgrowth of the counterculture's focus on nature and the self. It encouraged health. Proponents touted its spiritual side: the endorphins released on a long run, the opportunity to be
alone with one's thoughts, the nonlinear thinking it promoted, which
some likened to meditation. Running, one paper declared, "has taken
on a cult following." Even though football, baseball, and basketball remained immensely popular in the 1970s, those professional team sports
were million-dollar businesses and spectator sports for most. Golf, with
its upper-class associations, could not be an alternative sport for nonconformists. Running was outsider President Jimmy Carter's sport of
choice, although the one time he ran a ten-kilometer race he collapsed
in front of photographers. Jogging and running became alternative
sports venues and races places to feel good about yourself while bringing home a T-shirt that told others how you spent your free time. Like
Tony Manero's disco togs, running offered individual benefits as well as
providing an immediately recognizable identity.[38]

Track suits and nylon running shorts started as runners' gear but
quickly became commonplace leisure looks. At decade's end, running
shoes were outselling all other footwear, as indispensable to the younger
man's fashion statement as his pair of Levi's. By 1979, there were 25
million runners in the United States, plus another 10 million people
who did not run but wore running shoes. While cheap canvas sneakers
could still be had at Sears or the Thom McAn shoe chain, at mid-decade
serious runners and status seekers purchased German imports, Adidas
shoes. Adidas looked different from other brands of running shoes,
distinguished by three stripes on each side of the shoe. The company
carefully guarded its look from imitators, forcing McAn's "striper" to
add a fourth stripe. "I knew—all kids knew," recalled one runner, the
difference between Adidas and Stripers, suggesting that even the very
young discerned status differences their elders might miss. Adidas also
made shorts and track suits, clothing to help you "look nice when you
run," said one running coach, and "make you feel a little better about
yourself." Those same items could also make you feel good about yourself even if you didn't run. The distinctive three-stripe styling was so instantly recognizable that everyone wanted to wear it. "The cult of equipment," the *Chicago Tribune* announced early in 1977, "has begun," and
no part of running equipment was trendier than "the hottest 'life-style-
indicative' footgear since the Earth Shoe," the running shoe.[39]

Berry's World

"You're not wearing the right kind of shoes OR the right kind of outfit — where do you get off running?"

© 1978 by NEA, Inc.

Running required its own set of accoutrement and shoes in the 1970s, an acknowledgment that the act of running was a public performance of sorts. Cartoon courtesy of Jim Berry and United Feature Syndicate/NEA.

Obsolescence was a crucial part of the running costume. Annual races generated new T-shirts each year. Publicly recognized runners began endorsing their own lines of shoes. While previous brands of sneakers, like Keds, looked the same year to year, running shoe companies innovated, not for style, but to enhance performance, adding "design and state-of-the-art technology." That motivation, like Earth Shoes' ugly comfort, offered young anti-Establishment types legitimate reason for repeatedly purchasing shoes, even if, sometimes, it was only a justification for acquiring the newest, trendiest, product available. If, as marketers believed, younger consumers sought experiences rather than possessions; running shoes provided both an experience and a tangible status item. Like other consumer goods in the 1970s, the cost of clothing and shoes kept climbing, but Americans were willing to spend more on them. What they paid for was not just a shoe, but visual evidence of their passion. The average single American male worked fewer hours in 1975 than in 1965 and spent more time on individual recreational pursuits.[40] So when an American company, Blue Ribbon Sports, of Beaver-

ton, Oregon, produced a running shoe with a new type of sole beginning in 1974, millions of Americans were ready and willing to snap up
the item.

"Every religion needs its creation myth," *Runner's World* magazine explained, and Blue Ribbon Sports, manufacturer of Nike shoes, brought
together "running and tech." University of Oregon track coach Bill
Bowerman invented Nike's springier, road-gripping bottom using his
wife's waffle iron and put it on a shoe nicknamed the Waffle Trainer,
bright blue, with a trademark yellow "swoosh" on the shoe's side. The
shoes were more expensive than shoe-store knockoffs but not as expensive as Earth Shoes or "Birkies." Suddenly, everyone wanted the shoe,
including President Carter, who ran his ill-fated 10K in them. There
was plenty to like about Bowerman's anticorporate story, including the
fact that Nike was an American-made brand while its rival, Adidas, was
imported. Among runners, though, it was Bowerman's protégé, Steve
Prefontaine, who really sold Nikes. Pre, as he was commonly known,
was not only a fine runner but the epitome of a countercultural rebel.
Shaggy-haired and mustachioed, he challenged the sports establishment, lived in a trailer, partied hard, and, ultimately, died young in a car
crash. Pre "helped to give personality to the young company." He served
as "the living, breathing embodiment of what we were trying to create,"
explained Nike cofounder Phil Knight. His marketing style, noted the
man who replaced him at Blue Ribbon Sports, conveyed "a whole different attitude." Nike's consumer strategy enabled the company to capture
one-third of the vast running shoe market by 1979.[41]

Once younger men discovered that they could buy shoes that revealed their avocation from companies that seemed to "get" them, they
started to buy other items of apparel as well. As new looks trickled down
from early adopters to more casual consumers, the pedigree became
less important, especially since knockoffs were cheaper. Once-exclusive
brands either entered the mainstream or risked being co-opted by
copies sold at cut-rate chain stores. But as looks mainstreamed, they
ceased to conjure rebellion quite so distinctively. Levi Strauss and Company expanded "to a leisure wear manufacturer for the entire family,"
out of the Gap and into department stores. As Americans made leisure
a priority and used leisure clothing to help construct identities, denim
lost much of its rebellious reputation, ultimately symbolizing casualness.[42]

While the Levi Strauss Company dominated the market for denim,

French designers worked their influence on the product, offering alternatives to the unisex 501 in the later 1970s. American designers followed suit, branding their pants with their names across the back pocket: Calvin Klein, Jordache, Gloria Vanderbilt, and Ralph Lauren. Those men and women who shed Levi's 501s for designer jeans chased a different vibe than did the more-rebellious hippie of the 1960s, that of leisure and pleasure. Being tighter, the new pants were less comfortable than 501s. So-called designer jeans emphasized the wearer's sexuality. They came in different colors and luxurious fabrics and were marketed as lifestyle enhancements. "Is there a particular look being worn for roller-disco skating?," a young man queried the *Los Angeles Times* male fashion expert. Advertising suggested there was, Jordache jeans, the look "you want to know better," as the slogan promised in an ad set in a roller disco. Jordache manufactured jeans for men and women. Three young brothers owned the company, Joseph, Ralph, and Avi Nakash—they fused their names and added the "che" to sound French. They admired Levi's quality but felt that the "functional jean" lacked style. "We wanted a dressy jean," Avi Nakash explained.[43] Jordache advertised relentlessly, associating itself with lifestyle freedom and sexuality. Its most famous print ads featured men and women in skintight jeans and nothing else, the women's arms placed strategically across their breasts. Ads focused on derrieres to reveal the stitched name, Jordache, and the horse's head that was the company's logo. Plenty of American men did not succumb to the pitch. Others, however, bought Jordache jeans, recognizing the power of clothing to wordlessly convey to others—especially women—who they wanted to be.

Designer jeans reflected a different part of the sixties mentality, less anti-Establishment, more pro-sexuality. The unisex hippie look of the late 1960s and early 1970s lost favor by the late 1970s. The new style showed off a changing male body. Earlier in the decade, the ideal male figure for jeans was singer James Taylor's, a "long, lean, poetical stalk of a man," in wife Carly Simon's eyes, with his "long, lean legs" and "wishbone-slim" body. Taylor was thin but not muscular, and his appeal was his waifishness. The ideal young man of the latter 1970s, by contrast, had a mop of curly, possibly even permed, hair and wore his shirts fitted, with more than just the top button open in order to show off his medallion or gold chain and his hairy chest. His jeans were equally tight, oftentimes highlighting what was known familiarly as his "package," his genitals. This new man's presentation was deliberate, and his identity was more consciously masculine; but neither his job nor his income conveyed that masculinity. Instead, it was his energy. He was fit from biking or running or dancing or going to the gym. He was fit for looking good and having fun. He was ready for sex with the new, liberated woman whom singer-songwriters had helped to popularize.[44]

The sexual revolution reached what seemed a public peak in the late 1970s. Younger boomers, old enough to have consumer independence, proved more willing than their elders to follow a fashion establishment reinvigorated by new trends. In the popular culture, sexy blondes reigned: Suzanne Summers, Farrah Fawcett, Loni Anderson. In imitation of these women who excited men, young women scrambled out of unisex jeans and Earth Shoes and into designer jeans or clingy polyester disco dresses and Candies, high-heeled sandals. For both men and women, liberation from traditional gender roles revolved more and more around sexuality. The jacket and tie that men who were good husband material wore in 1955 made no sense at a time when one-night stands and relationships prevailed. The hippie look did not work any longer either; members of the younger half of the baby boom endorsed their elders' desire for casual clothes but also wanted to project more overt sexuality.

Marketers and ad agencies pursued them. Phrases like "'turn-on' togs" and "seducer robes" remade sleepwear into sexual inducements, and department stores began to sell nylon bikini briefs in a variety of colors and styles to men who expected women would see them. Half a decade or more after the women's underwear market sprouted new colors, fabrics, prints, and styles that emphasized sexuality, the "fashion underwear" trend spread to men. In an era of greater female sexual agency, a woman might buy her husband or boyfriend sexy briefs, often "as a gag," noted one merchant. However, those who donned the newer styles discovered that, as one middle-aged man confessed, "I feel young, I feel thin, I feel sexy." To escape the "sissy" label, Jockey, one of the largest manufacturers of men's underwear in the nation, enlisted top athletes to prove that "fashion underwear can be manly." Much of the intent of fashion underwear was to "turn on a lady," a nod toward mutuality and shared sexual pleasure. A National Organization for Women chapter in Los Angeles staged an underwear fashion show, with men as models and the women "doing the ogling." Explained one of the volunteer models, a construction worker by day, "women like men's bodies; men like women's bodies."[45]

Which leads us to the famous scene in *Saturday Night Fever* where Tony Manero dressed for a night at the disco. One commentator likened his routine to that of a "bullfighter ritually adorning himself for the ordeal." Women, he noted, found the scene puzzling, but men could relate, as "most 20-year-old males have clocked a lot of hours flexing and combing and just staring in the mirror." John Travolta's Tony took pride in his appearance and dressed to show off his sexy, masculine body. He was utterly comfortable preening and using tools and embellishments once designated female.[46] Far more than middle-aged 1960s fashion followers, Tony was a peacock who used his body and the clothing that adorned it to create a spectacle, to attract attention, especially female attention.

Tony's disco look did not originate with the college crowd. It began with "blue-collar working kids," African Americans, and Latinos. Identity politics enabled individualized ethnic looks. Disco drew from what *Ebony* called "black men's flamboyant fashions," including platform shoes, colorful flared-leg trousers, and polyester shirts. Alice Echols notes the deliberate nature of Tony's masculinity, "highly self-conscious and self-consciously performative." The costume-like elements of his look helped, as Jefferson Cowie has argued, "cover up" his class roots, liberating Tony to "create himself anew."[47] The disco look, thus, began with poorer men and men of color, which made it suspect to the traditional forerunners of the 1960s, college men. Some shunned the music as well as the look. Many found the whole culture of disco alien. But like Earth Shoes and running, it became a fad, one that invited a wide variety of Americans to try out at least elements of the style. While few men acquired full-scale, Tony Manero–style disco outfits, many incorporated parts of Tony's outfit, whether it was the black briefs, the heeled shoes, or the medallion around his neck, because disco definitely upped the sexual ante for men.

Disco's more sexual look also drew from another unlikely source whose visibility owed much to the 1960s, gay men. The gay liberation movement freed gay men from stereotypes that extended to dress. When he was closeted and living in New York City, San Francisco city supervisor Harvey Milk wore a business suit that connoted what he did for a living. When he came out and moved to California, he dressed like the counterculture with which he identified, in overalls and ponytail. However, as a distinctive gay community grew in his district, the Castro, Milk, like out gay men in other cities, became more expressive with his look. Although he wore suits to city hall, he favored vests, open-necked shirts in bold colors, T-shirts, and tight jeans at leisure. Other gay men took the possibilities opened up by the peacock revolution and younger men's fashion rebellions to dress in ways that subverted gender stereotypes of them. Although the gender of the partners they sought differed from that which straight men sought, like straight men, they increasingly dressed to attract attention and emphasize their sexuality.

Yet for gay men, dressing to attract attention and emphasize their sexuality was a conscious political act that commented on the social construction of masculinity. A *Village Voice* reporter dubbed one trend among late 1970s gay men "phys. ed fashion": jogging shorts, sleeveless tank tops, and running shoes that both called attention to the wearer's body and undermined the equation of homosexuality with physical weakness. Some gay clubs were so hot that dancers went bare-chested. To bare one's chest or wear shorts required a toned body, and gay men often worked hard to gain muscular bodies and then dressed them in ways that flaunted social assumptions about them as effeminate or inverts. The result, described by Michael Tolliver, the gay hero in Armistead Maupin's 1978 novel *Tales of the City*, was "a nice mustache, Levi's, a starched khaki army shirt . . . strong. . . . Somebody you could take back to Orlando and they'd never know the difference." Michael's look had several names but was best known as the clone, because the style was so common that, as humorist Fran Lebowitz observed, seeing a lot of gay men at a disco was "like being at a twins' convention." Clones wore tight jeans, tees, polo or flannel shirts, and running shoes. The "macho man" in the title of the 1978 Village People song dressed in "western shirts and leather" that expressed his "own life style and ideals." In throwaway lines, the group urged listeners to "dig the hair on my chest" and "see my big, thick mustache," which were also parts of the look.[48]

"Macho," a Spanish word that entered the American lexicon in the 1970s, described aggressive masculinity, a term feminists wielded as a disapproving commentary on male power. Macho was the name of a men's cologne by Fabergé that was bottled in such a phallic container that many magazines refused to carry the advertisement. Once the gay community appropriated the word, it symbolized a teasing and ironic version of masculinity, one that shared gendered attributes, like sexual aggressiveness, but not sexuality with heterosexual men. Boutiques catering to the gay community bore names like Man Alive or Machismo. Macho dressing, Alice Echols has noted, was the visible symbol of "changes in gay men's identity and subjectivity," signaling new visibility. Clone dressing allowed gay men to fashion their own images apart from the stereotypes society imposed on them, to play with traditional manhood. The clone style had two elements, according to Martin P. Levine, a sociologist who studied clone communities, "butch" and "hot." The former represented the macho aspect of the style, "both parody and emulation" in its representations of manhood. Hotness — sexual attractiveness — completed the look. Clones used their clothing to show off their bodies. Maupin's Michael wore his Levi's in the shower and used a wire brush to gain "that well-worn shading in just the right places," to highlight his crotch. Levine believed that gay men constructed their look more self-consciously than did straight men, who might wear exactly the same clothing only with less awareness of its meaning.[49] But whether straight or gay, the goal of male leisure dressing was to project masculinity and sexuality.

If peacocks, Earth Shoes, and designer jeans revealed anything, it was that the much-touted new 1970s man had a fundamentally changed attitude toward his outer self. His looks and his clothing mattered to him; he often discovered that how he looked affected how he felt about himself. Even those men who claimed to be oblivious to style might deliberately construct their public selves as antifashion or somehow make their "absence of style" "slightly ostentatious," as Carly Simon felt James Taylor did. Their refusal to wear certain items of apparel or their resistance to trends made their own statements about their identities. While on the job, men continued to dress to fit in. Away from their jobs, they had a new need to stand out. The clone might be the most blatant example of the connection between style and sexual attraction, but even straight men came to recognize that in a changed sexual marketplace, their looks mattered more and their jobs counted for less. Men's attention to fashion showed that they understood that, after the 1960s, "what it mean[t] to be a man" had changed. In a 1974 survey of young adults, three-quarters of them defined a real man as "concern[ed] with women's sexual satisfaction."[50] A gray flannel suit said "good provider" but was not sexy, and in a more sexualized, post-counterculture world, "the look you want to know better" counted for more.

"This is a man's world," singer James Brown proclaimed in 1966, but a decade later, it sure did not feel like it to a lot of men. While the sixties started out male dominated, the concept of liberation undermined the hierarchy of privilege that predominated in workplaces and homes.

The feminist-defined 1970s new man was a distressing phenomenon for a lot of ordinary males. His status always seemed lesser than his father's, negotiated not just against the rising expectations of women but against the realities of his economic possibilities. By decade's end, he was beginning to suspect he might not achieve his father's financial stature. His ambitious female peers, moreover, now competed against him. Every day, new experts seemed to tell him what he was doing wrong. Once feminism redefined women's roles, it freed men from some of the heavy social pressure to be breadwinners; however, freedom also meant anxiety for men who were not sure where they fit into the new order. Similarly, the sexual revolution offered freedom but raised social expectations about performance. As women changed, men had to examine their social responsibilities and roles.[51] The demographic changes precipitated by feminism and the sexual revolution meant that increasing numbers of 1970s American households did not resemble the 1950s ideal. Men, just like women, had been groomed for a world that no longer existed.

Certainly, millions of American men continued to make their careers their first priority; however, even those men often learned to see themselves as individuals rather than company men. What undercut the stereotype of the model of American masculinity predicated on breadwinning was not feminism or the bad economy or the rising divorce rate. It was all of those things together that made traditional masculinity less possible. So men began to improvise, trying on new possibilities and personae the same way they tried on new outfits and looks. Like women, they learned to move from role to role, mask to mask—corporate one moment and at leisure the next. Even Ronald Reagan, who championed traditional family values, looked equally at ease in a presidential dark suit and a cowboy hat and jeans. Having learned the language of clothes and the politics of style, men were able to present themselves more fluidly, dressing to suit the occasion, capture their moods, or convey their essences to others. For the price of a pair of shoes or a pair of jeans, they bought their safe piece of modernity.

But as clothing became the outer expression of the many different roles men played, it also marked the end of some aspects of the counterculture. Its anti-Establishment attitudes lived on in many but coexisted with a revived corporate marketplace. Eighties yuppies—young urban professionals—were that decade's trendsetters because they modeled liberated, comfort-heavy, status-conscious lifestyles. Big business loved yuppies because they consumed without the guilt or hesitation that often constrained older baby boomers. Yuppies willingly donned corporate uniforms, reserving expressive and comfortable clothing for their leisure times. To consume fully, yuppie men needed yuppie partners—the era of the two-income middle-class household had arrived. In the eighties workplace, men set the style norms as women dressed to fit in with suits, shoulder pads, and versions of ties. Still, everyone understood that while such work looks might express who a person had to be to earn a living, leisure dressing could be more expressive, individual, comfortable, or sexy.

Yuppies and their successors continue to consume expressive clothing. In 1982, menswear designer Calvin Klein test-marketed underwear that looked exactly like the white cotton briefs and T-shirts most American men had worn for decades, but fitting them tighter, adding his name to the waistbands, and using advertising to "make them appealing and sensual." He sold 400 pairs in two weeks, despite a price tag considerably higher than any store brand. One analyst observed another "fashion revolution" in the result, bringing "designer credibility" from jeans to underwear. When "casual Fridays" emerged in the 1990s, Levi-Strauss "saw . . . a way to save itself," explained former Levi's public relations man Rick Miller. With baby boomers "getting older and flabbier, they were not buying as many Levi's jeans," but by making and marketing a brand called Dockers, sensible khaki pants with considerably more freedom of movement than tight 501s, the company revived.[52] The success of Dockers demonstrates both the ongoing economic power of boomers and their continued willingness to express themselves through clothing. More than anything, though, the existence of both Dockers and casual Fridays indicates that, however much leisure, pleasure, and mindful consumption have been style watchwords, corporate capitalism drives our marketplace.

We live with the consequences, both good and bad, of what happened to fashion in the 1970s. We might value comfort, but we also love variety. We are style-conscious, constantly aware of how others might read our clothing. In ongoing pursuit of ever more self-expression, the average American in 2005 bought one new item of clothing every five and a half days. Trends shift quickly, requiring men as well as women to pay more attention to what is popular. Walk-in closets come standard in most new construction to accommodate our expanding and specialized wardrobes. The average American man now owns twelve pairs of shoes.[53] Lost in the process are some aspects of the countercultural ethos. Many of the same people who so religiously boycotted grapes in the 1970s to be mindful of the conditions farmworkers faced, buy for themselves—or for their grandchildren—running shoes or jeans made in factories in places like Vietnam or Bangladesh, where workers are poorly paid and exposed to all sorts of dangerous conditions.

Still, gender is a more fluid concept than it used to be, nudged along by men's fashion rebellions of the 1970s. Although the pursuit of style initially seemed unmasculine to some, it helped men adapt to a more gender-neutral, sexually expressive society. The spectrum of clothing choices suddenly available to men reflected their assimilation of new roles and identities shaped by the sixties. Nerd or peacock, disco dancer or clone, American men experimented with a lot of different roles in the 1970s, and the looks they donned to express themselves—whether stylish or awful—symbolized Americans' more-tolerant understanding of masculinity.

3 : You're Gonna Make It After All

The Mary Tyler Moore Show Helps Redefine Family

ilming the iconic moment at the end of *The Mary Tyler Moore Show*'s opening credits, the one where the lead character flings her beret into the air, did not begin auspiciously. It was unusually cold for February, even for Minneapolis, where the show was set and the scene shot. Reza Badiyi, who filmed the sequence, added the hat-tossing at the last minute, securing no permissions before instructing series star Mary Tyler Moore to rush into a busy downtown intersection and act "as if this is the happiest moment of your life." Moore did, and it was sheer luck that delivered the disapproving middle-aged woman behind her right shoulder, a visual reference to the generation gap. The raw footage did not impress the show's creators. With music and freeze-framing added during editing, though, the sequence transformed, evoking that final joyous moment at graduations when caps are tossed, which was precisely the feeling Badiyi was after. That few seconds of film captured the show's premise like no other, the main character's transformation into "a free woman for that era," as Badiyi later explained.[1] The first line of the series' theme song, though, posed as counterpoint to the character's giddy, perhaps gendered, liberation, one that echoed the concerns of millions of Americans: "How will you make it on your own?"

TV's Mary did not have to make it on her own. The series' lead character, Mary Richards, took her audience with her on her journey through a changing workplace and a changed life. Hers was the story of an independent woman, reflecting the lived experience of an increasingly coveted subset of viewers, younger single ones, especially women. The show juxtaposed its main character's independence and liberation against a situation comedy staple, the family, bridging the gap between old and new. TV's Mary had parents that were infrequently mentioned and seen in only three or four episodes during the series' eight-year run. The series was not about that family but about one that no one explicitly identified as a family until the show's last episode. Mary's most impor-

Mary tosses her hat in the air on the opening credits for The Mary Tyler Moore Show, *an act so culturally resonant that today a statue commemorates it. Photo courtesy of Photofest.*

tant family consisted of friends and coworkers who provided emotional and logistical support as she negotiated a modern single life. Behind the scenes, a similarly self-constructed family enabled cast and crew to create Mary and her friends differently than the networks imagined family, as nuclear, home-centered, and gendered. *The Mary Tyler Moore Show* helped Americans reimagine family in ways that would support the lived experiences of a new generation, and some of the older one.

Television in the 1950s presented families in idealized, gendered ways that suited a populace that wanted to fit in. "Our most powerful visions of traditional families derive . . . [from] 1950s television sitcoms," historian Stephanie Coontz explains.[2] Family, however, changed because of the 1960s, affected by rising divorce rates and a generation generally less eager to get married than their parents had been. Boomers savored the freedom to be alone longer, postponing the traditional markers of family construction, marriage and children. They resisted some of the gendering that existed in the families in which they were raised. Carving their own paths could alienate them from their parents, especially as they came of age and seemed not to settle down as it had been defined. Empowerment and liberation, key components of individual identity after the 1960s, made them seem selfish. *The Mary Tyler Moore Show* modeled and culturally reinforced the choices of a new generation. Mary's attractive qualities, manifest in her character, moreover, were nurtured, supported, and encouraged in the program not by parents or a husband, but by friends and coworkers.

Never before had a single female TV character struck such a public nerve. Newspapers featured stories about "our Mary." Women's magazines told Moore's life story and highlighted fictional Mary Richards's style. The M that hung on her apartment wall started a decorating trend. The Minneapolis post office received letters addressed to Mary Richards, and a stream of visitors knocked at the door of the Minneapolis house featured in the opening credits. Even the U.S. government treated the character as though she were a real person. When the series left the air in 1977, everyone from Gloria Steinem to Walter Cronkite speculated on what would happen to the character next. Later sitcom actors like Julia Louis-Dreyfus and Tina Fey credit watching the show as children with influencing their own comedic styles. Plenty of celebrities and thousands of ordinary people have paid their homages to her hat-in-the-air opening. The program "changed America," series regular Cloris Leachman recalled.[3] *The Mary Tyler Moore Show* had transcendent popularity because it so vividly captured the experience of work and life in a changed era. More cultural influence than sitcom, the program reassured Americans that, like another line in the theme song initially promised, they "might just make it, after all," in the complicated personal and professional terrain of post-1960s modernity.

Critics of the sixties decried the era for undermining American families. Some blamed the sexual revolution or the birth control pill for freeing couples from the responsibilities of marriage or children. Others held the women's movement responsible for undermining traditional gender roles, tempting women with careers instead of their traditional role nurturing their husbands and children. Many observed that counterculture hedonism worked against the kinds of long-term commitments family required. The generational rebellion, many a parent complained, constricted their influence over their offspring as they grew up. The age of "sex, drugs, and rock 'n' roll," conservatives argued, trumped old-fashioned values like hard work, loyalty, and obligation to something besides the self. Self-awareness or actualization movements, Christopher Lasch wrote, made many Americans too self-obsessed. Americans had, Natasha Zaretsky has argued, "a preoccupation with the family" in the 1970s, generally within a context of "national decline."[4]

The family-of-one emerged in the 1970s, to traditionalists perhaps a threat, but courted and catered to by advertisers and products and embraced by women like fictional Mary, single and working. These were the women who bought Carole King's *Tapestry*, who had relationships, spent money, and exercised relative freedom of choice over their lives. Of course, the members of this single-longer demographic group were also male, spending with more attention to leisure, pleasure, and fun. Because families-of-one had disposable income, marketers accommodated their unique needs. Food came in single-serving sizes, and compact cars accommodated them. New technologies like answering machines assumed that no one might be home to take a phone call for long swaths of the day. Families-of-one had consumer power disproportionate to their numbers. Families-of-one were also often Daniel Yankelovich's forerunners, forging new paths at home and in the workplace. Families-of-one generally needed to work, some students excepted, but enjoyed the luxury of not being responsible to anyone else, undoing a relationship that millions of young husbands and fathers had to their jobs in the 1950s. This was especially true of the millions of baby boomer women entering the workforce for the first time in the 1970s, not as married women looking for part-time or flexible work, but, to quote a seventies aphorism, as the first day of the rest of their lives. Yet families-of-one heretofore garnered little attention or reinforcement in the popular culture and, especially, on television.

When *The Mary Tyler Moore Show* first appeared in the fall of 1970, the women's movement pointed the way for family-of-one females to enter the workplace, sometimes in nontraditional jobs. The civil rights and feminist movements had opened up, at least theoretically, new possibilities for them and other traditionally underrepresented workers. The "entrenched culture of exclusion that long restricted to white men nearly every one of the nation's most desirable jobs," as Nancy MacLean has described it, was supposed to be in the process of giving way. Activists challenged companies to become more diverse and more democratic, to give women and members of minority groups opportunities and all workers more influence over their workplaces. Reality, however, rarely measured up to this ideal. Sixties values collided with a seventies economy, one visibly changing from "the most economically egalitarian time in U.S. history" to a more polarized one.[5] Many new workers started with Mary's trademark optimism only to discover that the real world was tougher than they imagined. Rather than experiencing work as empowering or liberating, they felt defeated, alone, and powerless. *The Mary Tyler Moore Show* and other 1970s workplace sitcoms explored for their many viewers the delicate balance between high hopes and real life. The show's heroine grew, mastering skills and authority and building networks of loving and supportive friends. But in the last episode of the series, she lost her job in an injustice even chipper Mary could not fix. It was a paradox to which many viewers could relate, a microcosm of the world of work that only partially changed in response to the sixties.

Mary's professional path forward, like real-life seventies women's, existed in tension with expectations about family. Sixties' changes trapped millions of Americans between eras. The social authorities of their youths, the institutions that shaped their early lives, even the television programs they watched, told baby boomers that adult life was desirable, started early, and involved marriage and children, and that earning a living was a responsibility men owed their families. Women, by contrast, were supposed to be naturally maternal and maintain the house and children, rewarding their spouses for all they did with well-run homes and well-raised children. When married women worked in the 1950s, which happened more frequently as time went on, family fictions explained those endeavors as temporary, for a specific purpose, different from men's careers, and to be fit into schedules that revolved around caring for family.[6] Boys grew up expecting to get jobs, have wives who would take care of them, and have children mostly tended by their wives. Girls grew up with toys aimed at their future roles as wife-and-mother, including baby dolls, toy kitchens, and miniature electric irons. But as a 1974 film so boldly declared, a lot of women did not live there anymore.

TV's Mary had a job, and not just any job; she was the associate producer of the six o'clock news. Even though her junior management position was at a second-tier TV station in a second-tier market, as her friend Rhoda once joked, it was "the kind of job Gloria Steinem wants you to have." Mary did not have a husband and did not want one. She was neither a picture-perfect TV mother nor a man-hungry spinster, a departure from sitcom norms. She was a family-of-one, single by choice, working for a living and living among friends and workplace colleagues. Watching Mary and her constructed family was instructive and satisfying for the series' large audience, a weekly appointment with "good company" that celebrated camaraderie, collaboration, and independence.[7]

The series was set against a bleak reality—a consistently bad economy that represented a significant change from the prosperity Americans Mary's age and race had experienced virtually their entire lives. After World War II, millions of people achieved middle-class status and all that it meant: single-family homes, consumer goods, family vacations, and new cars. Boomers matured, overall, in relative comfort, including many with working-class parents or in families of color. But by the 1970s, the costs of Lyndon Johnson's Great Society programs coupled with the Vietnam War started to impact the economy. The burdens of guns and butter were a growing federal debt and soaring prices. Oil politics added to the disarray, weakening one center of American innovation, the automobile. As the price of oil rose, so too did the cost of everything else. Japanese competition delivered a second blow to American industry, new practices that gave assembly-line workers elsewhere more incentive to work hard and produce reliable products. The percentage of workers in unions declined while the power of executives grew. As a bulge of new workers competed for fewer jobs, there was high unemployment and high inflation, stagflation in the parlance of the time, forcing workers to take what they could get. Even in the depths of the Great Depression of the 1930s, most Americans still proudly believed they were middle class; but in the 1970s, the middle class experienced a noticeable drop-off in its standard of living.[8] The era of relative economic equality was coming to an end, replaced by the polarization of income we continue to experience today.

Policies enacted in the 1960s and 1970s promised workers better lives through equal opportunity and government regulation: the Equal Pay Act, affirmative action, the creation of the Occupational Safety and Health Administration. Those ideals clashed with the entrenched bureaucracies and resistance to innovation that too often greeted new workers. Nepotism and sexism persisted in many companies. Younger women and members of minority groups discovered that their co-workers and superiors stereotyped them as quota fillers and treated them without respect. Unions lost power. A service economy required traits for which boomers' child-centered upbringings little prepared them, deference and obedience. 1960s protesters had optimism; 1970s job seekers were cynical. "When we were kids the United States was the wealthiest and strongest country in the world," noted Students for a Democratic Society's Port Huron Statement in 1962. Ten years later, Americans were tethered to a global economy seemingly controlled by others. "The Great Inflation," concluded Bruce J. Schulman, "produced its own generation, altering Americans' relationship to money, government, and each other."[9]

Boomers' opinions of their parents' lives made them concerned about more than paychecks. Family togetherness, a much-touted middle-class fifties ideal, functioned less ideally in real life, for which work was to blame. Singer Harry Chapin's 1974 hit, "Cat's in the Cradle," told of a father too busy to spend time with his son, a cultural symbol of the Establishment's hold over its employees. Forerunners often saw fathers who sacrificed time with family for long hours on the job or long commutes. Some resented their mothers' jobs as well for depriving them of the 1950s family dream or imposing additional household responsibilities upon them. One aspect of the counterculture's critique that resonated with a lot of middle-class youth was the idea that their parents had given them things rather than time. Many did not want to duplicate this perceived dynamic. Staying single and childless longer, on average, freed young people from the responsibilities their parents assumed at young ages.

High on lists of youth's priorities was "anything but a 9-to-5 job with two weeks' vacation a year," particularly "from a company whose activities I do not approve of." Antiwar protesters, hippies, and environmentalists challenged the ethics of corporate America. Foreign models of more-flexible, employee-centered, positively motivating workplaces contrasted with American capitalism. Factory managers reported high rates of absenteeism and turnover when workers felt their jobs were "unfulfilling." Boomers were not entrepreneurial. The number of college students interested in business majors reached its nadir in 1971. College graduates wanted to help others and "develop a meaningful philosophy of life," as one survey showed. Boomers believed "there must be something more to life than making a living," fearful of ending up in what then-activist Bernie Sanders called "moron work, monotonous work."[10]

The character of Mary Richards illustrated the unexpected trajectory many new female workers faced. Her work history resonated with many viewers. Like Carole King, circumstances thrust her into a more modern life. She had not finished college, was working as a secretary and helping a boyfriend get through medical school with the expectation that they would marry when he finished. Her Plan B began only after her boyfriend finished medical school and dumped her. As the series started, she has moved from a small town to a big city to begin a new life as an unencumbered working woman. Mary was not a flower child off to find herself or a feminist in a consciousness-raising group. Rather, out-side events plunged her into what historian Ruth Rosen called a "world split open" by feminism, and Mary went into her future, nervous and fearful but also excited.[11]

The workplace reality for Mary, as well as for her viewers, did not always merit her optimism. When *The Mary Tyler Moore Show* pre-miered, the unemployment rate was already higher than it had been for most of the previous twenty-five years, and it would go even higher before the last episode was filmed. Those lucky enough to have jobs often felt frustrated. "The communications gap between employees and company decision-makers," one 1977 survey found, was "a wide one." When the series ended in 1977, 80 percent of workers believed they were "locked-in" at their current places of employment, stuck where they were because they had no alternatives.[12] Like a lot of her real-life counterparts, Mary faced a sometimes-hostile workplace. Her viewers, thus, saw reflected in her fictional experiences variations on their own struggles with workplace authority.

In the series' first season, when the theme song still promised only that "you might just make it, after all," the opening montage leading up to Mary's hat-tossing began with goodbyes to an old job, old life, and old ways, symbolized by a going-away party, Mary fending off the ad-vances of an older male colleague, and a shot of her in her car driving into Minneapolis. Nowhere were there familiar female sitcom markers, no cute kids, no picket fence, no handsome husband. In the first epi-sode, she applied to be a secretary at TV station WJM but was offered a more challenging job previously occupied by a man, associate producer of the nightly news, for less money. Mary became, as her office mate in-formed her, a token, the sole woman in management. Indeed, her boss made all the decisions, telling her what to do, leaving the interpersonal matters to her more sensitive womanly touch. Mary struggled at first but grew increasingly assertive over the show's seven-year run. By the third year, the line in the theme song morphed to "you're gonna make it after all" in recognition of Mary's growth. Regular viewers became invested in that process, as well as bonded to Mary's "support group," coworkers and friends who "eclips[ed]," television scholar David Marc has noted, the "once . . . energy-giving center of the sitcom universe," the nuclear family. Crucial to Mary's workplace experiences were colleagues who embodied what baby boomers wanted the most from their jobs, "friendly, helpful co-workers."[13]

Because work and the workplace were central aspects of American life, novels, movies, and radio and television programs featured them in stories often full of lessons. Cultural renderings of work reinforced social understandings about power dynamics and workplace practices. As such, they supported a status quo where employers had invisible disproportionate power while, as popular culture often does, allowing viewers the temporary fantasy of subversion and resistance. Narratives typically attributed workplace success to hard work and wise choices, while subplots sometimes hinted at the unevenness of the playing field. The didactic arc even had a name, Horatio Alger stories, after a prolific author of books for boys featuring heroes who rose from the lowliest of positions through clean living and utter dedication. Implicit in the plots, though, was the cultural normalization of an individual get-ahead philosophy that largely excluded women, whose nature was nurturing others in the domestic realm. Cultural working girls were temporary employees waiting to be rescued from the horrors of the workplace and their spinsterhood.

In the 1950s and 1960s, situation comedies focused on the family outnumbered any set in the workplace. "They showed us how to be moms, dads, and kids in post-war America," television scholar Laura R. Linder tells us, and provided weekly check-ins "that we were doing okay.[14] Work outside the home distracted from the family stories and so appeared mainly as an afterthought. Generally, the only characters viewers saw working on early TV were single. Married women did not work at all. In perhaps the most famous single television rerun of boomers' young lives, *I Love Lucy* showed that anarchy reigned when housewives Lucy and Ethel went to work making chocolates on an assembly line while their husbands struggled to cook dinner and clean their apartments.

In the 1950s, TV's working women were secretaries, teachers, and assistants, subordinates to men in their workplaces, which mirrored reality. Women of color, who only rarely appeared on sitcoms, served as maids, subordinate to white women. Series replicated working women's economic realities as well as their likely job categories. TV women made less money than did men, and, in consequence, their material lives were lesser. Stories reinforced social assumptions about marriage too.

Although most Americans believed people needed to be married to be happy, TV bachelors enjoyed and actively fought to maintain their single status, often against predatory women, while their spinster coworkers "plott[ed], plann[ed] and relentlessly track[ed]" men.[15] Television in the 1950s suggested women were competent, even exceptionally skilled, at their jobs. Still, they always had a hidden agenda: find a man, get married, and abandon the workplace for housewifery. It was a social message reinforced by songs, movies, and advertisements. TV spinsterhood was lonely and unsatisfying.

Although the workplace became more visible in 1960s television, the bulk of baby boomers were asleep when TV's earnest doctors, lawyers, and private eyes fought for others, supported by female nurses and secretaries. Their glimpses of the workplace continued to come from sitcoms, most notably from *The Dick Van Dyke Show*, a consistent top-ten program between 1961 and 1966 and a popularly syndicated daytime rerun thereafter. The series split its stories between workplace and home. It also featured a female worker with a "man's" job. The show told the story of Rob Petrie (Van Dyke), the head writer of a fictional television variety show. His wife, Laura, played by Mary Tyler Moore, was often hailed as a different kind of TV helpmate, sexier but, like other housewives, cutely ditzy and emotional. At work, Rob and fellow writers Buddy Sorrell and Sally Rogers wrote comedy sketches for an unreasonable star/boss. Consequently, they experienced work as "alienating."[16] The series confirmed what other sitcoms suggested: that bosses were authoritarian and demanding, with negative implications for workers' home lives. Because *The Dick Van Dyke Show* was not just a family sitcom but one that included stories about the office, Rob, Buddy, and Sally built the rudiments of a workplace family to cope, a device that made the show both popular and unique.

Yet Sally's reality was distinctly different from her male colleagues'. They counted on her to type their scripts and keep the peace. They went home to wives, while she went home to a cat. The qualities that made Sally successful at work made her unfeminine and unappealing to men, which made her sad, because Sally wanted a husband. On another baby boomer must-see, *The Beverly Hillbillies*, executive secretary (and plain) Jane Hathaway embodied all the cultural clichés about working women. Stiff of manner, completely lacking femininity or a bosom, she was a tweed-suited model of both efficiency and misery. Such attitudes reflected the mixed messages baby boomer girls got about the workplace, that it could be glamorous, that it undermined your femininity, and that it was, ultimately, not as satisfying as having a family.

Sixties changes undermined shows like the *Hillbillies*. That program and others like it did well in the Nielsen ratings, although their primary audiences of children, rural viewers, and the elderly were not big spenders overall, which mattered to advertisers. Baby boomers loved the imaginary worlds of shows like *Hillbillies* only until they hit their teens, especially once the sixties offered them a fully realized peer culture built around the idea of rebellion. Teenagers and young adults who would grow up to buy Carly Simon records and Earth Shoes were already willing and practiced consumers but increasingly critical television viewers. As a version of this new culture trickled down to ever-younger boomers, network executives realized TV was going to have to change to hold onto the lucrative boomer market. The way back to young peoples' hearts, they decided, not surprisingly given the era, was to become hip.

Programming targeted at youth brought rock music, space exploration, and stylish spy dramas to late-1960s television, but most sitcoms remained stuck in nostalgic family or fantasy settings. One exception was *That Girl*, introduced by ABC in 1966. Aimed at teen and young-adult female viewers, the series starred Marlo Thomas as fledgling actress Ann Marie. Ann lived in New York and supported herself with temporary jobs. The program was not really about work, but about female independence, carefully contained by Ann's constantly meddling father and her much-more-stable boyfriend (later fiancé). The series provided a family-friendly version of the single working-girl image presented in *Cosmopolitan* magazine, one without sex, where the heroine often needed rescuing from the consequences of her nurturing instinct. Yet even this constrained version of a modern woman affected the show's disproportionately female audience hungry for models. "*That Girl* got me to New York," one working woman recalled. Savvier viewers might concede that "no temp job could pay for all those clothes" but liked the fantasy of Ann's independence nonetheless. By the end of its run, 1971, Thomas had enough clout to dictate what would and would not happen in the finale. There was no big wedding to bring traditional closure to a working girl's life. Instead, the last episode found still-single Ann arguing with her boyfriend about women's rights.[17] *That Girl*'s five-year run straddled the great divide of the late 1960s. Although it was groundbreaking in 1966 in its representation of a woman who was independent and career-ambitious, by 1971, Ann's limited independence no longer resonated with the audience segments the networks sought.

The same social forces that made Ann a less compelling character nurtured *The Mary Tyler Moore Show*. By the late 1960s, ABC and NBC had started to siphon off urban viewers from first-place CBS with more contemporary shows that Yankelovich's forerunners would enjoy. In 1970, CBS president Robert Woods made the executive decision to cancel still well-performing rural-based series in order to pursue an increasingly prized audience segment, those elusive forerunners— between eighteen and thirty-four, living in cities, and college educated. What these viewers wanted to see, he concluded, were renderings of 1960s-inspired change, "social significance" programing that was "relevant and youthful," or as *Time* magazine quipped, "aflame, or at least perspiring, with social consciousness."[18]

Two independent television production companies spearheaded the effort to incorporate sixties changes into programming, Norman Lear's Tandem Productions and Mary Tyler Moore and husband Grant Tinker's MTM Enterprises. Independence from the networks was crucial to the success of both. Neither wanted to create idealized TV families; both, instead, sought authenticity. In sitcoms like *Good Times* and *All in the Family*, Lear showcased families Americans did not often see on TV, working class, poor, divorced, or members of minority groups, in "transgressive" situations. Contemporary issues like abortion, feminism, racism, violence, and drug use affected these families, generally not the subjects of comedies. MTM focused more on changing values and the ways primarily middle-class people negotiated change. Its series, including *Rhoda* and *WKRP in Cincinnati*, featured characters struggling to reconcile their upbringings, values, and choices. Workplace was generally more central to MTM series, and biological family was downplayed.[19] The different foci addressed two aspects of modern life relevant to the privileged boomer audience, family conflict and workplace struggles.

CBS signed Mary Tyler Moore for a series in the fall of 1969. Her contract guaranteed that whatever show she made would air for thirteen weeks. Moore wanted to make a situation comedy about a divorcée. Like Carole King, she had married young and then divorced and hoped to represent someone with this increasingly common experience. The creative team she and Tinker hired to produce her vehicle, James L. Brooks and Allan Burns, fought a losing battle with CBS to bring her vision to life. CBS executives opined that the public would "never accept a divorcee as a funny heroine" because divorce "implied a woman of lesser morals." So Brooks and Burns made their lead a single woman instead, imagining for her a history that quietly shaped their product: that she had lived with her boyfriend before their breakup and was "no wide-eyed virgin," as Burns insisted. The shift, Brooks noted, moved the story into the office because "a single lady's job is as important as her private life." The goal was to represent what Moore called "truth," but CBS kept arguing for clichés. The network suggested that someone "pretty" play opposite Mary, a handsome newscaster who offered a "chance for romance" and maybe marriage before the first season ended. Instead, Brooks and Burns made the news anchor, Ted Baxter, vain and dim-witted. Conveniently, the vice president most opposed to the project departed CBS, replaced by someone who felt the series had enough appeal to position it prominently on the network's fall 1970 schedule.[20]

It was not just a single-but-sexually-experienced working woman lead that set apart the series. Brooks and Burns desired to give viewers a "sense of [the characters] living in the time," Allan Burns remembers. Its characters were "'everyday' people," according to Mary Tyler Moore.[21] Its locale was real, Minneapolis, its exteriors were filmed there, and characters made references to real streets and real weather. Its sets were deep in order to look like actual rooms rather than stages. The director of photography deliberately avoided the even brightness typical of theatrical shows, instead employing varied lighting to add depth. Microphones positioned around the set allowed the actors greater freedom of movement, which added naturalism. The three-camera method of shooting also provided flexibility of view, invisibly moving the viewer around Mary Richards's studio apartment or workplace. Characters did not break the fourth wall or offer commentary to the audience; actors inhabited their personae entirely. The series' style gave Mary an authenticity most previous sitcom characters lacked.

Its comedic style also set the series apart from other sitcoms. The show lacked the attention-getting "zingers" even Norman Lear employed in his series. It avoided "zany antics just for a laugh." Its humor started "with a relatable premise," like being audited, having to work on Christmas Eve, or hosting a brunch. Its plots unfolded leisurely; its jokes often derived from experiences characters and audience shared. "Mary's world would always be a bit unstable," sitcom historian Gerard Jones has noted, which drove plots forward with gentle jokes along the way. The series did something rare in 1970 but common today; it rewarded regular viewers, who better understood continuing story lines or personal quirks, like Mary's tendency to throw horrible parties. Thirty-five years after the series left the air, it might seem "not that funny" to today's viewers, but it is still compelling in its construction of what its creators wanted most, relatability. What *The Mary Tyler Moore Show* did better than nearly any show around was to provide weekly portraits of lovable-but-flawed characters who "seem[ed] like real people."[22]

Mary's realness was crucial to the series' success. She was a "mimetic" character, "one of us," as contemporary television writer James W. Chesebro defined her, someone who represented her audience's best impulses and some of their flaws. Although such characters rarely existed before the 1970s, after Mary, more and more did. What the public liked about these characters was that they were multifaceted rather than ever-so-perfect *Father Knows Best* models or *I Love Lucy* crazies. Mary's authenticity was rooted in the character-driven nature of her series, a format "generally considered to be more feminine."[23] Making Mary "one of us" was a gendered enterprise tasked to a writing staff that included women. From the first season on, *Mary Tyler Moore* employed female writers. By 1973, half the series' scripts were written by women, and in 1974 Treva Silverman became the series' story editor, a woman in television living a version of fictional Mary's behind-the-scenes TV career. Several of the writers began as Mary did, as secretaries, bringing additional verisimilitude to the scripts. Female writers Mary's age knew firsthand how it felt to fight for new responsibilities on the job or define their own sexual values as single women. They brought their experiences into the writing room and turned them into episodes, whether it was ugly bridesmaid dresses or "the wonderful thing that happens once a month." Writer Susan Silver "identified with Mary," she has noted, and was able to make the character satisfyingly familiar to lots of women.[24]

Even the smallest details helped the audience relate to Mary Richards and her life. Unlike *That Girl*, Mary's living standard was commensurate with her actual job. Her studio apartment was meant to look familiar and "affordable." Indeed, lacking any other, it was the standard by which my own mother judged my first studio apartment. Mary slept on a foldout couch and cooked in a cramped kitchenette. The set's furniture came from thrift stores. Her office had the same gunmetal-gray desks found in offices across the country. Only her boss got his own tiny office. The character wore what Moore called "realistic working girl" clothing. The costumer selected each season's outfits at once, mixing and matching from episode to episode as if to affirm that Mary's clothing budget was limited. Her style influenced younger women, who began tying scarves around their ponytails or wearing pantsuits to their offices. The opening credits after the series' first year documented the ordinary things Mary (and millions of singletons) did: wash her car, shop for groceries, or take a walk.[25]

More resonant, especially with female viewers, than how Mary's apartment looked was how she spent her time there. Traditionally, female TV characters performed domestic tasks in domestic spaces, and their conversations were mostly about others. Mary, by contrast, was responsible only for herself. Yet she was never lonely. Her best friend, Rhoda, another single woman, lived upstairs. The two friends spent a lot of time together, hanging out, borrowing each other's clothes, exercising, complaining about their mothers, and telling stories about their pasts. Those conversations were unprecedented. They offered commentary and perspective on the parameters of the lives millions of young women were starting to live. Those conversations passed what later scholars call the Bechdel test (after cartoonist Alison Bechdel): at least two women having a conversation that is not about a man.[26] They set the precedent for a host of female sitcom interactions since then. There was an engaging intimacy about Rhoda and Mary. They knew each other's lives and insecurities, as did the audience, who was vicariously invited to participate in these ongoing conversations, which were enhanced by continued viewing. Mary, Rhoda, and the other females who stopped by her place constituted what contemporary feminists would have called a sisterhood, which consciously and overtly dissected the female experience in America.

The character of Rhoda helped to highlight Mary's independence, ironically by providing her with a sitcom staple, a sidekick. Like most television sidekicks, Rhoda was neither as attractive nor as successful as Mary. She fought an ongoing battle with her weight and had an overbearing mother and a self-deprecating manner. Yet her role in the series was not to assist Mary in situational high jinks. Rather, Rhoda served as Mary's sounding board, offering reassurance or questioning her choices as both women negotiated the etiquette of modern life. Rhoda was wonderfully individual, "loopy, colorful, neurotically self-expressed." "Women really identified with Rhoda," noted the performer who played her, Valerie Harper, "because her problems and fears were theirs." "Rhoda is who you probably are."[27] Like Mary, Rhoda was a mimetic character, and the combination of the two women whose attitudes and values felt so familiar facilitated a deeper bond than usual between series and viewers. Mary's neighbor Phyllis (Cloris Leachman) was not a mimetic character but one whose quirky self-absorption validated Mary's status as a single working woman. Phyllis was a relatively privileged stay-at-home wife, but hardly one of those much-beloved 1950s sitcom moms. In one episode, she articulated, with some resentment, precisely the twist on sitcom conventions that made the series so innovative, noting that because of the women's movement, she lost status, while Mary went from "lost little lamb" to a modern trendsetter, the "single girl, free, independent, self-sufficient."[28] Traditionally on family sitcoms, mothers enjoyed exalted status. Phyllis, however, experienced quite a different reality. Her never-seen husband had an affair, and her daughter chose Mary as her role model. The series inverted *The Dick Van Dyke Show*'s familiar female hierarchy, privileging the single working woman while suggesting that being "just a housewife," as Betty Friedan's *Feminine Mystique* put it, was not the satisfying family role earlier TV suggested it was. Phyllis was, at best, an unofficial member of Rhoda and Mary's sisterhood because of her status as wife and mother.

Other characters also enhanced Mary and Rhoda's sisterhood from its fringes. Anchorman Ted's girlfriend-then-wife Georgette (Georgia Engel) stopped by now and again, mostly so that Mary and Rhoda could raise her consciousness and self-esteem, plainly articulating the ideal of the equal relationship for the audience. Mary's parents appeared only rarely, but when they did, their old-fashioned expectations revealed why she needed a peer group to help her forge a nontraditional path. Mary's father urged her boyfriend to hurry up and propose. Mary told him she was not "living my life waiting to get married." When her mother asked where she had been all night, Mary refused to tell her.[29] Even an occasional viewer of the series understood that Mary's relationship with her parents was loving-but-distant and that her state of adulthood required, on some level, that she outgrow her parents' need to protect her. The series did not criticize traditional family so much as demonstrate that it was a relatively unimportant aspect of many younger Americans' lives, less compelling than their friends, peers, or roommates.

Augmenting and sometimes interacting with Mary's home-based sisterhood was her workplace family. The series followed the split model of *The Dick Van Dyke Show* but gave the workplace more importance than Mary's home life. As such, the WJM news office could not function as previous sitcom workplaces had, as afterthoughts that disrupted domestic life or as angst-inducing spaces ruled by unyielding bosses. Instead, it had to be a place of collaborations, friendships, and general harmony. The workplace family metaphor meant that *The Mary Tyler Moore Show* borrowed its basic comedic premise from the family sitcom, a formula that began with a functioning community disrupted in some way from inside or out that must then be restored to its previous status. To make it authentic, the sitcom workplace needed to be peopled with a variety of different types who, like family members, did not always get along because their individual interests sometimes clashed with the greater good. Quirky-but-familiar characters worked alongside Mary, legitimating an experience that was pretty central to most American adults' lives, one that was becoming relevant to boomers entering the workforce for the first time. For those viewers in particular, it was reassuring and pleasurable to imagine your future as an extension of what you experienced growing up or in college, being surrounded by friends who had your back.

Leading Mary's workplace family was Lou Grant (Ed Asner). He served as a father figure to Mary, someone to nurture her and recognize her value as a person. Lou was experienced and professional but could also be gruff, insensitive, and sexist. He taught Mary about journalism, and she educated him about the modern workplace. Lou fought familiar battles against those above him keen on maximizing profits and minimizing costs. Real-life journalists loved Lou, because he stood for old-fashioned journalistic integrity at a moment when the profession was changing. Lou was not infallible, so counted on Mary to help him negotiate the sixties and the decade's impact on his personal life as his marriage failed and he learned to live alone and date again. Their relationship was far more equal than earlier TV workers' interactions with their bosses. His respect for Mary and hers for him offered a pleasing picture of the workplace as a collaborative enterprise and something more meaningful than whatever it officially produced. How could you not want a boss/workplace father like Lou?

Mary's best friend at work, newswriter Murray Slaughter, was her greatest ally and champion. He was her workplace Rhoda, the person to whom she confided her hopes, dreams, and fears. Their relationship existed because the 1960s made it possible for men and women to

Mary's office family was headed by her gruff boss, Lou Grant, played by Ed Asner. Lou taught Mary about television journalism, and she taught him the etiquette of the modern workplace. Photo courtesy of Photofest.

interact with one another beyond a dating arc, liberating them from the gendered preparation and training that would lead them to contrasting marital roles. Mary was not husband-hunting Murray, who was in any case already happily married. Mary and Murray's deep workplace friendship was built on mutual esteem, unerring faith in the other, and what Murray characterized in one episode as "pure love" rather than sexual love. Their intimacy was radical, but neither character was, which made the arrangement safe and mainstream. The network hoped that Mary would find love, like all good TV working women, in her workplace, but like a lot of real workers, on the job she found a friend.

Ted Baxter (Ted Knight) and Sue Ann Nivens (Betty White) were more contentious parts of Mary's workplace family, "mismatched misfits" who "play[ed] to type." Ted "combine[d] all the frailties of man" into a single character, Knight noted. As such, he became a convenient driver of plots but not a particularly relatable character. "A pompous bore with nothing between his ears . . . [who] lucked out," Ted was a familiar workplace type. "We all got one just like him," as one headline noted. In the 1970s, less than half of all Americans thought that "hard work will always pay off," considerably down from the decade before. Ted epitomized the central thesis of a humorous 1969 best seller, *The Peter Principle: Why Things Always Go Wrong*, that individuals rose to the "level of their incompetence."[30] Deep voiced and handsome, he got by on these superficial qualifications for his job, much to the frustration of all of his coworkers. He disrupted the communal ethos of the group, to borrow from another 1970s book title, by looking out for number one.

Sue Ann was similarly selfish and similarly disruptive, although she served to remind the discerning viewer how much had changed since the 1950s. Like Ted, she was unrelentingly self-promoting; but her most distinguishing characteristic was her sexual excess. The juxtaposition of someone whose job description was *Happy Homemaker*, the name of Sue Ann's fictional WJM program, with her general randiness and constant pursuit of men allowed the series to consider once-taboo topics the target audience found relevant, like office affairs and sexual chemistry. Yet Sue Ann was also Mary in another era, a woman whose most logical career possibility in television was on a program for and about housewives, one whose perhaps best avenue for success also required her to flatter and flirt with male executives and sponsors. As she aged, and as she watched a new generation of women achieve because of the women's movement, she bolstered her fragile sense of self-esteem with bluster and competitiveness. Mary, of course, bested Sue Ann regularly, being younger, more attractive to men, well liked by everyone, nicer, and employed in the more male-defined, higher-prestige arena of news broadcasting. Sue Ann's failures reinforced the audience's sense of a just world where new values triumphed and fairness (and youth) prevailed. When it absolutely mattered, Mary and her workplace family helped Sue Ann, and on occasion she helped them. Yet for the most part, she also performed an old-fashioned role in a new-style family, disrupting "domestic harmony" with her selfishness until the "wisdom of the group" was reaffirmed. Sue Ann's transgressive nature, like Ted's, helped viewers see the power and wisdom of the workplace family.[31]

Although temporary disharmony did sometimes prevail, *The Mary Tyler Moore Show*'s rendering of coworkers as family helped to conjure a space where, as Ella Taylor has noted, "human worth was measured by loyalty and humanistic values." Mary's fictional work experience validated many of her viewers' frustrations with their jobs. So too did it "create a symbolic mastery" of concerns they might feel about having to function in environments about which they felt morally ambivalent. This was what *The Mary Tyler Moore Show* did best; it affirmed workers' suspicions that the workplace could be unfair, unyielding, unethical, and inhumane but still be peopled with caring, honest individuals. The workplace family metaphor reassured viewers that they could coexist with corporate values they did not fully endorse so long as they had people around them who mostly shared their concerns and their commitment to do their jobs well anyway.[32]

When the show premiered in September 1970, however, that was not a message audiences expected in a series with a female lead. CBS executives sometimes seemed to think the show ought to be an extension of *The Dick Van Dyke Show*, with Mary Tyler Moore as helpmate. Critics did not seem to understand its premise either. One described Rhoda and Phyllis as "bloodthirsty, man-eating single females." *Time* magazine assessed the show as a "disaster," calling Mary "an inadvertent career girl, jilted by the rounder she put through medical school." The preview audiences gave the network little reason to be optimistic about the series' future. They thought Rhoda was too Jewish, Phyllis "annoying," and Mary a "loser," since she was over thirty and not married. They were kinder about the workplace side of Mary but imagined her in a subservient, nurturing position, solving all the problems, just like the classic working girls of sitcoms always did. Early on, the series did pay more attention to Mary's dating habits than it would later, and it took a while for the workplace family to congeal. The situational humor created by bad dates, though, swiftly gave way to more sophisticated, character-driven stories about modern life. By the end of its first season, the series had edged out its ABC and NBC competition in the ratings, hinting at the cultural reference point it would shortly become.[33] That fall, Valerie Harper and Ed Asner won Emmys for their portrayals of Rhoda and Lou. In both of their acceptance speeches, they referred to the show's ensemble cast as their "family."

The series benefited from its timing, premiering just as "the wave . . . of feminism" began to reach the mainstream. "Things started to change for the women in the workplace," Allan Burns observed, and that worked to Mary's advantage.[34] The show relied on an audience familiar with feminism, at least in its popular manifestations. Much of its humor derived from that awkward moment of transition when a practice once normalized suddenly becomes something else. By simply presenting generally invisible and deeply entrenched workplace sexism through a female lead, the series nudged its viewers to see the unfairness of those acts. Workplace family could not fully exist in a space where women were objectified or treated as second-class citizens. It became, as one recent scholar said, "the mother ship of television postfeminism in the United States."[35]

For female viewers, what they saw could be revelatory. Other than teachers, nurses, secretaries, and store clerks, girls grew up without female workplace models. *The Mary Tyler Moore Show* was neither extreme nor militant in its feminism, but it featured a lead character who clearly believed in workplace equality. Making and fetching coffee, acts that occurred so seamlessly in other TV workplaces, became occasional series' "flashpoint[s] about the differences between service and servility." Other stories explored sexual dynamics, pay inequities, tokenism, even appropriate office wear. Mary was on a rocky path to leadership, one that required her to adopt qualities different from those associated with the secretary she used to be. The federal government recognized the power of the program to shape viewers' sense of emerging office norms, but also Mary's difficulty adjusting. A 1977 U.S. Commission on Civil Rights report chided Mary for calling her boss "'Mr. Grant' even though everyone else calls him 'Lou.'" Yet Mary's fans understood that, as one said, the choice was "in keeping with her personality," and the series responded by having her try and fail to call him by his first name.[36] The writers recognized their role in commenting on contemporary workplace issues, but they also insisted on making their main character individual.

Collective action or legal appeals might have been choices real-life workers made to ensure more-equal workplaces, but strikes were incompatible with a family metaphor. In that sense, the WJM workplace family was conservative, reconfiguring for the audience paternalism as a shared endeavor. The show endorsed older network renderings of unions as inflexible and implied that agencies like the Commission on Civil Rights were disruptive rather than helpful. Mary was, as one episode title suggested, "thoroughly un-militant." She resolved what would seem to be a violation of the Equal Pay Act of 1963 without the aid of the Equal Employment Opportunity Commission. The show emphasized what Susan Douglas called "legitimate feminism," fairness in the workplace reified by classic American values like justice or democracy. *Maude*, a Norman Lear comedy, provided viewers with a more dogmatic ideologue than Mary was, reinforcing, Douglas argues, "the stereotype of the feminist as a strident, loud, unfeminine bruiser."[37] Mary's moderate reactions to sexism respected younger women's basic working knowledge of feminist ideals without alienating the parts of the viewing audience who might find a character like Maude off-putting. Mary's modernity synched with the version of liberation female singer-songwriters sang about. She was hip to the modern world but had one foot in the old one.

Mary's experience was gendered, but it was also more universal because the values of family rather than feminism shaped her workplace. Most sitcom leads were male; for Mary to be a universal character required a certain amount of ambiguity where feminist values were concerned. Over the show's seven-year span, as Mary Tyler Moore herself noted, Mary became "more assertive, more mature." But what enhanced her confidence, feminism or experience? Viewers could use gendered, generational, or other lenses to assess Mary's growth. Her obvious discomfort with being in authority and eagerness to please revealed a lack of confidence feminists ascribed to gender socialization, but plenty of males also felt uncomfortable assuming authority. Regular viewers could see that Mary's competence grew as she gained experience and received encouragement from her peers, especially Lou. In the fifth season, her job title changed to producer of the six o'clock news. She hired and fired on-air talent, delivered editorials, and produced documentaries, no longer the "glorified secretary" some feminists found initially problematic. By series' end, Mary was a different worker than when she started at WJM because she had been encouraged by her workplace family to achieve.[38] However much the show might address gendered concerns, its ultimate message was that the workplace should be gender-neutral and that success or failure are individual.

What really enabled the universality of Mary's story was its villain, the Establishment. Regular viewers of the series could recognize the many ways the "suits" that ran Mary's station tried to streamline, economize, and generally extract more from employees whom they wanted to pay less, all in the name of higher ratings. While the specifics of broadcast journalism might be different, the expectation was the same, that the WJM news team should compromise its integrity for larger corporate profits. Conservative critic Ben Stein complained that Brooks's and Burns's antibusiness sentiments permeated their product, yet that attitude was crucial to the program's success. Without the threat of Establishment exploitation, Mary's workplace family might not exist and would not look like such a humane alternative to the more competitive offices that previous popular culture had featured. The members of the audience segment the program most desired, younger, urban, and well-educated, were the least likely to feel loyalty to their companies or believe that they were "treated fairly" by them. The series explored many facets of growing workplace dissatisfaction, whether it mocked the arbitrariness of decisions at the top or captured the pathos of being middle-aged and afraid of being replaced by some bright young thing. Brooks and Burns used the newsroom to capture a "common work experience" that commented on contemporary society. The series' premise of a workplace family struggling against a larger, more problematic institution remains the norm in TV workplaces today.[39]

At the series' end, though, the loving WJM workplace family could not triumph over corporate America. A new station owner, concerned by low ratings, concluded that the fault lay behind the camera and fired the whole workplace family except inept Ted. The end reaffirmed the series' long-standing critical renderings of the Establishment, as one commentator noted, since "the man in charge is made to look like a fool because all present, including the audience, know that his instincts are uneducated and wrong." The crew members accepted their fate and mourned their soon-to-be-broken family with a group hug, while Mary delivered one of the most quoted speeches of this—or any—series: "Sometimes I get concerned about being a career woman. I get to thinking that my job is too important to me. And I tell myself that the people I work with are just the people I work with. But last night I thought, what is a family anyway? It's the people who make you feel less alone and really loved." And then, singing "It's a Long Way to Tipperary," they departed the newsroom, and Mary turned off the light.[40] Ultimately, the system won and the world was unjust. The show was one of the first to offer closure to its audience in the form of a finale, and it was telling that its resolution was bittersweet. Even the celebrities who commented on the series' end expressed concern about how Mary and her workplace family would fare alone in the cold, cruel world. Still, as the cast's absurdly illogical snatch of song suggested, when life dealt you a raw deal, there was nothing else you could do but accept it, maybe appreciate the irony, cry, and then move on.

In the end, whatever Mary Richards learned about producing the six o'clock news was less important than what she learned about herself and taught her viewers about being on your own while being part of a family. The new "social anthropology" of human interaction, one contemporary commentator noted, was as much a part of Mary's skill set as mastering budgets and schedules. Workplace family was an important aspect of the series, but so too were those elements that showed Mary learning to be a family-of-one. There was both a gendered and a more universal aspect to Mary's single status. Mary was "a child of the 50s" raised "as a Girl" rather than a woman. At the same time, men coming of age when Mary did also experienced a gap between the norms with which they were raised and the reality they inhabited. The choices she faced "reflect[ed] the real world and help[ed] viewers form their own opinions on contemporary issues," its producer noted. Indeed, Mary Richards "ratified a pattern of liberal social behavior" not yet covered in classrooms or job training.[41]

Like other 1970s sitcoms, milestone episodes rendered visible topics television comedy had not covered before that offered insight into the changing lifestyles of both men and women. The series tackled a host of interpersonal challenges brought about by sixties social changes, each handled, to some degree, by one or another of Mary's circles of friends. Ted discovers his mother has moved in with her boyfriend in one episode; in another, Phyllis's brother is revealed to be gay. In one late-series episode that could have been the subject of a Carly Simon song, Mary tells her boyfriend she loves him, only to find out that he has been sleeping with other women. Although she lays out her values very clearly to him ("I can't accept that"), he fixes the situation by saying "I love you," she backtracks, and as the scene fades, it is clear she intends to go to bed with him. In one of the series' most famous episodes, Lou's wife leaves him "to learn more about the rest of me, not just the part that's your wife." The *Los Angeles Times* called the story a "breakthrough," honest and touching rather than funny.[42] Fifties sitcoms modeled normative ways of being for young couples trying to figure out family life. *The Mary Tyler Moore Show*, by contrast, spoke to Americans trying to figure out the sixties and their own interpersonal lives relatively untethered from nuclear family.

The series helped to anchor CBS's new-style programming precisely because it offered a different kind of television experience. The characters and situations were familiar, the humor was intelligent, and the stories felt real. Along with two other nontraditional sitcoms, *All in the Family* and *M*A*S*H*, the series ran on Saturday night. As Tina Fey has noted, the three shows in a row made Saturday evening a powerful night of programming. What Fey did not note, having been only a child when these series aired, was that all this modern programming ran on what was traditionally date night in America. Although all three programs ranked in the Nielsen top ten, their placement on Saturday night suggested that something else had changed. "Our favorite Saturday night of all is spent watching *The Mary Tyler Moore Show* [and] ordering pizza," one viewer recalled. All across America, in family rooms, dorm lounges, and apartments that did not look so different from Mary's, young people clustered around television sets, watching within constructed families of their own, making or finding solace in the fact that if they were home alone on a Saturday night, as Nora Ephron noted, "Mary Tyler Moore was at home, too." The series' "literate" humor and recognition of the importance of "the friends we worked with [more] than the men [or women] we loved" deeply affected young, white, middle-class viewers, Yankelovich's forerunners. "Many experts . . . think it's not entirely coincidental that the increase in the number of people living alone has paralleled the increase in happy, well-adjusted live-alone characters depicted on such television programs as the *Mary Tyler Moore Show*," the *Los Angeles Times* reported in 1977.[43]

Indeed, Mary's experience was so satisfying and so resonant that dozens of sitcoms since have borrowed from its formula. The self-contained circle of very-close friends-as-family drove such series as *Friends*, *How I Met Your Mother*, *The Big Bang Theory*, and even *Seinfeld*. Workplace sitcoms like *Murphy Brown*, *Cheers*, *Scrubs*, and *The Mindy Project* have introduced us to a myriad of work situations where women might excel or fail but form tight bonds with coworkers. In either case, the closeness of the community is reassuring and pleasing, especially to young people on the cusp of adulthood, ready to venture out for the first time into the "real" world. *The Mary Tyler Moore Show*'s venue was important. Mary's life was too ordinary for the big screen, and its ongoing developmental arc made it unsuitable for a film. But sitting at home watching Mary in her home or in the office invited viewers into the charmed circles of her sisterhood and workplace family.

For female viewers of a certain age especially, Mary offered a blueprint, a way of living single for longer than they had ever been prepared to live, one that was positive and affirming. The bond between those viewers and Mary was particularly strong. "Thank you for Mary Richards," one fan letter to Mary Tyler Moore read. Its author explained: "I am 35, unmarried and not looking very hard. Since your program came on the air, people have begun to understand that there is a life for women like me." Minneapolis resident Erin Geiser left college and moved from Ohio to Mary's town, reasoning that if it worked for Mary, it could work for her too. Oprah Winfrey, who says she has seen every episode of the program, searched for years for a job in Minneapolis in emulation of Mary. The character reassured a generation of women struggling against pervasive social conditioning to marry and have families. "I'm proudest of the show for giving women the opportunity to choose what they want to do with their lives by emulation," Moore once said.[44]

Mary's efforts extended to the cast and crew. Mary Tyler Moore wanted a "happy" set, which led to a constructed family behind the scenes as well as in front of the camera. United by their distance from CBS network executives and the common anti-Establishment frame of mind that came with that distance, those working on the set felt ownership and enormous pride in what they produced. Moore and Harper shared lunchtime ballet lessons, and Harper and Gavin MacLeod (Murray) joined Weight Watchers together, widely reported in the press. Although initially conceived by two men, from the moment Mary Tyler Moore demanded a single female lead an informal sisterhood emerged behind the scenes. Mary's female creators were feminists, reading feminist texts, joining women's groups, and bringing those ideas into the writing room, but constructing them so that they had broad appeal. The show's female writers took seriously their role as pioneers, organizing within the Writers Guild so that, like Mary Richards, they could be more assertive to their television bosses. The men who ran the networks, noted Susan Silver, "have preconceived notions, and they're not sure that the audience is ready to see a strong or liberated woman on television yet."[45] To those executives, nothing was as persuasive as success, and Silverman's two Emmys for writing the series, and, in particular, the episode when Lou's marriage ended, encouraged the networks to hire more women. MTM Productions not only brought a version of workplace feminism into American homes; so too did they help bring feminist ideas, gender equity, and a family model into the sitcom business.

The series likewise nurtured its female family members to challenge stereotypes, break down barriers, and grow as professionals. Although Ethel Winant—a real-life Rosie the Riveter during World War II—was a CBS vice president, she was so excited by the *Mary Tyler Moore Show*'s premise that she cast it herself and defended it when CBS wavered over it. Female cast and crew got directing opportunities, including Moore herself. Women would go on to write and direct other MTM shows, including *Rhoda*, *Phyllis*, *WKRP in Cincinnati*, and *Lou Grant*. Newspaper and magazine articles, especially in publications that targeted female consumers, touted the progress of the series' behind-the-scenes female workers and lauded MTM Productions for offering them new opportunities.

Yet neither Mary was a "militant feminist." The character was intended to be modern but not too radical, someone who did not compromise Moore's own beliefs or create too much tension within the workplace family. Because of its popularity and the effectiveness with which it dispatched its message, however, it came to represent workplace feminism, much as 1950s sitcoms like *Father Knows Best* and *Leave It to Beaver* shorthanded domesticity to many Americans. CBS capitalized on the series' symbolic meaning. The network asked Moore to narrate its "We the Women" special and used a clip from her series to illustrate the proposed equal rights amendment. In 1975, the *Los Angeles Times* named her its woman of the year, showcasing her belief in "women's rights" and her admiration for feminist Gloria Steinem. "Small wonder," assessed the *Times'* TV critic, "that many women equate ERA with MTM."[46] The popular association of a satisfying, nonthreatening television workplace with the scary concept of feminism helped to mainstream some workplace feminist values, particularly gender neutrality and equality of opportunity.

While most viewers did, as the *Times* asserted, regard Mary Richards as a model of feminist workplace achievement, some chafed at her timidity and traditionalism, confirming that the show was mainstream rather than radical. One feminist who watched a few early episodes of the series complained that Mary only worked because she had to, had no experience that would justify her position in the newsroom, and "frankly views the station as manhunting ground." Another wondered why Mary's job consisted of waiting on the men in her office, an oft-repeated criticism that missed the many responsibilities Mary quietly undertook. *Ms.* magazine conceded that "white middle-class men" and their "social attitudes" dominated network programming but thought that the show was "the best example of how things have changed." *Ms.* editor Steinem believed the program "really broke through a boundary on TV." Still, the vice president in charge of CBS programming, Perry Lafferty, insisted that "women do not want to see bright, intellectual females who understand all the overtones and complications of a woman's position in relation to society" on television.[47]

Threatened by audience losses to cable television, the mostly male network hierarchy grew uneasy with Mary Richards's realism. The audience did decline in the series' last years, although it was still viable when Brooks and Burns decided to end it. Producers claimed that "the public wants to see pretty young women in comedic situations or in jeopardy situations." The networks gambled on shows like *Three's Company*, which conveyed its modernity through risqué humor while perpetuating older stereotypes about the differences between men and women. Critics argued that the men in charge reached their decisions "unscientifically" and that, as one female executive at Twentieth Century Fox concluded, such choices hurt the women's movement. A *Glamour* magazine poll targeting precisely the female forerunner demographic that producers claimed to court suggested that women were divided over the late-1970s style, with 59 percent contending that television featured too much sex and that, in the words of one respondent, the sheer number of curvaceous blondes on TV "makes young girls today very anxious."[48] In a very real sense, the series' demise was a case of life imitating art, a potentially incorrect programming decision encouraged by male executives who lacked perspective.

The year after *The Mary Tyler Moore Show* ended, a new MTM Enterprises product, *WKRP in Cincinnati*, "compromise[d]" the production company's trademark style, nowhere more "egregiously," *TV Guide* opined, than in the character of Jennifer Marlowe (Loni Anderson). Jennifer was the receptionist at the radio station, and she, unlike Mary Richards, aspired to be nothing more. Although smart, the character strove to remain aloof from workplace drama, and her platinum blonde hair and clingy costumes emphasized her looks rather than her brains or ambition. She refused to fetch coffee or take shorthand, but feminism was just an excuse. Her office philosophy sounded like Ted's: "Do your job, but don't do too much of it." Jennifer dated older wealthy men who showered her with gifts, so no one expected her wardrobe or apartment to look ordinary and familiar. She was only a disengaged member of her workplace family. Anderson explained that she portrayed Jennifer as if she were "a modern-day courtesan. She accepts gifts for being talented and beautiful and wonderful, but she gives nothing back." While Mary Richards was a "role model," Jennifer inspired two posters and a Loni doll. The second female character on the program, journalism school graduate Bailey Quarters (Jan Smathers), embodied more Mary-like qualities — a career focus, a concern for how others saw her, an eagerness to fit in — but she was a secondary character. By 1981, TV columnists had begun to lament "the decline of women on TV."[49]

In the 1980s, there were a lot of workplace families on shows like *Designing Women*, *Cheers*, *Night Court*, and *Murphy Brown*, but the place of women in the constructed families varied, and there was considerably more shaming of female characters with ambition and feminist values, reflecting the Reagan-era backlash. On *Cheers*, feisty barmaid Carla rejected educated feminist Diane's attempts to build a workplace sisterhood. In much the same way, feminist news-magazine anchor Murphy Brown was appalled by her new coanchor, a former Miss America hired to do cute human interest stories. Both series mocked the pretentions of educated women; *Cheers* celebrated a very guy-centric world filled with what Diane characterized as "bimbettes." What scholar Bonnie Dow calls "lifestyle feminism" was the network take-away from *The Mary Tyler Moore Show*, but it proved to make for more contentious constructed-family dynamics, as the liberated women — rather than traditional values — became the disruptive forces.[50]

Still, *The Mary Tyler Moore Show* had a profound impact on programming. "Its DNA is still all over TV," one contemporary writer has noted, especially affecting workplace sitcoms and stories about single women. It was, notes another scholar, "a different kind of show." The 1997 film *Romy and Michelle's High School Reunion* included a fight over who was the Mary and who was the Rhoda in their friendship, a plot point that only worked because the audience understood the reference to a television series that had ended twenty years before. "Hey, Rhoda, calm down," cautions a character in the 2012 series *The Mindy Project*, even though series' creator Mindy Kaling had not even been born when *The Mary Tyler Moore Show* went off the air. The show's skill at bonding audience and stories "not [over] large, dramatic public events, but small personal crises and confusions," accounts for its transcendence. The stories were familiar and comforting — messing up at work, struggling with a budget, failing to get the recognition you deserved. So too were the characters — the crusty boss, the bitchy coworker, the slightly competitive best friend, the cynical office mate. For the millions of viewers whose lives in 1975 were different from what they had imagined they would be like ten or fifteen years before, those small similarities were reassuring and their impact lasting. "Oh my God," Oprah Winfrey recently said, "I wanted to be Mare," invoking Rhoda's nickname for the series' lead. Mary and colleagues spoke to a generation that went on to create television that was about families, whether they were biological or constructed. Today, "as work claims more and more of our lives," the *New York Times* has noted, "so does the lived texture of work occupy an ever larger place in the pop-cultural imagination."[51]

In a world where values, practices, and norms seemed to be changing rapidly, Mary Richards modeled everything from affordable boots to an attitude. "She showed me how to pursue a career, how to keep romance in perspective, how to suffer fools, how to face my own foolishness," one fan remembered.[52] Yet, while modeling a family-of-one, Mary showed a broad range of Americans how those families-of-one also fit into other kinds of families. Mary's TV sisterhood and her friends at work functioned as constructed families that were, by turns, nurturing, meddlesome, or somewhere in between, but always doing battle with the status quo. They suggested that liberation did not mean aloneness. Mary and company concretized modernity in gentle ways for a viewing public struggling with the outcomes, both good and bad, of sixties changes, whether it was Lou's divorce, Phyllis's response to her husband's affair, or Mary's defense of her choices to her father. These characters made viewers feel, to quote Mary's final speech, "less alone and really loved."

Mary, her friends and coworkers, and the many people who helped create them also epitomized a relationship to their jobs many American workers cultivated. They committed themselves to principles, but not to employers, and to one another. Constructed family eased their ways into unrelenting bureaucracies—the Establishment—and provided them with personal satisfaction. With the buffer of a workplace family for protection, Americans learned to coexist within a society over which they felt they had little control. Workplace family reinforced important sixties practices like rebellion and communalism on a modest, conventional scale. It helped to revive and expand the family's reputation at a time when the central institution of American life seemed to be breaking down. Thanks at least in part to *The Mary Tyler Moore Show*, Americans learned how to be in their workplaces, but not necessarily of them, the kind of studied distance we exhibit today toward realities we cannot change but likewise cannot fully endorse. That attitude took American workers into the 1980s and a corporate arena of enhanced power. That same attitude prevails in modern America and with a new generation, Millennials, who expect, above all else, that their workplaces will be communal and their bosses fatherly (or motherly, a whole new style of modern corporate leadership) and are as skeptical as their parents were about their ability to fit into the Establishment.

4 : Different Strokes for Different Folks

Roots, Family, and History

Like the rest of the country, G. B. Trudeau, the creator of *Doonesbury*, the au courant newspaper comic strip, got caught up in the popular frenzy that followed the broadcast of the miniseries based on author Alex Haley's best-selling book, *Roots*, in January 1977. Trudeau specialized in translating current events into humorous vignettes laced with social truth. The *Roots*-inspired sequence he drew featured no-nonsense, Afro-wearing law student Ginny and her boyfriend, Clyde, whom Trudeau depicted as a jive-talking huckster. *Roots* inspired Clyde to follow in author Alex Haley's footsteps, to research his roots. "I want to know where my family's comin' from," Clyde said, while Ginny tried to figure out his angle or scam. "I want to get in touch with some *serious* personal heritage, dig?" But while Haley's saga told of the ways his ancestors resisted slavery and racial oppression, Clyde was not after that sort of usable past. Rather, he wanted, as *Doonesbury*'s punchline noted, "a beer mug with our crest on it."[1]

Clyde was not alone in seeking "some *serious* personal heritage." Millions of Americans embarked upon personal quests to find out about their ancestors after watching *Roots*. That they did so at a moment when conservatives bemoaned the decline of the traditional American family confirmed what *The Mary Tyler Moore Show* also demonstrated, that many Americans no longer believed that families had to look like fifties TV stereotypes to fulfill the functions traditionally assigned to families. That Clyde could be a stereotype of a particular kind of post–civil rights new black man and at the same time want a symbol of Anglo-Saxon heritage affirms the fluidity of identity as a construct in the 1970s. Haley's enthusiasm for his family history invited Americans of diverse backgrounds and family experiences to see how they were, as Haley said of his family, "part and parcel of the American saga." His book and the miniseries it spawned served as affirmative social catalysts encouraging Americans to accept and even celebrate diversity. *Roots*' protagonists were black, and the majority of its audience was white, something very new in American culture. The popularity of both the book and the miniseries demonstrates that in 1970s America the off-quoted lyric from a song by the multiracial musical group Sly and the Family Stone, "different strokes for different folks," had become a social value embraced by a lot of people.[2] Yet, just as Clyde's quest for a family crest seemed comically misguided, so too did some whites watching *Roots* appear to look past the racial elements of the book and program in search of more individual and, sometimes, contrived pasts.

Until the 1950s, the Caucasian majority in the United States tended to regard families that did not look like them as poorer versions of themselves. So long as a single cultural norm dominated the landscape, they would be its focus. Consequently, the books whites read and the movies they watched presented a middle-class family structure that their government and psychologists, ministers, teachers, and advertisers told them was normal and desirable—and implicitly white. That same dominant monoculture excluded or problematized African American families. Most white Americans believed that strong families with two opposite-sex parents in traditional gender roles produced model citizens. Black families, stereotyped as fractured and with confused gender models, were lesser in many whites' eyes. The civil rights struggle and other sixties movements challenged those assumptions by demonstrating how inequality reshaped families. In the sixties, liberals and radicals alike believed in some version of the Yoruba proverb that it takes a village to raise a child. Certainly Lyndon Johnson's War on Poverty recognized that "the crippling legacy of bigotry and injustice" thwarted many Americans, not bad families or bad values.[3]

Alex Haley's family story centered on a black family, until the 1970s rarely a popular cultural subject. It was set in the past, in the antebellum South. It was not, however, set in a genteel plantation house but instead in the cabins of the enslaved, drawing attention to the evils of slavery. *Roots* "occupies a singular place in American cultural history and remains one of the most popular television series ever," a *New York Times* columnist opined nearly forty years after the fact. That white audiences would be interested in such a story suggests how much had changed. Diversity was a strong social value borne of the sixties, with its many ethnic, racial, and gendered movements. Interrogating the past, moreover, had become another expression of the rampant anti-Establishment mind-set. Forerunners—in this instance, younger historians—had begun the process; Haley's work would popularize it. By the time *Roots* aired, the civil rights movement already held a cherished place in liberal mythology. It represented the sixties' best side by modeling responsible protest. It fused means and ends into a satisfying story of moral triumph. It represented the full realization of the ideals on which the nation was founded, that all Americans were created equal. "Reason and right seemed to triumph," as historian Manning Marable observed in 1984.[4]

What followed in official legal equality's wake, though, divided white Americans considerably. Riots and assassinations blunted the optimism civil rights generated within the white majority, and busing in the early 1970s infuriated working-class whites especially, who regarded their children as cannon fodder for social change. Conservatives feared that the fragmentation that came with celebrating diversity threatened the nation. Tolerance for other ways of being, they insisted, had its limits, and cultural pluralism took the focus off the great achievements of founding fathers and "Americanness." "The seventies," Marable assessed at decade's end, "brought a basic cultural and political reaction which reversed many of the gains made during the mid-sixties."[5]

Trudeau's creations, Clyde and Ginny, reflected popular white understandings of the outcomes of the civil rights movement, complicated by gender and class. Ginny was pulling herself up, perhaps through the advantages that affirmative action offered, toward mainstream success, which meant that although she celebrated her heritage with an Afro, she planned to fit into a society that remained invisibly white dominant. Her implicit status reflected one contemporary assessment of the challenges faced by members of her race. In his famous 1978 treatise, *The Declining Significance of Race*, sociologist William Julius Wilson argued that the 1960s caused a shift from "racial inequalities to class inequalities" within the nation, producing black haves and have-nots, the latter lacking education or economic possibilities. Ginny's likely outcome was as part of a "black elite," which was disproportionately female.[6] Clyde, by contrast, lacked any visible means of support, mooching off Ginny, spending money on foolish status items, and hoping for sex, behaviors traditionally attributed to African American males. Liberals argued that the culture failed to provide men like Clyde with an environment that would facilitate their success, but conservatives blamed Clyde. According to economist George Gilder, most African American men were "less able to defer gratification, less interested in achievement, more prone to crime."[7]

While Wilson would argue that what separated Ginny from Clyde was education, Daniel Patrick Moynihan, then working in the Department of Labor, suggested it was the African American family structure that produced more Clydes than Ginnys. Moynihan's famous 1965 report, "The Negro Family: The Case for National Action," drew from Department of Labor statistics, but also from history, for its interpretation. At the beginning of African Americans' new world sojourn, he explained, enslavement created only contingent families. Without the legal institution of marriage or economic exchanges for wages, enslaved men had no authority within their families, while bonds-of-necessity connected women and their children. After emancipation, Moynihan continued, the situation worsened. Little encouraged a stronger father figure. Indeed, discrimination and welfare programs further estranged black fathers from their families. This left the modern black family a "tangle of pathology," as the report's most infamous phrase put it, a dysfunctional unit of too-strong females and absent males. By the late 1970s, conservatives used Moynihan's thesis to argue that social programs encouraged women to have children out of wedlock and made African Americans dependent on government. The consequence was "social deviancy." Black men, conservatives claimed, fathered children but did not provide for them, lacked jobs, joined gangs, or did drugs. To a white majority already worried about what a 1973 *Newsweek* cover story called "The Broken Family," the idea that African Americans might exhibit a more extreme and concerning version of family dysfunction often made sense.[8]

In some very important ways, though, the stereotypical black family's alleged social pathology was becoming more the norm in the United States, as the divorce rate climbed and the out-of-wedlock birthrate followed, more women worked, and women headed more families, especially poor ones. The changed reality generated awareness of and sympathy for what had heretofore been known as "broken homes," families that failed to match up with the glowing fifties sitcom stereotype. In a tough economy seemingly dominated by an unresponsive Establishment and at a moment of changing cultural conventions, it was possible to walk in one another's skin, as a beloved fictional character of the era, Atticus Finch, in *To Kill a Mockingbird*, suggested to his daughter, Scout.

At the same time, politics discouraged racial empathy. While celebrations of diversity and culture prevailed in some circles, backlashes built in others, as conservatives contended that affirmative action was unfair to white male breadwinners. Richard Nixon deployed a deliberately divisive "Southern strategy" to gain white Democrat votes. Republican political strategist Kevin Phillips advised him to use "social upheaval" to create an "emerging Republican majority" of whites disenchanted with racial politics. Phrases like "anti-busing" or "law and order" became coded ways of engaging whites fearful that attempts to codify equality overcompensated in ways that lessened their privilege. Many "were simply tired of talking about race," historian Eric Porter noted, "and were tired of the critiques that implicated them in the social inequalities that still pervaded American society." As civil rights activist John Lewis observed, the 1960s revolutions did not carry African Americans far enough, and "when it got to hard things, and when the problem started to touch the North, the whites turned around."[9]

How African Americans experienced the 1970s varied. "Empowerment," as Robert J. Norrell has asserted, was one takeaway from the black power and pride movements, a way of perhaps gaining more control over one's possibilities.[10] For someone like *Doonesbury*'s Ginny or Alex Haley himself, a life that carefully balanced a distinctive racial identity with mainstream success seemed both desirable and possible. After the civil rights movement, American society appeared at least superficially inclusive. There were black mayors, black admirals, and black bishops. In 1972, a black woman, Shirley Chisholm, became the first of her gender to seek the Democratic presidential nomination. Black musicians and comics and actors captured the rhythms, speech patterns, and challenges of African American life. There were even new terms to describe oneself, "Afro-American" or "black." "We became aware of ourselves," one Detroit resident explained, including African American history and culture.[11] Alex Haley gained national prominence coauthoring a book about black nationalism, *The Autobiography of Malcolm X*, but also wrote for mainstream periodicals like *Reader's Digest*. Trudeau's fictional Ginny attended the University of California's prestigious Boalt Hall law school and had a white roommate and a black boyfriend. For some African Americans, the civil rights movement and other 1960s changes made it possible to be in the majority culture and still be racially authentic.

For others, the 1960s brought less access to mainstream, white-defined success. With baby boomers flooding the job market in the 1970s, more people competed for jobs, and, as Wilson argued, the African American underclass suffered because the economy changed. World War II helped to bring more black workers into unions and factory jobs, but as American manufacturing declined in the 1970s, the black working class lost power. Rising unemployment undermined a lot of the idealistic commitment to racial quotas and affirmative action measures by liberal politicians, typically stigmatizing their recipients as less able or qualified. Economic disparities between blacks and whites dramatically slowed equality, shunting blacks into poorer housing and schools. The decline of the Rustbelt cities where many African Americans had sought better lives during the Great Migration revealed the loss of working-class jobs and union power. As sex outside of marriage lost some of its stigma, the unmarried birthrate for African American women rose to 51.7 percent in 1979, significantly higher than the white rate, which was also growing. Young African American males like Clyde became scapegoats for rising urban crime rates and symbols of angry radicalism. "While the black elite advanced," Manning Marable has argued, "the social and economic conditions for the majority of blacks remained the same, and in some respects grew worse."[12]

Media framed the evolution from Negro to Black, revealing, for those paying attention, an increasingly assertive black voice commenting on the limits of white-majority culture. The 1960s marked the era of the superlatively credentialed, unfailingly polite, token African American character positioned to fit into dominant white society, like Sidney Poitier in *Guess Who's Coming to Dinner*. The first blacks in lead roles in movies and television were white-defined and inoffensive, "a black version of the man in the gray flannel suit," one critic complained. Soon many TV dramas had a diverse cast member. African Americans, however, did not want to be tokens or secondary characters. Black playwright Clifford Mason complained that the "Sidney Poitier syndrome" ("a good guy in a totally white world . . . helping the white man solve the white man's problem") predominated on network TV, a new normal for majority-white audiences but unsatisfying to African Americans.[13]

By the time *Roots* appeared on television in 1977, there were more characters of color for Americans to watch, but since whites generally defined those characters, "TV still evade[d] the nitty-gritty truth" about blacks, as one 1974 *TV Guide* story complained. Unlike sixties tokens, these characters had fully fleshed-out families and home lives; they were the stars of the show. Most were engaged in pursuing some version of the American dream in difficult circumstances. *Sanford and Son* was set in Watts, while the family in *Good Times* lived in Chicago's projects. Only the Jeffersons (*The Jeffersons*) succeeded in "movin' on up," as their theme song said, to a "deluxe apartment in the sky." The song's patois revealed how Norman Lear's disproportionately white production staff imagined the modern black man, as a carefully policed balance between a mainstream character with relatable goals and a cluster of stereotypical traits that might include laziness, cockiness, and chicanery. Another Lear creation, Fred Sanford, projected the image of the "consummate trickster" figure, "shiftless and lazy," to many activists. The onus of rendering a fully developed character of color often fell on the performers. The actor who played George Jefferson, Sherman Hemsley, "was careful to keep George from being a cartoon,"[14] but the character's hard-fought upward mobility was often undercut by his foolhardy confidence. George's wife, Louise, as sensible as *Doonesbury*'s Ginny, tartly exposed her spouse's schemes and conceits.

Like George Jefferson—or *Doonesbury*'s Clyde—other popular culture black men found themselves put in their places by critical black women, who were sometimes emboldened even more by feminism. It was a familiar cultural convention, the sassy African American woman who verbally undermined her man and reined in his more antisocial tendencies, a fusion of Moynihan's female-dominated black family with stereotypes borne of the radio series *Amos 'n' Andy*. Feminism reinforced the anger the modern black woman was assumed to possess. Despite some strides forward, early 1970s culture still often emasculated black male characters into comic impotence in order to reassure white audiences that no race war or riot was forthcoming. Overall, white society remained more comfortable with achievement and assertion by black women than by black men.

The Moynihan thesis was as embedded in the white-dominated popular culture as it was in policy making, a stereotype that whites often believed and that black performers keen to offer real role models to black viewers fought. The actor who played *Good Times*' matriarch Esther Rolle insisted that her character have a spouse; she wanted the audience to see an intact African American family. Yet when son J.J. (Jimmie Walker) became the breakout series' star portraying a character that Rolle described as "18 and he doesn't work. He can't read or write. He doesn't think," Lear gave J.J. more airtime. Soon, all over America, children imitated J.J.'s phrase "dyn-o-mite," while his younger brother Michael, intelligent and engaged by contemporary black politics and culture, faded into the background. Rolle's TV husband, played by John Amos, complained and lost his job, and then the program, in Amos's words, "revert[ed] to the matriarchal thing." A few years later, Rolle too would disappear from the sitcom, leaving the younger generation to fend for itself. "There just are not enough positive black male images," Amos concluded.[15]

Black authenticity came more black-constructed to the 1970s film industry in the hypermasculine urban male character who countered "Poitier syndrome" with a new formula "of the black winning and being triumphant," as the creator of the first of the so-called Blaxploitation films, Mario Van Peebles, explained. His creation, *Sweet Sweetback's Baadasssss Song* (1971), was independently funded, including $50,000 from Bill Cosby. Its success inspired *Shaft* (1971) and *Super Fly* (1972), both written and directed by African American males. The main characters in these films defied stereotypes of African American men as shiftless and emasculated. They featured "a particular kind of neo-Black masculine hero [who was] recuperative, redemptive," and very sexual. Crucial to Shaft's appeal was his "cool putdown of The Man and the film's insistent image of a virile black man in action," or so speculated one reviewer. Blaxploitation films made money without gaining much of a positive artistic reputation along the way, with white or black reviewers. "A swift fist and a stiff penis . . . [was] the Shaftian way," one African American writing in the *New York Times* complained.[16]

The representations of modern manhood that *Shaft* and *Superfly* put forward were strutting and angry, celebrating physical violence and male sexuality. They reinforced a theme of black masculinity emanating from power movements that challenged black men to claim the responsibilities of leadership for their families and their communities. But as Black Panther Huey Newton pointed out, that community-minded goal quickly became "individualistic [and] self-indulgent," until their lead characters' "chemically-straightened locks, . . . gaudy clothes and customized Cadillacs" made them look like inner-city denizens with criminal intent. The "vulgarity, violence and vanity" of Blaxploitation, the Reverend Jesse Jackson declared, failed the African American community.[17] Blaxploitation films provided an alternative venue for black culture rather than challenging the dominant one. Mainstream cinema, dominated by white men, could continue to ignore African Americans as subject and audience.

Both black and white critics lauded *Sounder* (1972) as one successful film with African American lead actors, crossover racial appeal, strong production values, and a positive message about the importance of family. Based on a Newberry Award–winning book for younger readers about a sharecropper family during the Depression, the film followed a popular 1970s narrative arc of the underdog's triumph over adversity. Reviewers commonly contrasted *Sounder* with *Shaft* and *Super Fly*, describing those films as exploitative, particularly of women. In *Sounder*, Cecily Tyson played a "stalwart sharecropper's wife who keeps the family together when her husband is jailed." Carefully tiptoeing around stereotypes of too-powerful African American matriarchs and their missing mates, she justified her role as someone who "had to come forward" because of circumstances. Overall, she pronounced herself satisfied that the film showed African American family life to be strong and positive.[18] *Sounder*'s modest success as a family film, however, did not generate a rush of copycat productions.

Part of *Sounder*'s success resulted from its historical setting. Perhaps because the present felt so contentious, Americans retreated into the past in the 1970s, sometimes as nostalgia, but often in search of ordinary heroes. One of the more successful television dramas of the decade, *The Waltons*, was, like *Sounder*, set in the 1930s, and popular movies, including *The Way We Were* and *Cabaret*, also featured that decade, which was already characterized in popular mythology as a time when individuals needed to exercise initiative and responsibility to survive. In 1976, Americans celebrated their bicentennial as a "do-it-yourself" series of events that planners envisioned would draw in lots of volunteers, engaging people with stories about revolution and freedom. A sense of the past was important to sixties activists as well, who taught black history as part of Freedom Summer in 1964 and later pressed for multicultural and women's history courses on campuses. One of their goals was to find a usable past to give legitimacy to their endeavors. History became a "tool for social redemption," according to historian Andrew Hartman.[19] New versions of the past reached the big screen as well. Arthur Penn's *Little Big Man* (1970) challenged the classic frontier narrative of wild Indians defeated by frontiersmen, while 1969's *Butch Cassidy and the Sundance Kid* turned robbers into funny, hip good guys.

Mel Brooks's popular film *Blazing Saddles* (1974) took on racism along with old Western myths. What appealed about these films in part was their irreverence toward historical sacred cows. They upended American history in ways that made sense to audiences who had lived through the 1960s.

In the sexually liberal seventies, one way slavery served a usable past was for filmmakers interested in including kinky or taboo sexual themes in their productions. A glistening male slave with well-defined muscles and astounding sexuality was central to the plot of *Melinda* (1972), *Quadroon* (1972), and *Mandingo* (1975). *Mandingo*, starring boxer Ken Norton, told the story of a slave-breeding plantation and included "floggings, hangings, slave auctions . . . gory combats . . . sadistic assaults on prepubescent black girls and a good deal of bother about incest," according to film critic Richard Schickel, who pronounced the result "tasteless." The "militant thinking, language, and aspirations of the Black Power movement" produced a different rendering of black masculinity, according to scholar Ed Guerrero, one that generated fear and awe but not respect.[20] Norton's character's sexual prowess gave him power over his enslavers, the white mistress who pursued him sexually, and the impotent master who needed him to make his plantation profitable. Physical strength, sexual stamina, and a rebellious attitude, though, were all the film offered. *Mandingo* was Blaxploitation set in the past.

Mandingo did not shape anyone's image of slavery, but until *Roots* came along, the film *Gone with the Wind* (1939) often did. The popular film, periodically rereleased, presented what a *Time* magazine essay called a "Magnolias-and-Banjos" version of history, where slaves were a logical and harmonious aspect of the Southern way of life.[21] The film first showed on television in 1976. The two-night event set a record for the number of viewers watching. Millions of Americans tuned in, most caught up in the drama of "cavaliers and cotton fields," as the film's opening crawl promised, which never questioned the naturally servile slaves and cooperative freed people who took care of the film's flawed heroine. As portrayed in the film, the Civil War's end brought a dramatic change to the status of white Southerners; blacks, by contrast, seemed not to want and only barely acknowledged freedom.

History education confirmed, often by omission, a version of slavery not unlike that of *Gone with the Wind*, a version that *Roots* would ultimately challenge. In the 1950s and 1960s, America's public schools

Roots *did not shy away from depictions of slavery as brutal. Here, LeVar
Burton, playing a young Kunta Kinte, is in chains after being captured.
Photo courtesy of Photofest.*

swelled with baby boomers, yet neither the environment nor the curriculum encouraged serious analysis of African American history. Long after *Brown v. Board of Education*, the vast majority of American children attended schools where members of their own race predominated and textbooks represented U.S. history as an unending triumph of democracy and white males. The cold war spurred innovation in math and science education but made the social sciences more conservative, as teachers celebrated the wonders of American capitalism, "hiding," one African American woman noted, inequality and conflict. In the 1970s, the civil rights revolution had yet to find its way into public school curricula, there was no Martin Luther King Jr. holiday to commemorate, and U.S. history classes rarely made it past World War II. The most commonly used history texts devoted scant attention to African Americans. Historical consciousness generated by the Bicentennial converted what had been a February week devoted to "Negro history" into Black History Month, but within the realm of popular history, a traditional narrative still prevailed.[22] Only around the edges, in works like *The Autobiography of Malcolm X*, did a different version of the American past exist.

The Civil War remained the main moment when history classes might discuss African Americans, yet the curricular emphasis on battles and legislation rendered their experiences invisible. Textbooks hailed Abraham Lincoln as the president who freed the slaves, just as they summarized the constitutional amendments that gave African Americans freedom, rights, and the vote. For most of the rest of American history, blacks were absent from the texts, while white men conquered frontiers, fought Redcoats and Nazis, built railroads, and delivered heroic speeches in the Senate. Consequently, white students, like their parents, learned their racial history in a more resonant popular culture still filled with plantation verandas where white-jacketed butlers silently delivered mint juleps, mammies who knew best laced beautiful white girls into corsets, and silly young house servants with bulging eyes and high voices served as comic relief.

But within the academy, 1960s freedom struggles upended the notion that American history should celebrate triumph in ways that would enable *Roots* to offer a different kind of story about slavery. A new generation of historians decentered institutions and focused on the history of ordinary people: factory workers, immigrants, women, and members of minority groups. Revisionism, a reexamining of historical assumptions, dominated the field in the 1960s, moving the profession beyond narratives of American exceptionalism. Statisticians and economists shone a different light on the American past. The history of race relations was one of the first fields to change. Until after World War II, white Southerners wrote Southern history, many of them trained by William A. Dunning of Columbia University, who worked early in the century. Dunning assessed Reconstruction as a disaster, a crass Northern attempt to disturb the South's natural structure. Georgian Ulrich B. Phillips added social detail, suggesting that the slave system was as much a burden as an economic success necessary because African Americans were "more or less contentedly slaves, with grievances from time to time but not ambition." "Nearly all the books," historian Eric Foner has noted, "took as a given black inferiority."[23]

These scholarly interpretations dominated popular culture representations of slavery, the Civil War, and Reconstruction. Its scholarship influenced D. W. Griffith's landmark 1915 film, *Birth of a Nation*. Once freed, the cinematic African Americans who peopled the movie — many of them played by whites in black face — stuffed ballot boxes, chased white women, and sought revenge on the kindly people who had fed and clothed them. Klansmen redeemed the white South at *Birth of a Nation*'s end, while blacks cowered in fear. *Gone with the Wind* provided a less fractious version of history than did Griffith's epic. Its ex-slaves were less sullen and more loyal, especially strict-but-protective Mammy, who enforced propriety within the O'Hara family that had owned her. Mammy did not even have a name, just a label that denoted her relationship to whites.

Long before the 1960s triggered a reassessment of American history, African American historians questioned academic assumptions about daily life in the plantation South, first W. E. B. Du Bois and later John Hope Franklin. In the postwar era and, most especially, the 1960s, younger white historians joined them in their quest to challenge the complacent racial assumptions of traditional history. With different tools and civil rights movement–inspired ideals, they examined slavery from the perspective of the enslaved. Kenneth Stampp's *The Peculiar Institution* (1956) directly upended Phillip's vision of the childlike slave and the benevolent slave master. Other historians followed, piecing together information from plantation logs, runaway slave ads, census data, and Freedmen's Bureau records. They found evidence of a strong culture of the enslaved, shaped by African carryovers, family bonds, religious beliefs, and a careful negotiation between black accommodation to enslavement and resistance. These studies redeemed African American history and implicitly supported the civil rights movement. It was only after Americans' faith in traditional institutions began to decline that this new version of history moved outside the academy.[24]

When Haley began his research in 1964, black history was just becoming a separate subfield; but by the time he finished *Roots*, a host of specialized studies proved that the enslaved had constructed communities of vigor and complexity. John Blassingame's *The Slave Community* (1972), Albert Raboteau's *Slave Religion* (1978), Lawrence Levine's *Black Culture, Black Consciousness* (1977), Eugene Genovese's *Roll, Jordan, Roll* (1974), and Herbert Gutman's *The Black Family in Slavery and Freedom* (1976) showed that a people that previous generations of historians regarded as simplistic had built moral and spiritual yet practical communities beyond the white gaze. Gutman explicitly challenged the Moynihan thesis claim that slavery undermined black families, using alternative evidence like naming patterns to demonstrate that family bonds persisted, even when families were physically separated or constructed via ritual alone.[25] Such histories emphasized the humanity and determination of individuals and the strength and diversity of American families. Historians' views of slavery changed; history textbooks, however, generally did not.

African American leaders understood that the popular culture rather than the academy demarcated black history for the white majority and for that reason were vigilant about negative images and stereotypes in the public arena. As early as 1915, the National Association for the Advancement of Colored People (NAACP) campaigned to stop *Birth of a Nation*'s racist renderings. In the 1950s, pressure from the NAACP altered *Amos 'n' Andy* as it transformed from a radio program to a television comedy. "Ethnic characteristics were toned down and admirable aspects heightened," sitcom historian Gerard Jones noted, turning the stereotypical title characters into generic "funny dopes." In the 1970s, watchdog groups like the National Black Media Coalition monitored the airwaves to make sure a rich and varied picture of African American life prevailed, a picture to which African American writers, directors, producers, and actors contributed in meaningful ways. That group protested that John Amos's departure from the sitcom *Good Times* left the Evans family a clichéd "fatherless black family," for example.[26] Still, African Americans' minority status ascribed an upper limit on the majority culture's willingness to bend. When Haley began writing his saga, he sold his paperback rights for a "pittance" to help fund the work,[27] which initially gave every sign of having limited marketability. His book included white characters, but they were not the focus of the story. They were also its villains, which likewise seemed to minimize its mainstream possibilities.

"The revolution will not be televised," singer Gil Scott-Heron proclaimed in his 1970 song of the same name, although glimpses of a more assertive African American presence and identity occasionally broke through TV's predominant whiteness. Bill Cosby narrated a 1968 CBS news special called *Black History: Lost, Stolen or Strayed*, which depicted history through the lens of media. Cosby minced no words in assessing the country's "psychological history": "There was a master race, and there was a slave race—and though there's no political slavery anymore, those same old attitudes have hung around." CBS did so well with the documentary that it repeated it three weeks after its original airing, although it originally ran in July, the middle of the slow summer rerun season. That same year, PBS began its monthly *Black Journal*, which explored controversial contemporary political issues, culture, and history from an African American perspective.[28] In 1974, CBS had tremendous success dramatizing Ernest Gaines's novel of an African American woman's life from slavery to civil rights, *The Autobiography of Miss Jane Pittman*. Viewers wept as the title character, played by Cecily Tyson, approached the whites-only drinking fountain as a very old woman to sample a taste of equality. Some 42 million Americans watched that night, 47 percent of the viewing audience, and the TV movie won nine Emmy Awards.[29] *Black Journal* was a niche program with a limited audience, but *Miss Jane Pittman* suggested the broader possibilities of black history as entertainment television.

Haley's family research bridged the 1960s and 1970s, with his process begun immediately after his work on *The Autobiography of Malcolm X* in 1964, attracting attention in part due to *Miss Jane Pittman*'s success, and finishing with the publication of *Roots* in 1976. His endeavor spanned two eras, one characterized by civil rights and integration and one focused on diversity and individual identity. His interest began as a child, listening to his grandmother telling "pieces and patches of family history" on the front porch. Those tales provided powerful proof of African carryovers and their oral transmission over centuries, as well as demonstrating the strength of Haley's family. She told her grandchildren of "the African" and the way slave traders snatched him. She taught them a few words in an unfamiliar tongue. While scholars have since disputed Haley's emotional version of *Roots'* history, in his mind, the project was a magical, personal quest that began when he wandered into the National Archives on a whim and found some family names on census records. With the help of a linguist, he claimed, he learned the likely location of the language of the words he was taught as a child, somewhere near the Gambian village of Juffure. A *griot*, a keeper of oral traditions, obtained by the Gambian government, met with Haley and told him a folktale that matched in significant dimensions the story told by Haley's grandmother, giving "the African" a name, Kunta Kinte. Examining ships' logs in London provided the link between the old world and the new, the manifest of a ship Haley believed carried Kinte to Virginia.[30] It took Haley more than a decade to research and write his family's history.

The 1960s brought a vibrant new source of culture and history to Haley and to other African Americans—Africa. White Americans' knowledge of the continent was spotty and quirky, bounded by assumptions brought from the *National Geographic* about its people (exotic and tribal) and news stories about their many contemporary problems. Haley knew little of Africa, although the continent was just beginning to represent for African Americans the possibilities of black-majority cultures. Malcolm X's travels, included in the autobiography Haley helped him write, set conversations about race in a global human rights context. Interest in Islam, also sparked by Malcolm, encouraged others to see themselves as world citizens. Civil-rights-activist-turned-black-power-advocate Stokely Carmichael (Kwame Toure) and poet and playwright LeRoi Jones (Amiri Baraka) used their resonant voices to call attention to Africa. In 1966, Maulana Karenga, an academic, created Kwanzaa, a holiday for African Americans intended to "affirm and reaffirm . . . rootedness in African culture."[31] By 1970, Afros and African-inspired shirts called dashikis publicly identified their wearers as attuned to an African past, and colleges offered courses in African history. Alex Haley's desire to find his own ancestors, including those in Africa, both drew from and encouraged black pride in a part of black history separate from everyone else's, an African past.

As Haley himself was fond of noting, his research might not have been all that compelling to others when he began it, but it resonated better in the 1970s. His was a story of identity, family, and community,

Roots *author Alex Haley on the set of the miniseries in Georgia,*
which stood in for Gambia. Photo courtesy of Photofest.

a search for his own usable past. Haley's family background was "atypical," whether measured by black stereotypes or white norms. His parents were poor, professional, and college-educated; a stepmother and
grandparents helped raise him. His father expected him to earn a college degree and enter a profession. Haley's brother became an attorney,
but Haley dropped out of college, enlisted in the Merchant Marines,
married at twenty, and left a pregnant wife at home while he put out to
sea. Desegregation of the military facilitated his upward mobility from
cook to working journalist. Haley's personal and professional life revealed someone who both challenged stereotypes of irresponsible, hus-
tling black men and fell into them. He married three times, spent little
time with his children, and was a "womanizer." Yet he was ambitious
and hardworking. *Roots* was a very personal project for him, focusing
on the part of the writing process he loved the most, research. As the
project grew bigger and bigger and his editor more insistent he complete it, he relied on others to organize and even write drafts of portions
of the work. Thus, the book was often improvised, although he was confident that "every statement in *Roots* is accurate in terms of authen-

ticity." Still, he declared the outcome a "faction," an amalgam of fact and fiction, or "heightened history."[32]

The book took considerably longer to complete than Haley imagined, but it became "the Big Book of this bicentennial year," as one reviewer called it. By Christmas 1976, it stood atop lists of best sellers, generally in the category of nonfiction. Literary critic Leslie Fiedler called it "a popular epic." Most reviewers lauded the "monumental effort" involved and the scope of his "persistent detective work," the "fact" part of Haley's hybrid product. The "fiction" aspects fared less well because Haley was no novelist. Many reviewers likened the book to a soap opera and suggested that the writing read like a romance novel— "very conventional," in one's opinion. Some found the integration of the "fact" with the "fiction" clumsy. His use of dialogue to explicate historical events disturbed several. The research process intrigued nearly everyone. Most reviewers acknowledged that Haley had managed to do "something extraordinary" by providing a sort of communal heritage for African Americans. One particularly singled out the unorthodox and almost mystical African sources the author used, noting that "the narrow discipline of documentation" was inappropriate for groups like "the American Indian and the black African." Nearly all reported that the book was being made into a television program.[33]

Haley was still at work on the book when producer David L. Wolper learned of the project from actors Ruby Dee and Ossie Davis. Wolper's forte was documentary films, and his work helped define the genre of the docudrama. He also had a reputation for working with diverse casts and stories. Once he learned of Haley's project, Wolper obtained the rights and sought a commitment from ABC to fund and air the program. ABC proved reluctant until after *Miss Jane Pittman*'s critical and ratings success but thereafter agreed to the project, with executives reasoning, "What have you got to lose?"[34]

Wolper modulated the project to suit a "white middle-class sensibility." Haley oversaw the story, but white screenwriters crafted it, affecting particularly the African portions of the story. Gambia became a "Garden of Eden" where Haley's African ancestor, Kunta Kinte, lost his innocence to slave traders. The director of the African sections was especially careful to make Kinte "a young man everyone could identify with." ABC executive Brandon Stoddard urged the production to get "out of Africa as fast as we could" to hold white interest. Kinte's grandmother was played by famed poet Maya Angelou, providing intellectual cachet. A new white character appeared, the captain of the slave ship that carried Kinte to America, Christian and troubled by his job and one of a series of what Haley's son William called "good white people" added to the story. Head screenwriter William Blinn outlined "an amazing adventure story" more than an explicitly racial one.[35] Like the previous season's successful miniseries *Rich Man, Poor Man*, *Roots* was peopled with familiar television stars: Ed Asner, Lorne Greene, Sandy Duncan, and Robert Reed, white actors purposefully showcased in series advertisements. Still, Wolper's crew was committed to capturing the spirit of the story if not always getting the details right, showing the Middle Passage, whippings, and enslavement's impact on family relations.

The contours of the developing *Roots* project also reflected ABC's success with big television events with a particular format, miniseries full of "lots of soft-core sex, blood, sadism, greed, big-star cameos and end-of-episode teasers," as *Newsweek*'s television critic explained. Haley's book seemed ideally suited for such a project, with its "pulpy style that smacks of conventional historical romance" and "the excesses of flamboyant Gothic fiction." The strategy that ultimately helped ABC gain ratings dominance over CBS's programming guaranteed a lot of attention to the sexual side of the story. Indeed, much of the prepublicity that *Roots* received concerned Wolper's insistence that the African females be bare breasted.[36] To up the sexual quotient, the script also featured the kinds of violence that served *Mandingo* so well, rapes, brandings, and whippings. At a time when cable television could offer audiences racier fare and no commercials, *Roots* had to be both a classy offering and a soap opera to succeed.

The project was originally edited as twelve one-hour programs to be run once a week, following *Rich Man, Poor Man*'s successful model as a limited series that overlapped with the February sweeps period. But ABC executives got nervous about *Roots*' marketability, worrying that it might make "no profits whatsoever." He had only recently arrived at the network, yet programming executive Fred Silverman made a bold decision to run the show over eight consecutive evenings in January. If the program failed to attract viewers, he reasoned, the consequences would not extend into a sweeps' month. Silverman, moreover, scheduled *Roots* in the last hour or two of prime time, providing it with popular ABC lead-in programming, like its highest-rated sitcoms, *Happy Days* and *Laverne and Shirley*. ABC's motives in presenting *Roots* in this unorthodox manner reflected executives' assumptions that white viewers might not

The birthing scene for Haley's hero, Kunta Kinte, featured two of the era's more famous African Americans, actor Cicely Tyson and poet Maya Angelou, bringing gravitas to the production. Photo courtesy of Photofest.

watch a program featuring whites as the oppressors. Ironically, these decisions turned the miniseries into a piece of not-to-be-missed programming, something discussed in offices and classrooms and among commuters on their trains, so that the audience built night after night.[37] With *Roots*, ABC discovered a new way to capture and hold a diverse audience's attention.

Roots premiered on a Sunday night, and by the next morning it was clear ABC had a hit, "one of the highest ratings of the television season," with more and more viewers each night it aired. By the series end, some 140 million viewers—more than half of all Americans—had seen at least part of *Roots*, eclipsing *Gone with the Wind*'s TV performance a few months before. Bars reported having to turn their TVs from sporting events to the program or lose patrons; stores and restaurants closed; theaters rescheduled performances. "This is better than the Super Bowl," one tavern owner told ABC. Colleges across the country promised students extra credit for viewing episodes and writing summaries. Parents allowed young children to stay up late and watch. Clearly, *Roots* had captured the public's imagination.[38] For months afterward, different groups of Americans parsed the series' popularity and meaning, wondering why so many whites watched and how the story affected African Americans.

Anticipating the airing of this big television event, a host of experts speculated on its impact. Advocates of all sorts of racial agendas stood ready to use the program to support their points of view. Southern stations braced for protest and hate mail but ended up logging only a few complaints, which critics read as a "sign of change." "The world has changed down here since I arrived fifteen years ago," declared the president of one North Carolina ABC affiliate. Pollsters asked, after the fact, whether people had expected an "inflammatory" response, and 42 percent said they had, providing another opportunity for the media to emphasize American progress. The *New York Times* insisted that "most reports of scuffles could not be verified," downplaying the sporadic violence that did occur after some episodes. Newspapers eagerly reported what civil rights leaders thought of the program, although some also recorded Ku Klux Klan head David Duke's opinion that *Roots* was "a wholly contrived bit of propaganda" that drew its large audience only because the talk shows hyped Haley's book in advance. Roger Wilkins, who had worked for the NAACP and the Justice Department and was part of the *New York Times'* editorial board, believed that *Roots* "may have been the most significant civil rights event since the Selma-to-Montgomery march of 1965."[39] Despite the ubiquity of commentary, however, the media had trouble finding ways to harness the post-*Roots* frenzy to a particular political agenda.

Instead, much of the attention focused on the man who conceived this major TV event, Alex Haley. Within the span of a few weeks, he went from being just another working journalist to a national celebrity. He dined with President Gerald Ford, met Henry Kissinger, penned Jimmy Carter's biography for the official inaugural brochure, and appeared on *The Tonight Show*. The Senate honored his work with a special resolution, while both the National Book Award and Pulitzer Award committees created a new category for his work of "faction." "Will success spoil Alex Haley?," one newspaper columnist wondered.[40] The answer depended on whom you asked. Many African Americans credited him with providing "the basis for all black identity." He confirmed their confidence in him as a cultural hero by turning down a host of endorsement offers, including Kunta Kinte dolls and replicas, deeming the "dignity" of his family story "just not consistent with overt commercialism." Among African American youth, Haley soon ranked as the third-most-admired man in America, following Muhammad Ali and Stevie Wonder.[41] To the African American community, Haley represented a desirable blending of racial authenticity, service, and achievement in a world where whites still held most of the power.

The white-dominated press, however, cast a more critical eye on Haley, with some journalists looking for signs of the stereotypical black hustler, while others measured him against the superlatives of the exemplary black overachiever that Sidney Poitier represented. His April 1977 suit for $5 million against his publisher, Doubleday and Company, a "symbolic" gesture he claimed to make on behalf of "black people and others struggling to make it in the country and writers who are like sharecroppers," raised enough controversy that Haley formed the Roots Foundation to fund "multi-ethnic, needy students." That same month, a British journalist investigated his research methods and concluded that "the factual core of the Kunta Kinte story is more tenuous than anyone had thought." Haley initially conceded in response that he had enough doubts about the veracity of the African story to contemplate writing a work of fiction but justified his choices once again as "symbolic" and his role as a spokesman for black Americans: "My people need a Pilgrim's Rock," he explained. Before the month was out, two American authors sued Haley, alleging that he had plagiarized parts of their works and included them in his book.[42]

These attacks cut into Haley's marketability as an author and his credibility as an amateur historian. In the more than 1,000 lectures he had delivered, his quest sounded mystical. He told audiences that "something impelled" him to go into the National Archives and talked about the giddy elation of finding his ancestors on census rolls and the way he wept uncontrollably when he heard the *griot*'s tale. Even when reviewers of the book emphasized the scope of his efforts as he "scoured libraries and archives in two continents, consulted university professors . . . and read widely," it was always in the context of his deeply personal need "to connect the stories his grandmother told . . . with the remote African homeland." Haley's "dedicated search" was "a powerful story in itself," enhanced by Doubleday's efforts to promote *Search*, a companion how-to book to be written by Haley about finding one's roots. It was quickly evident that a lot of Haley's research methods were sloppy. While the British journalist turned up errors of judgment, inconsistencies, and confusions about archives, the charges in one of the plagiarism suits, filed by Harold Courlander, author of the 1967 novel *The African*, were more damning. Haley settled out of court, paying Courlander $650,000 and explaining the common passages as the result of some notes "somebody had given me . . . [that] somehow or another . . . ended up in the book," conceding poor research methods and a much more casual relationship to the end product than the stories of his long-time quest indicated. Indeed, having accepted advances from his publisher and missed several deadlines, Haley's frenzied efforts to complete the book bore little relationship to the romantic and inspirational story he told. Doubleday shelved plans for the companion how-to volume.[43]

Professional historians divided over *Roots*, although few regarded it as legitimate historical scholarship. Most agreed with Bernard Bailyn's assessment of it as "fiction" that popularized history. Leon Litwak welcomed it as a "much-needed antidote to the sweetness of *Gone with the Wind*," a like-with-like comparison that emphasized both the fictional and the popular cultural elements of the work. Oscar Handlin, an opponent of historical revisionism, called out his colleagues as "cowardly" for failing to concede that *Roots* was "a fraud." The scholarly discussion raged for years. Some specialists who examined the American sections of the book, which reviewers tended to find drier precisely because they appeared so fully documented ("a recitation of historical jottings, deaths and births," one reviewer said), also questioned whether Haley got the details right or was familiar enough with the historical context to construct lives from those facts. Yet, in 1994, an African American scholar conceded "Haley's shortcomings as a historian and scholar" but still insisted that *Roots* "cannot be measured by the same conventional standards" as other texts on slavery. Most 1970s historians shared that view, that *Roots* was historically inaccurate but provided, as Manning Marable said in 1980, the decade's "most significant example of 'living history.'"[44]

What made *Roots* so significant in the long run was its popularization of a narrative contemporary historians were writing, one that presented America's history from a post-1960s revisionist perspective. Whether or not the enslaved people depicted in the book and miniseries were Haley's ancestors, a majority of viewers of the TV show believed its representations of slavery to be "accurate." By depicting slavery from the perspective of the enslaved, Haley contributed to a growing body of literature about the mechanisms of oppression. His version of a usable past gave African Americans agency. One explained that "the black people in *Roots* won in the end. It really made me feel good." "I want to be able to tell my children," a mother waiting in a long line to obtain Haley's autograph noted, "I want them to know what it was really like." For several years before the *Roots'* broadcast, Americans had been primed via daily CBS Bicentennial Minutes characterized by a "seriousness bordering on scolding" to see history as a suffering, a battle, but also a triumph of the Colonial underdog over the British overlord.[45] So too were many experiencing the present as a place where ordinary people bucked an Establishment they could never quite beat. Haley's ancestors never fully triumphed over the system, but they struggled to protect a version of their family so tenaciously that generations later a little boy would hear family history on his grandmother's knee. It was a satisfying story.

Yet, in many cases, the racial story took a backseat to its family-history model. Doubleday and ABC both promoted Haley's work in a race-blind way. "Searching for his roots," one advertisement read, "Alex Haley helps us discover our own." The word "roots" ubiquitously marketed everything from *TV Guide* to trips to Israel. Americans by the score sought to document their family stories, visiting archives and paging through census records. Genealogy became, in one paper's estimation, "the most voguish obsession of the decade," the more personal part of a "nostalgia craze"[46] that made TV shows like *Happy Days* and feature films like *Grease* popular. Whites understood that the centerpiece of Haley's work was enslavement, but what they wanted to know more about was *their* families' stories. Like *Doonesbury*'s Clyde, they wanted something tangible that might reflect their personal heritage.

For a lot of whites, *Roots* was one piece of a larger 1970s enterprise, affirmative celebrations of diversity that took very personal forms: learning about your own family heritage and, in many cases, the struggles your own ancestors survived. Bicentennial planners "refashion[ed]" the event, Natasha Zaretsky has argued, "to highlight . . . localism, cultural pluralism, diversity, and difference." In many communities, that included hands-on events that let people experience a specific past through food, costume, or ritual. "The ethnic revival," historians Thomas J. Sugrue and John D. Skrentny have concluded, "became a sort of counterculture—an attempt to restore 'authenticity' into a soulless modernity," to see diversity as a democratic counterbalance to the Establishment. Many Americans went searching for their own personal

Juffures, the "'exotic,' premodern villages" of their ancestors. Minus actual slavery, the narrative arc of Haley's family story was suitable for any family who had overcome adversity, whether their roots were Irish, Polish, Italian, Mexican, or a mixture. Ethnic pride movements, though, erased the difference between voluntary and involuntary migrations and institutional and informal forms of oppression. White Americans watching *Roots* often felt little guilt over what had happened to Haley's ancestors because, after all, someone else was to blame, especially some past version of the Establishment. By claiming ancestors who did not own slaves or who had come to this country after slavery ended, whites could disassociate themselves from *Roots'* actual history. As "megastar" Ben Affleck recently discovered, when PBS's *Finding Your Roots* turned up not just the evidence of the familial interest in "social justice" he had hoped for, but also a slaveholding ancestor, being part of a slave-owning establishment is "embarrassing."[47]

Consequently, Haley's work was often read as less about history and more about the persistence of family at a historical moment when conservatives suggested it had been fatally weakened by sixties-inspired individualism. People identified with the motives and values of Haley's ancestors and saw reflected in their struggles some version of their own efforts to stay together in the face of enormous challenges. While that outcome may seem narcissistic or self-absorbed, behind it lay a more-noteworthy accomplishment: large numbers of white Americans identified with African Americans rather than with whites. Conditioned by anti-Establishment fervor to be suspicious of those with power, to root for the Native Americans or the train robbers over the cavalry or the sheriff, putting the mechanics of enslavement front and center made it difficult to feel common cause with slave owners. They saw what it cost to maintain the plantation myth. Many recognized the centrality of family to Haley's sagas and their own lives. Historian Eric Foner likened *Roots* to *The Waltons*. Both families, he said, manifested "unity, self-reliance, and moral fortitude, to face and overcome adversity." "Haley's ancestors," he concluded, "'made it' as a family."[48] Underneath the diversity that separated people, *Roots* suggested, was a cultural value that united them, and that value was family.

Haley's family story, moreover, directly challenged conservative claims that fathers were losing their authority because of feminism, blurring gender roles, and the decreasing ability of men to be sole family supports, as well as stereotypes of feckless black men. What one scholar called *Roots'* "extraordinary emphasis on maleness" undermined the cultural stereotype of the black family as fatherless and African American males as irresponsible and oversexed. Contrary to what the Moynihan report implied about black men, *Roots'* patriarchs were authoritative and powerful, not shiftless or invisible. Kunta Kinte provided "a nurturing father, a cultural tradition, a proud family heritage . . . and an exceptional personal pride" for his slave family, "everything American slaves were assumed to lack," one English professor noted, embodied in one mythic male human being. He loved and honored a family he could not legally head, demonstrating better family values than the white men who sold his daughter away from him or raped her. Haley's patriarchs were recognizable and admirable to all races, and yet not the sort of stud showcased in *Mandingo*, so reassuring to white viewers and affirming to black ones. Feminists, however, did notice that "Haley's myth . . . glorif[ied] maleness."[49]

Most viewers noticed the myth rather than the maleness. Myths tell universal stories, generally about heroes who suffer, struggle, and finally triumph, and it was that narrative arc that appealed to viewers in 1977, whatever their color. Psychologists studying *Roots'* reception noted that audiences appreciated its "historical and educational value," its story of family, and its depiction of progress in the face of adversity. Many "felt a heightened identity with their own family" as a result. Haley intended his work to be read and viewed by both whites and blacks. Some whites, however, suspected he wanted "to make whites feel guilty." Few, though, received the story that way, identifying with Haley's black family narrative of assertion and triumph. "Who can forget the grandeur of the young father holding up his newborn daughter to the Heavens?," asked one self-professed "middle class white" from Malibu, California, who celebrated Kinte's triumphs rather than feeling racial "guilt" over slavery.[50] Instead, what audiences enjoyed and appreciated was the resistance characters practiced and their determination to endure together despite almost-impossible odds.

Resistance was at the heart of *Roots*, a sixties-inspired quality that transcended race. Researchers noted that whites who chose to watch the show had less respect for traditional authority than those who did not. Studies also showed that while white "liberals" learned about slavery from *Roots*, the rest of the white viewing audience felt "a strong[er] emotional involvement" in the story.[51] Victimhood, thus, was less interesting than the characters' efforts to maintain their humanity. Haley invented the personalities of his characters, emphasizing their rebellious spirits. Kunta Kinte resisted his slave name, Toby, and ran away so many times that one owner maimed his foot. Kinte's daughter, Kizzy, spit in her mistress's cup and changed "Toby" to "Kunta Kinte" on her father's grave marker. These acts modeled one way to exist in relation to authority, to resist it whenever you could. Yet seventies racial politics did not fall into the easy categories presented by *Roots*, and some aspects of contemporary black resistance made whites uncomfortable and scared. The past was a much safer arena for identifying with the morally correct cause. Vicariously resisting an earlier version of the Establishment by celebrating Kinte's rebelliousness proved a gratifying experience whatever one's race.

After *Roots*' success, the racial and economic composition of TV families changed. If early-1970s comedies like *Sanford and Son* or *Good Times* were supposed to show white audiences what ordinary life was like for African Americans and confirm a shared core of values, later-1970s sitcoms were more likely to bring together the races in constructed multiracial families living in comfortable or luxurious circumstances. *The Jeffersons* already featured TV's first interracial married couple. Beginning in the fall of 1978, Norman Lear introduced the blended family of wealthy widower Philip Drummond, who adopted his black housekeeper's two young sons. Its title, *Diff'rent Strokes*, borrowed from the Sly and the Family Stone song. *Gimme a Break!* (1981–87) featured a white policeman — another widower — with a black housekeeper raising his three daughters. In 1983, ex–pro football player George Papadopoulis (Alex Karras) and his wife adopted his black teammate's orphaned son in *Webster*. Although these shows generally proceeded from assumptions about white largesse, and in the case of *Gimme a Break!*, a large, sassy black Mammy type, they also assumed that their audiences would have no trouble accepting multiracial constructed families. The shows reflected liberalizing attitudes about interracial marriage and interracial adoption and what constituted a family.

While Alex Haley's scrappy and struggling family symbolized American notions of family in the 1970s, in the 1980s the most famous American family on television was the Huxtables (*The Cosby Show*). The program's message was not about struggle but offered viewers a reassuring message about the centrality of family life as a launching pad for individual achievement and just happened to be about a black family. *The Cosby Show*'s large audiences could see the Huxtables as a successful multigenerational family or as a successful multigenerational African American family, some of whose members attended a historically black college, whose grandchild was named after Nelson Mandela, and whose parents could reminisce about the 1963 March on Washington. Either way, what stood out was the glue of family life, the rituals, the loyalty, the sorrows, and the triumphs. Certainly, when viewers watched *Roots*, the immorality of the slave system came through either way; yet the more engaging aspect of the story was its familiar narrative of overcoming adversity. *Roots* was, as one scholar noted, a "surprisingly upbeat" drama given its subject matter—most episodes ended "with a minor triumph or on a note of promise," and the series ended with Reconstruction. Its stories offered "proof of human will, of the persistence of identity," individual achievements supported by family members working together and, sometimes, putting others' needs before their own.[52] Like *The Waltons*, *Miss Jane Pittman*, or a book used widely in American schools, Anne Frank's *Diary of a Young Girl*, *Roots* and its historical setting gave viewers distance enough to look beyond the specifics to the heroic nature of everyday life under stress. In an era with lesser, but still significant, social distress, watching *Roots* was reassuring.

At the same time, however, what happened after *Roots* aired in 1977 confirmed what the Kerner Report of 1968 had warned, that America was becoming "two societies, one black and one white."[53] African Americans like *Doonesbury*'s Ginny, with education and opportunity, gained entrée into the middle class, but a lot of Clydes remained stuck in neighborhoods with deteriorating infrastructures and services. Measures of individual well-being, including employment, incarceration rates, graduation rates, and life expectancy, continued to reveal significant gaps between whites and blacks. Even television became stratified, with stories about African Americans consigned to smaller cable channels or, like *Cosby* or the more recent *black-ish*, depicting upper-class black families functioning in a diverse and generally accepting world. Inequality remained a contentious subject, a reality not fully solved by the civil rights movement or celebrations of cultural diversity.

Still, *Roots* provided African Americans with new ways to forge racial identities and to see connections to Africa. Black parents named their children after Kinte or Kizzy, hoping to pass pride and determination to their offspring. "We're going to do all we can to make him be somebody," one young father said of his new son. A teacher told of a young boy who insisted that he be called Kunta Kinte, warning, "Don't call me anything else." A mother got her sleepy four-year-old out of bed by urging her "Mandinka warrior" that it was "time to go hunting in the forest." A father was delighted to see his black son and a white classmate "rooting together for Chicken George [another of Kinte's descendants] to prevail over his mean master-father." *Roots'* stubbornly autonomous slaves were a source of pride for African Americans, and seeing even one view of their African origins was inspiring. Haley "retrieved the African past of black Americans for the benefit of all people," Robert J. Norrell concluded in his biography of the author, "adding depth to our understanding of the experiences of African Americans." Even today, the series remains "almost a rite of passage" for blacks. "Somebody will sit you down in front of *Roots* and say 'you need to watch this,'" notes an actor in the 2016 remake of the program.[54]

As history, *Roots* did have some impact. Haley was not a forerunner in this regard so much as a popularizer. His work became part of a new popular narrative of American history, a more diverse one that replaced the heroic recounting of great men who passed laws, invented things, or led troops into battles with stories of ordinary and diverse people. The same anti-Establishment sentiment that accepted Kunta Kinte as a rebel against the system made Americans eager to read and hear about their founders' flaws and learn about the many ways farmers and factory workers, conscientious objectors, civil rights volunteers, Rosie the Riveters, and other brave souls bucked convention and made America a better place. Alex Haley's stories about Kinte, Kizzy, and other slaves who struggled to retain their identities, families, and as much of their dignity as possible fit this new historical paradigm. Increasingly, this more humanized version of American history would find expression by other popularizers besides Haley, among documentary filmmakers and novelists or amateur historians. Popular history remains popular, as any Ken Burns documentary demonstrates.

As history curricula and textbooks began to reflect revisionism, *Roots* became a cultural document that spanned the popular and scholarly versions of history and served as an accessible visual resource for teachers. Although racist assumptions no longer shaped the historical narrative about slavery and Reconstruction, textbooks still, as one scholar has noted, "catered to conservative White Southerners." The enslaved appeared as "historical objects," passive and victimized. Despite the late hour of its broadcast and the sex and violence contained within the series, teachers across the country urged their students to watch

Roots. One study of suburban high school students found that more than four-fifths of them saw it and from it learned about slavery and African customs and developed sympathy and a better understanding of the challenges that faced their ancestors, whether they were black or white. The show arrived at a point when history education was becoming more visual, a change reflected in newer texts full of pictures and graphics. Haley's story helped to personalize abstract issues for younger learners, and actually seeing what the hold of a slave ship or a slave market looked like further concretized history. A photo in a *Newsweek* story a week after *Roots* aired suggested its classroom impact. A young African American boy stood at a chalkboard, a timeline and a map juxtaposing the slave trade with Kunta Kinte's personal history.[55] A few years later, with the routine use of video cassette recorders in American classrooms, a new generation of schoolchildren would learn about Kinte and Haley's other relatives.

U.S. history textbooks written after *Roots* aired "reflect[ed] a society trying to end discrimination." Educators sought to explicate America's past in all its messiness, which many educators believed was a necessity for shaping modern—post-1960s—citizens. Haley's presentation echoed a curriculum laced with stories of high-minded individuals of different races, ethnicities, and classes who resisted authority and, together, built the nation. Native Americans, women, immigrants, African Americans, and their families gained voices in these texts, just as *Roots* presented a story of enslavement and resistance. Textbook authors emphasized African cultures as "high civilization" and described the Middle Passage as a traumatic event. Texts also introduced the notion that some slaves fought back, while still talking about victimization and exploitation. Social history, as Nathan Glazer and Reed Ueda noted, did not easily match the more traditional narrative of "history as a success story."[56] *Roots* sent teachers and learners into the new textbooks looking for answers, evidence, and examples.

Roots' stress on slave resistance no longer always prevails within the academy. The current emphasis on slavery as an economic system tends to stress slaveholders' deliberate cultivations of violence, fear, and ignorance. Yet, in classrooms, "it's important to show that African-Americans did not just bow down to the oppression," notes historian Daina Ramey Berry. In 2016, original *Roots'* producer David Wolper's son, Mark, set out to remake *Roots* for a new generation, to "deliver a visceral punch of the past to a younger demographic, consumed anew by questions of race, inequality and heritage." No one expects the re-make to carry the cultural power of the original, which functioned as historical theater, "making history less 'abstract,'" as the original series' newest chronicler, Matthew F. Delmot, recently noted. The original series provided "a new kind of textbook, according to one of its stars."[57] The genre Haley called "faction" is the basis for virtually all historical films we watch today.

Roots also challenged several different kinds of stereotypes about race and family. No longer perfect and no longer only white and middle class, the families Americans saw in the seventies media were persistent, resilient, and individual, and they fought oppression. Whether multigenerational like Haley's or temporarily constructed like Mary Richards's, these families modeled resistance to authority and, in particular, to the Establishment. Such portraits directly contradicted conservatives' vision of American families under siege by the forces of modernity and the changes that followed 1960s activism. *Roots* affirmed family survival under the worst of circumstances.

5 : Obviously Queer

Gay-Themed Television, the Remaking of Sexual Identity, and the Family-Values Backlash

One evening in 1971, President Richard Nixon settled in to watch television and stumbled upon a new program airing its fifth episode, *All in the Family*, a detail that survives thanks to the White House tapes. On this evening, the show's plot featured a case of mistaken sexual identity, one where, Nixon complained to soon-to-be-infamous aides John Ehrlichman and H. R. Haldeman, an "obviously queer" character turned out not to be, while a "virile, strong" football player was. "I don't mind homosexuality," he insisted, "[but] . . . I don't think you glorify it on public television. . . . What do you think that does to kids?" What Nixon saw on that February evening was a milestone moment in the history of television for Americans with minority sexual identities. *All in the Family* was the first situation comedy to depict an out gay man, specifically on the "polariz[ing]" genre of what was becoming known as relevancy TV. The sudden frankness about subjects heretofore absent from the sitcom entertained some Americans and disturbed others, including Nixon, who equated the episode's message with "immorality" and other "enemies of strong societies." Homosexuality, he contended—and he was not the first person to so assert—had led to the fall of ancient Greece and was likely to weaken American society and, particularly, the family.[1]

What singer-songwriter music and more expressive clothing did for straight men and women television helped to do for gays, lesbians, bisexual, and transgender individuals, that is, provide them with a public space to try out new identities. But while many Americans celebrated the sexual liberation of straight men and women, others considered the liberation of sexual minorities as a threat. Experts' understandings of sexual identity shifted rapidly during the 1970s. They did so while another sort of debate occurred: what was and was not an appropriate topic for television, a medium nearly everybody watched. Concern about family decline focused on the nature of sexual identity, but also on the content of television. Social conservatives feared many of the sexual and gendered outcomes of the sixties, but none scared them more than did the emergence of a public gay community supported by a new media establishment. They could muster no live-and-let-live tolerance for a kind of diversity that they believed was neither benign nor natural. Nixon was not the only TV viewer worried about America's children and what they might see and learn from networks increasingly willing to tackle controversial issues. Television became one of the primary fronts in conservatives' war against the sexual and gender changes sparked by the sixties, and public discourse about gays was perhaps the most pitched battle of all.

Television that placed some version of modern life before the public provided a social vehicle for informing citizens about changing mores; but such educating ran contrary to the family-friendly programming of the medium's traditions. Burglaries, impotence, unemployment, and miscarriages did not happen to 1950s TV families, but they did to the Bunkers, the multigenerational family featured in *All in the Family*. Was television's function to "deal with real issues," as Ed. Weinberger, the executive producer of *The Mary Tyler Moore Show*, suggested,[2] or merely to entertain? The question was especially complicated because television was a domestic medium freely available to children. During the 1970s, commentary about TV focused on its biases and impacts and existed within a broader conversation about the consequences of a more open society. Stories about sexual minorities, more than any other kind of television, challenged at least some people's notions of protecting innocence and sheltering young people, just as they challenged their beliefs about sexuality, gender, and family.

Seventies television commented on the nation America was in the process of becoming, a more diverse and tolerant one. Some of this new style of TV was gentle and character driven, like *The Mary Tyler Moore Show*. Other shows, like *All in the Family*, were intentionally controversial, scripted programs tackling issues traditionally discussed via news and documentaries. Like *Roots*, such programming blurred the line between fact and fiction. New production companies, especially Norman Lear's, which made *All in the Family*, privileged liberal sixties values. Their work also signaled a different function for programming. Television had, heretofore, reinforced social hierarchies, majority norms, and traditional values. In the 1950s, sponsors "owned" programs in ways that allowed them to at least partially control the end product. In the 1960s, networks assumed control over content. ABC, NBC, and CBS established Standards and Practices offices to monitor scripts and performances, assuming a protective role. By the late 1960s, series like *The Smothers Brothers Comedy Hour* and *Laugh-In* pushed hard against TV taboos, and their popularity meant that the networks loosened up in response. *All in the Family*'s success further opened up television's possibilities.[3]

Still, television's sexual revolution was heteronormative. Most historians identify World War II as the moment when gays and lesbians began to build the mechanisms of community. In the 1950s, two homophile groups, the Mattachine Society and the Daughters of Bilitis, pursued an "accommodationist strategy," asking for public tolerance and providing support for members. Community helped gays articulate their sexual identities not as perversions but as alternatives. Drawing on the civil rights model, they began to advocate for equal treatment and an end to majority oppression. The 1969 battle between police and the gay clientele of the Stonewall Inn in Greenwich Village launched a powerful, public fight for gay rights and community. When gay men resisted arrest at Stonewall, they also resisted clinical, scientific, and cultural understandings of themselves as deviant. By then, they were well on their way to constructing a "sense of minority identity."[4]

The battle at the Stonewall Inn may have stirred gays and lesbians into action, but the straight majority resisted the idea that being gay was not a choice. David Reuben's famous 1969 sex manual, *Everything You Always Wanted to Know about Sex, but Were Afraid to Ask*, portrayed gay men as promiscuous and homosexuality as a condition that could be "renounce[d]" with the help of a psychiatrist. As Dr. Reuben's statement suggested, most clinicians believed that psychiatric treatment could "cure" homosexuality. What the *New York Times* called the "sick theory" was "the orthodox view of the medical profession" for several years after Stonewall, despite pressure from activist groups and the opinions of researchers like Alfred Kinsey. Only at the end of 1973 would the American Psychiatric Association remove homosexuality from its list of personality disorders like fetishes and compulsions.[5]

Given the clinical opinion of homosexuality as deviance, the topic remained generally off-limits in mainstream America. When discussed at all, the focus was clinical, on the etiology of the "disorder." "Close-binding mothers" and "detached, rejecting fathers," one 1962 study claimed, created homosexuals.[6] Cultural assumptions that same-sexualities were unnatural implied that gays and lesbians were tormented by their urges. Many Americans believed they were also sexual predators driven by their pathologies to commit unspeakable acts. Majority understandings of what homosexuality was reduced gays to gender opposites of heterosexuals: effeminate men, drag queens, and butch women. Sigmund Freud called them sexual inverts. Those whose sexual desires and impulses did not conform to the enforced social norm had to come to terms with that crucial aspect of their identities without support. Yet, particularly after Stonewall, gay communities began to build, helping their members define their own sexual identities apart from stereotypes or notions of sexual inversion. Clothing, as we have seen, was part of this new identity, and constructing families gave gays support networks. Changing the mainstream narrative, however, was an enormous challenge.

The media offered little commentary on sexual identity, simply assuming heterosexuality as a universal norm. Movies never showed gays or lesbians except by innuendo; they were forbidden to by the industry's code. Early TV had its share of flamboyant males of seemingly confused sexuality, like wrestler Gorgeous George or pianist Liberace, who doted on his mother. These representations affected gays and straights alike. Beginning in the early 1960s, occasional TV documentaries purported to explain homosexuality, but the renderings were horrifying rather than enlightening.[7] Since few Americans knew any self-identified gays, the media's few portraits helped to shape most people's notions of what sexual minority status meant.

As the sixties ended, freer public notions of sexuality still did not include gays. Several months after the Stonewall battle, *Time* magazine's cover story on sexual minorities provided no real insight or empathy. The story explained that homosexuality was caused by "emotionally disturbing experiences." It cited Harris poll statistics "that most straight Americans" feared gays and that 63 percent thought them "harmful to American life." The authors did acknowledge that since Stonewall, "male and female inverts have been organizing to claim civil rights for themselves as an aggrieved minority," although 90 percent of American gays were "secret lifer[s]" who still hid their identities. Stonewall may have launched a civil rights–like gay liberation movement, but the popular culture featured only what one scholar called "pitiful gays."[8]

Seventies television, however, changed that. *All in the Family* took on gay stereotypes, just as it did other stereotypes, validating tolerance. As

*Archie arm-wrestles with his buddy, former professional football player Steve,
on* All in the Family. *Later, he will discover that "real man" Steve is also gay.
Photo courtesy of Photofest.*

Nixon noted, the show's episode juxtaposed two characters, one who
manifested the traditional tropes of a culturally constructed gay man
and another who was all man. Working-class patriarch Archie Bunker
complained about the gay-seeming one, a young man named Roger,
much as Nixon did, zeroing in on his purple shirt, ascot, and vocabulary
as proof he was a "fairy," a "queer," and a "pansy." Archie's son-in-law,
Michael, articulated the liberal viewpoint series creator Norman Lear
endorsed, that being "sensitive and . . . an intellectual" did not mean a
man was "queer." To emphasize the point, Lear's writers conjured the
anti-Roger, Steve, a former pro football player who was also Archie's
drinking buddy. The bar owner told Michael he tolerated Steve because
he was a local businessman: "He don't camp it up . . . and he don't bring
in none of his friends." When Steve came out to Archie, Archie thought
it was a joke, refusing to believe that his friend was "a fruit." But the
episode ended in a close-up of Archie's face as the possibility that everything he had assumed about gays was wrong started to register.[9]

Steve represented the first real type of gay television character, inoffensive, as the bar owner suggested, because he neither camped it

up nor congregated with other gays. To the extent that he was relatively open and comfortable with his sexuality, he could be a positive role model for gay viewers. That, of course, was not Steve's purpose. He was a minority character defined by the majority, someone who by his public existence showed Lear's liberal audience how a modern person should understand minority sexualities. Steve was like civil-rights-era African American characters from a few years before, exemplary and inoffensive, a simplistic, mainstreamed version of the modern gay male worthy of being included in the social definition of diversity. Steve's fictional existence was bounded by what heterosexuals thought of him. He could not be a sissy, sexually active, or assertive.

In the next few years, other sitcoms offered other exemplary gay men. Another gay former pro football player, Jack, turned up on *Alice*, confounding her young son's hearsay version of sexual difference. "From the way kids talk, I thought you could always tell," he said. "I didn't care, though, Jack's a great guy." On *M*A*S*H*, the gay man was a much-decorated soldier beaten by his comrades, along with a "colored" one, equating race and sexual identity as diversity categories. On *The Mary Tyler Moore Show*, he was an affable concert pianist, so wonderful that his unknowing sister tried to fix him up with Mary. Each of these gay characters deserved inclusion into mainstream society because each was careful not to offend. All seemed eager—even preferred—to socialize with heterosexuals. If any of these characters had an actual sex life or a group of gay friends, it was not part of the episode.

These stories privileged tolerance over real education about sexual identity. *All in the Family* fumbled for terms, using slurs rather than actually uttering a word that might send children scurrying to their parents to ask, "What does that mean?" *Sanford and Son* avoided words altogether, merely using hand gestures to convey sexual identity. The words, or lack of them, did not matter, as the audience was being taught that gays and lesbians were not that different from anybody else and that both the labels and the differences were best avoided. Although Steve was supposed to be Archie's friend, the audience never saw him again. Nor did the audience understand anything about the difficulties that came unbidden because of Steve's sexual identity. Archie Bunker was "a lovable bigot," as author Laura Z. Hobson argued,[10] but an impotent one. In real life, homophobes had power Archie lacked, the power to arrest, harass, or even kill those who offended them.

By 1977, *TV Guide* reported, "half the sitcoms on television had done a positive ('pro-social') gay show." On show after show, nice people encountered gay characters, and, while surprised, few were discombobulated by sexual difference. The representations made gay liberation "just another of those liberation movements which are so popular at present," adding sexual minorities to the list of differences Americans should tolerate, like race, gender, age, or disability status. While simplistic, publicly acknowledging gays' humanity began a process of social evolution, undercutting notions of deviance and, on television, turning them into mimetic characters. Once people learned to imagine gays and lesbians as people who "feel and think as we do," historian Lynn Hunt has argued, they could recognize their humanity and accord them civil rights.[11] While there were additional venues for showcasing racial minorities' humanity, relevancy sitcoms became one of the primary vehicles for representing gays and lesbians as ordinary people with quietly different sexualities.

Gay activists recognized that media was crucial to their movement and created strategies to gain positive visibility. More militant gays used "zaps" (disruptions) to gain publicity, while others pursued an antidefamation strategy already practiced by representatives of racial and ethnic groups. The Gay Media Task Force, founded in 1973, set about ensuring that media portrayed gays and lesbians fairly. The GMTF sought to raise "network consciousness to the point that GMTF is no longer necessary," as leader Newton Dieter explained. Its policy statement urged the networks to extend to gay and lesbian characters and story lines "the same rules you have for other minorities." The more liberal production companies quickly responded. Deiter consulted with scriptwriters and actors, and another GMTF representative spent two weeks during the summer of 1975 meeting with TV executives, including Norman Lear and Ed. Weinberger. By the fall of 1972, one activist reported that gays had become "a legitimate minority" on television, a sign of maturing American sexual tolerance.[12]

The networks, meanwhile, expanded their exploration of gay life through different genres, with mixed results. News and documentaries reported on the gay liberation movement itself. Talk shows served as forums for discussing discrimination against sexual minorities. In 1972, ABC presented the first made-for-TV movie with a gay main character, *That Certain Summer*, which told the story of a divorced father whose visiting teenage son unexpectedly confronts his father's new gay life. Writers Richard Levinson and William Link's first drafts read like a

The 1972 made-for-TV movie That Certain Summer *starred Hal Holbrook as a loving father, who also happened to be gay. Scott Jacoby won an Emmy for his portrayal of his distressed son. Photo courtesy of Photofest.*

"soap opera," but through revision and consultation, they achieved a human story "without moralizing and without the reassurance of an inevitable happy ending," the *Los Angeles Times* reported. ABC vetted the program, asking the writers to balance out its liberal tone by having the father note that some people regarded homosexuality as a "sickness."[13] The show earned decent ratings and received several Emmy nominations. ABC affiliates noted no surge of complaints about the film, and only one declined to show it. The gay community divided over the program, with the "sickness" speech and the lack of affection between the same-sex couple being two points of contention. Still, *Summer* asked viewers to empathize with a father who loved his son and another man.

The next year, the Public Broadcasting System (PBS) unknowingly took on sexual identity as a theme when it contracted with documentarian Craig Gilbert to produce a multipart portrait of a real American family. Gilbert's family of choice, the Louds, of Santa Barbara, California, were affluent and attractive. His goal with the series, titled *An American Family*, was to reveal "how a man and a woman and children live in America in the 1970s" and coped with "what the American culture is becoming." Gilbert's slice of reality was hardly reassuring. Before the cameras, the Louds' marriage came apart, paterfamilias Bill had affairs, and the children did drugs and drifted from good time to good time. The Louds' oldest son, Lance, was gay—not sensitively gay like *That Certain Summer*'s main character—but flamboyantly gay, with a host of psychological and substance-abuse problems. The most talked-about series episode featured matriarch Pat Loud's visit to New York to stay with her son at the seedy hotel where he lived among drug addicts and drag queens.[14]

Lance Loud's sexuality became the center of public conversations about the series, eclipsing the elder Louds' divorce, the children's self-absorption, and the whole family's "failures to communicate." PBS recognized the ratings windfall he represented, warning in advertisements that his story "might shock a lot of people." Novelist Anne Roiphe, in an oft-cited *New York Times* commentary, called him "the evil flower" who "dominate[d] the drama" with his outrageous outfits, "campy wit," and "leechlike" personality. As the series progressed, she believed, Lance became "more disruptive and irritating," until no "professional intervention" could correct "his manipulative connections to other people." Roiphe professed to have no "understanding of what combination of biology and environment produced Lance." She did, however, stress that his impact on the family was negative, pitting parent against parent. Ultimately, the debate over Lance "smother[ed] . . . [the program's] content," senior *New York Times* TV commentator John O'Connor opined.[15] *An American Family* might as well have carried as its subtitle, "Undone by Gay Liberation."

Two contradictory gay types emerged in those early days of television representations, one looking a lot like Lance and the other like Archie's friend Steve. What often determined which appeared where was the genre. Sitcoms generally gave their audiences Steve-variants. On dramas, by contrast, gay characters symbolized the dangers of a more-permissive and tolerant society. Audience, genre structure, and creators significantly shaped dramas' worldviews, presenting modern America as a scary place. Situated primarily in workplaces, their stories suggested that 1960s social changes threatened individuals and their families. The same present that sitcoms portrayed as inviting, exciting, and enhancing, dramas represented as so bleak as to require professional intervention. Those who watched a steady diet of dramas "see the real world as more dangerous and frightening," a congressional subcommittee investigating violence and obscenity on television concluded in 1977. Dramas reflected a 1970s political trend that historian Philip Jenkins has defined as especially focused on "the threats posed to children by relaxed attitudes toward sex and drugs."[16]

Resolution in dramas required heroes. Sitcoms employed relatable mimetic characters like Mary Richards. Such "one of us" characters coped affirmatively with modernity. They existed in nearly half of all serial programs by 1978. Dramatic leads, by contrast, were better than us, rescuing guest stars from infidelity, divorce, drugs, and hippies. The leads of 1970s sitcoms were diverse and often unconventional. Dramas' hero-figures were older males who protected traditional values. At a time when many Americans believed their nation was in the midst of what Natasha Zaretsky described as "a figurative crisis of father absence," father figures predominated on medical and police programs.[17] When a gay character showed up on a sitcom, his sexuality did not matter. But when a gay character appeared in a drama, it generally signaled some threat to the traditional family to be fixed by a heroic father figure.

Consider, for example, the differences between two doctors, one in a sitcom and one in a drama, and their encounters with a gay patient. Dr. Robert Hartley, the lead character on *The Bob Newhart Show*, an MTM Enterprises production, was a Chicago-based psychologist with a working wife, no children, and a wardrobe of plaid jackets and leisure suits, each of which made him a modern, if mainstream, man. Even his forte, group therapy, represented a modern psychological method. When a new member, Craig Plager, joined one of Bob's groups, the others welcomed him, until he began to talk quite matter-of-factly about a recent breakup with a same-sex partner. Only Plager showed up for the next group session. Bob stuttered over the word "gay" but urged his group to accept Plager as they would any other member. The group returned, and by the end of the episode an elderly group member wanted to set him up with her nephew. The story acknowledged that adopting a modern attitude about sexual identity was not always easy or comfortable, but the right thing to do. It also suggested that a gay man's emotional life was familiar and relatable, so much so that others began to see him as "one of us."[18]

Marcus Welby was not a modern psychologist but an old-fashioned family doctor, described by the executive producer, David Victor, as "the father confessor, the family friend." Welby represented an idealized past, with his family practice located in his house, which looked a lot like where the title character had lived in his previous television incarnation, as Jim Anderson on *Father Knows Best*. Welby knew best too. When he treated a diabetic patient, Martin Loring, he initially assumed his reckless health choices were collateral damage from a failing marriage. Probing deeper, he discerned the real reason for Loring's problems: "A sensitive, lonely boy with a cold and distant father you couldn't relate to and a mother who tried to fill the roles of both parents." "All right," Loring snarled, "so you guessed it." What followed was a lurid confession, the story of a man fighting the "loathsome and degrading" side of himself, repressing his impulses, marrying, having a child, and then, after his father died, succumbing to desires he could not control. Martin Loring was as tragic and conflicted as Craig Plager was open and comfortable with himself. Dr. Hartley modeled tolerance for his group. Dr. Welby prescribed psychiatric intervention so that Loring could overcome the "self-hatred and repression" that caused his homosexuality. With psychiatric help and a good dose of self-discipline, Welby assured him he would "learn to enjoy a normal marital relationship." At a time when the Gay Media Task Force was pressing for representations of homosexuality as "a natural variant of human sexuality," the *Marcus Welby* episode, with its paternalistic lead character and insistence that Loring's sexuality was perverted, offered Americans a very different image of sexual minorities.[19]

The differences between Plager and Loring were immense, suggesting that there was no cultural consensus about the nature of sexual difference in the early 1970s. Plager's sexuality was part of who he was, while Loring's was something to be fought, something that destroyed his family. *The Bob Newhart Show* depicted homosexuality as it was understood by a growing chorus of real-life experts. *Welby*'s version reflected an older explanation. Yet *Welby*'s primary audiences, women over fifty and adolescent girls, were not all that interested in learning whether being gay was a sickness or a natural state. They preferred the fantasy that any family could be healed. The program's sponsors, mainly cosmetic and health-related companies, did not feel threatened if a few GMTF members tried to organize a boycott.[20] *Welby*'s audience wanted to believe that homosexuality was as curable as other modern challenges to the American family.

Doctors were not the only dramatic leads to put right the world by protecting the American family from sixties fallout; so too did police and detectives. Along with drug addicts, hippies, and serial killers, the occasional gay villain threatened the natural order of the TV drama. Police dramas often blamed America's rising crime rate on social permissiveness and the evil people who capitalized on it—hippie drug dealers, Charles Manson–like serial killers, and runaway-exploiting pimps. Gay characters were part of the mix. They committed crimes for psychological reasons and selected their victims because no 1950s family protected them. As antidefamation groups protested associations of racial minorities with criminal behaviors, sexual minorities became a substitute category of social misfits. Homosexuality, which many Americans believed was unnatural, became the perfect explanation for sociopathic criminal acts.

No television crime was more deviant or threatening to the family than child molestation, and police and medical programs' creepiest villains were gay men preying on young boys. The decline of nuclear families with traditional gender roles often facilitated their heinous crimes. On *Marcus Welby*, a teacher assaulted a depressed child of divorce, while on *Kojak*, a young boy was easily separated from his distracted father, who was babysitting while his mother worked. Both episodes also commented on the erosion of traditional masculinity that conservatives feared. On *Welby*, the father saw his son as contaminated; a real man, after all, would have repelled the attack. Once Welby counseled him, he acknowledged how difficult it must have been for his son to name his assailant, equating courage with masculinity: "You acted like a man."[21] The contrast between the pedophile on *Kojak* and the muscular police pursuing him was jarring. The police ran fast and drove quickly. The pedophile was slight, foreign, wore glasses, and played chess. While sitcom gays were he-men, gays on dramas were, to borrow Nixon's phrase, "obviously queer."

TV dramas reinforced stereotypes. A trio of lesbian criminals on *Policewoman* featured "the butch, the bitch, and . . . the femme," as one lesbian publication complained. The "butch," Mame, wore men's shirts buttoned up to her chin, short hair, and no makeup. She "looks like she oughta be driving a diesel truck," opined the police sergeant, as he and policewoman Pepper Anderson exchanged knowing glances. Fay Spain, the actress who played Mame, reported that she was asked to cut her hair, bind her breasts, and deepen her voice. "I've never played anyone less attractive," she concluded. Her look marked her as different, unnatural, and, as Spain noted, possessed of "no redeeming virtues."[22]

TV dramas told their audiences that gay sexuality was not normal. If sitcom gays seemed undersexed, gay characters on dramas were sexually voracious and predatory, threats to the established social order. On *Policewoman*, the "bitch" tried to seduce the heroine, running her hand across her back during an innuendo-filled job interview. Later, she lingered as the policewoman changed clothes. Such assertive sexuality reinforced evangelical preacher Jerry Falwell's contention that gays and lesbians recruited because they "do not reproduce." One study of TV crime shows found that they "promoted . . . intolerance rather than tolerance of outgroups,"[23] in the case of sexual minorities reinforcing some viewers' fears that they might be recruited by a gay person. The overuse of violence on 1970s TV generated a lot of media discussion. The primary voices pondering the social implications of negative and inaccurate renderings of gays and lesbians, by contrast, were gay activists.

Still, the television audience, in the aggregate, preferred liberal and relevant programming to more conservative series. Dramas made for powerful television in the late 1960s, but kindly Dr. Welby had trouble holding his own against socially conscious TV. In four short years, the series went from being the top-rated show in the country to relative TV obscurity. Since their audiences were not as large as those for comedies, early 1970s dramas functioned as counterprogramming, a new scheduling strategy networks used to pursue niche audiences, in this case older viewers. President Gerald Ford, for example, enjoyed *Kojak* and *Policewoman*. So *Welby* ran opposite *All in the Family*, which displaced it from the top of the Nielsens. Producers cast older film actors like Karl Malden or Robert Young as leads. While women wrote and occasionally directed 1970s sitcoms, white, middle-aged men shaped dramas, creating "Republican supersleuths."[24] Television dramas, thus, were both made by and pitched at people uncomfortable with the many social changes the 1960s wrought.

The sorts of stories dramas told, with their fragile families, social permissiveness, and hippie-esque villains, reinforced the fears of coalescing social conservatives. The sexual revolution, the women's movement, and the gay liberation movement, they believed, challenged traditional family roles. Television had been a powerful arbiter of norms that touted whole, happy, white, middle-class families as desirable and everyone else as lesser. Suddenly, after 1970, it was full of constructed families, divorces, affairs, and generation gaps. Conservatives panicked at social relativity and lashed out at the culture that appeared to support it. The gay liberation movement seemed to pose, Matthew D. Lassiter has noted, "an external political threat to the traditional family" altogether.[25] Dr. Welby alone could not protect Americans from predatory gays or a post-1960s culture of moral relativity. In the second half of the 1970s, conservatives mustered to protect their values and privilege them as national norms.

The notion that so ubiquitous a medium as television must affect developing minds was broadly shared. Relevancy programming showcased sixties ideals, ideals not shared by the whole nation. So long as the networks censored their own programming, parents felt little need to exert control over the dial. As relevance predominated and censorship declined, prime time became less child friendly. A 1969 study by the Commission on the Causes and Prevention of Violence concluded that "exposure [to TV violence] tends to *stimulate* violent behavior." By the middle of the decade, evidence that watching violent acts on TV could trigger aggressive behavior in children seemed, one Health and Human Services report said, "overwhelming."[26] But who was responsible for protecting children from potentially problematic programs, parents or networks?

The controversy over violence and television viewing by children reached a crisis in 1974 with the NBC made-for-television movie *Born Innocent*. The story of a chronic teenage runaway sentenced to a juvenile detention facility for girls, the film's most controversial scene featured a gang rape of the runaway in the facility's communal shower. The scene, which *Los Angeles Times* critic Cecil Smith noted appeared at 8:20 P.M., was unusually graphic even for the era, alternating between shots of the girl's terrified face and the motion of the mop handle as it penetrated her. That evening, NBC affiliates logged "a surge of complaints" about the program. At the Nashville affiliate, a weary official called the story "filthy, disgusting, degrading." Critics were kinder, lauding its "glimpse of reality," and NBC defended itself, despite the "very real pressure" a spokesperson for the network acknowledged. "I'm sure we're going to bother these people in Nashville again," he predicted. Everything changed a few weeks later, however, when a parent filed an $11 million lawsuit against NBC's San Francisco affiliate alleging that *Born Innocent* provoked a copycat assault against her nine-year-old daughter by a group of slightly older children. As media scholar Kathryn Montgomery noted, the battle over *Born Innocent* put a face on dozens of governmental hearings about the impact of violence on American youth.[27]

Born Innocent became a rallying point for parents concerned about the impact of violence, particularly sexual violence, on children still forming their notions of the ways the world worked. Some expressed helplessness over the stream of profane images coming into their living rooms. Yet, while conservatives had once urged parents to counter "permissive" parenting by enforcing rules, limits, and punishments, by mid-decade they concluded that parents alone were not strong enough to fight the tide of cultural relativity. Thus, when responding to a concern expressed by a mother whose nine-year-old son was "afraid of grown men, even his teacher, ever since he saw a man rape a boy on 'Marcus Welby,'" popular psychologist Dr. Joyce Brothers did not suggest that the mother regulate her son's viewing or send him to bed before such adult-themed programming ran. Instead, she called for a television rating system to limit children's exposure to small-screen violence.[28]

She was not the only person to do so. Parents' groups began to talk about sponsor boycotts, borrowing a successful civil rights tool. Congress and the Federal Communications Commission launched investigations into the amount of violence on television, seemingly a prelude to imposing guidelines or regulations. Executives at the three major networks panicked and put their own hastily constructed solution into play. They would honor a Family Viewing Hour each evening during the first sixty minutes of network programming, beginning with the 1975/76 season. But the Family Viewing Hour created more problems than it solved. The networks competed with new cable counterparts, like Home Box Office (HBO), which could run movies full of sex and violence at any time. Rather than lose audience, the networks shifted their violent programming into what a *Los Angeles Times* reporter called the "crime ghetto,"[29] later in the evening, and front-loaded their schedules with comedies. The Family Viewing Hour did little to stanch the flow of TV violence. It did, however, affect those comedies unfortunate enough to be shown during it, not because they were violent, but because of their sexual content.

Suddenly *Rhoda*, a comedy about a married couple, could not show the couple in bed or talk about birth control, and Hawkeye, the libidinous surgeon on *M*A*S*H*, found even his implied sexual exploits curbed. As interpreted by the networks, the Family Viewing Hour also meant no confusing alternative sexualities. Marty, a recurring gay character on a comedy about a New York City police precinct, *Barney Miller*, "would have to go," ABC's Standards and Practices Department warned the producer, who, the censor noted, "became hostile and refused to co-operate." Behind the censor's back, the *Miller* cast and crew filmed another episode with Marty in it and justified it to the network as a useful opportunity for parents and children to discuss homosexuality. At ABC headquarters in New York City, the business part of the network, executives acquiesced,[30] but it required a convoluted process to do a story that would have been routine the season before. Tales of battles over a word, a gesture, or an idea filled dozens of newspaper columns, with critics complaining that the Family Viewing Hour inhibited grown-up television.

The Family Viewing Hour lasted only a season. Ratings showed that viewers turned off their TVs, particularly during the hour itself. By the spring of 1976, there was a 5 percent decline in the number of households watching television. The Writers Guild of America sued the networks over the restrictions they collectively imposed on their productions as violations of writers' free speech. In the fall of 1976, a judge ruled that the Family Viewing Hour violated writers' First Amendment rights, freeing up the networks to offer more adult fare. In the end, the experiment accomplished little, except to leave all parties involved in programming wary. Critics wondered, as *Newsweek* asked in 1976, "Why is TV so bad?" Was it the ratings wars or the "profit squeeze" or something more profound that lowered television's quality?[31]

Newly appointed ABC programming head Fred Silverman cared less about the perceived quality of network television than its declining viewership. Earlier in the decade, he was instrumental in shifting CBS from rural comedies to sitcoms like *The Mary Tyler Moore Show*, but over time, he came to believe that sex, rather than relatable characters, represented what the modern viewer wanted to see. As always with series television, his innovations begat copycats on the other networks. In consequence, the "frequency of normative sexual content" on network TV rose significantly. Late 1970s programming was visibly different from the thoughtful explorations of modern life that had proved so popular in the early 1970s. "They're pushing their way up through the TV ranks now," warned a 1978 *Los Angeles Times* story, "pom-pom girls, roller derby queens, reckless coeds, bronzed bikinied beach beauties, slapstick blondes and underdressed agents. Wriggling in and out of fun, trouble and temptation."[32]

As female singer-songwriters discovered in the late 1970s, sexual liberation was a potent and popular idea. Silverman championed *Three's*

Company, a sitcom based on the British series *Man about the House*. Its premise was that a heterosexual male had to pretend to be gay so his landlord would allow him to room with two women. The program contributed little to the public's understanding of minority sexuality. The kind of sex the main character, Jack, thought about constantly was heterosexual, as he leered at his roommates, Janet and Chrissy. An NBC executive complained that this new kind of TV had nothing to do with writing or stories; people watched "because the girls jiggle,"[33] forever branding the style "jiggle TV." *Three's Company* reflected ABC's determination to gain ratings dominance. Its popularity with audiences, though, rested on a new willingness to talk about sex.

One consequence of this new openness was that when it came to incorporating stories of sexual minorities on television, the major networks willingly moved beyond the "prissy tentativeness" of *That Certain Summer*.[34] Gay characters not only received more visibility in the second half of the decade; so too did they get fuller lives. Programs brought Americans into a public space most had never seen before, the gay bar. "Gay people shouldn't be out at a bar having a good time," explained conservative character Arthur Harmon (*Maude*) to studio-audience laughter. "They should be home, alone, being ashamed that they are gay."[35] But television's gays were not home and ashamed; they were donning their designer jeans to dance to disco at their neighborhood watering holes. Thanks to a culture more willing to explore once-taboo topics, they did not have to be inoffensively asexual anymore. Instead, like straight Americans, they lived at a moment when sexuality could be more freely expressed. As the core of the gay movement shifted from rights to liberation, television followed.

Gay characters also gained assertiveness on TV, becoming less exemplary and more multidimensional, following the pattern of African American characters. There was, certainly, an element of stereotypical flamboyance involved, but with an ironic undertone that assumed viewer sophistication and comfort. *Barney Miller*'s Marty and his partner, Darryl, were TV's first gay couple who cared about one another and lived together. Their backstories probably were not what audiences expected: Marty wanted to be a policeman, and Darryl had been married and had a son. They dressed in pastels and bracelets, extended their pinkies, and stood out, as Darryl put it, by "being unique." While earlier gay characters did not "camp it up," Darryl and Marty were deliberately provocative around those who were uncomfortable around them.

Knowing that one of the detectives was nervous about gays, Darryl extended a limp hand to provoke a response, making the detective the butt of the joke and Darryl the viewers' co-conspirator. Neither inverts nor asexual, these more-complex gay characters existed at a moment of quickly changing public acceptance of sexual minorities as human beings whose communities did not quite parallel straight communities but were equal, meaningful, and affirming to their members.

Complexity helped to undermine older gender assumptions. Clothing no longer signified gender or sexual identity. *Soap*'s gay Jodie wore a dress, but *M*A*S*H*'s Corporal Klinger wore one far more enthusiastically and with a better eye to detail, and he was straight. Jodie quickly gave up the feminine clothing, but Klinger kept wearing his because the audience loved the juxtaposition of his masculine and feminine sides. Two gay men shared a seedy room in *Hot L Baltimore*, bickering like an old married couple, and that is how the hotel's other residents treated them. Homophobia got skewered on *Maude* when one male character dreamed of kissing another and the object of his affection became suddenly self-conscious about his every phrase or gesture. As TV programs found the freedom to expand their sexual repertoires, TV audiences were challenged to consider what gender meant and how it related to sexual identities.

Gays also gained defenders and advocates, as dramas and TV movies explored the consequences of homophobia, including institutional and legal discriminations. Dramas revealed that however comfortable individuals might be with their sexual identities, they were not treated equally by society. A made-for-TV movie reenacted the Air Force's response to the first openly gay man in its ranks, Leonard Matlovich, which was to dismiss him. In *A Question of Love*, an ABC movie, a lesbian fought for custody of her children. These were nuanced accounts, and their legal aspects generally emphasized equal rights for sexual minorities, much as TV programs insisted on equal rights for women and racial minorities. Most critics agreed that TV's sexual revolution of the late 1970s was exploitative and often tasteless. At the same time, though, its renderings of sexual minorities invited more of those characters to become "one of us."

There were limits to the trend toward more relatable gay characters, however. Lesbian characters, never as plentiful on television as gay males, failed to gain much visibility. When they did, it tended to be for the titillation of male viewers. The female prison warden became a stock TV character, kinky and sadistic. On *Charlie's Angels*, her name was Maxine, "Maxie" to the male guards she clearly loathed. She presided over the Angels' intake, watching them strip and shower, promising a guard, "I'll try not to bruise her skin too hard," as she gestured to audience favorite Farrah Fawcett. One critic called the result "porno chic,"[36] putting beautiful women in sexual danger that excited male viewers.

The networks' exploitation of sexual themes also led to a bumper crop of transgender characters. The real-life story of Richard Raskind, an ophthalmologist and former professional tennis player who transitioned into Renee Richards in 1975, put the experience before the public and suggested story possibilities to producers and writers eager to create television drawn from real life. *Medical Center* used the Richards case as inspiration for its two-part story about a doctor who sought to correct the "ghastly joke" nature played on him by giving him male genitalia. The series' choice for its star was Robert Reed, a closeted gay man whose most famous role was as the father in a corny throwback sitcom, *The Brady Bunch*. In *Medical Center*, Reed also played a husband and father, under very different circumstances. The show acknowledged the difficult impact of his decision to seek sex-reassignment surgery on his family but ultimately concluded that the choice was his to make. The episode informed viewers that gender identity is "all in your mind," as the transitioning man declared.[37] It was an early statement of the idea that gender was a social construction, a set of learned behaviors that existed distinct from a person's sexual identity.

On sitcoms, stories about transgender persons became opportunities for playful commentary on the meaning of modern masculinity. Both *The Jeffersons* and *WKRP in Cincinnati* featured plots where old buddies of continuing characters returned as women to whom they were drawn. *WKRP* explained the attraction as logical because the two men had been friends. Between 1975 and 1980, a half-dozen transgender characters appeared on prime-time television, and while the initial reactions might have been shock, audiences saw heterosexual men like Herb Tarlek (*WKRP*) ponder the question, "If a guy dates a girl who used to be a guy but isn't anymore, what does that make the guy who dates the girl who used to be a guy?"[38] Gently and gradually, 1970s television separated characters' sexual and gender identities. While it is highly unlikely that most viewers thought about the deeper meaning of seeing Herb's old football buddy as a woman, that most laughed at the idea rather than write letters to *WKRP*'s sponsors suggests that sexual and gender categories were becoming fluid in real life as well.

Stories about sexual minorities encouraged understandings of gender as social constructions, what feminist theorist Judith Butler would shortly call "performances." In the sexually active world of contemporary series television, most viewers enjoyed the slightly naughty humor of questions like whether a character was "FM" instead of "AM," as Ted Baxter suggested on *The Mary Tyler Moore Show*. Having been told that comely receptionist Jennifer used to be a man, *WKRP*'s Herb merely altered his standard come-on to her, inviting her to "go bowling." Straight characters sometimes played gay, generally to discomfort characters presented as snooty or conservative. And when *Taxi* lead Alex Reiger showed up in a gay bar to "set . . . straight, as it were," a bisexual man dating a female cabbie while interested in a male one, he shortly found himself dancing with a man. At first he resisted, but he ended up on top of the bar in full disco mode, reveling in the pleasure of the performance and winning a trophy.[39] Such programs took their humor from parallel behavior, women behaving as stereotypical men, men behaving as stereotypical women, and same-sex partners behaving like stereotypical married couples. Today, such story lines are common; but they can only exist because Americans let go of the notion of fixed gender characteristics beginning in the late 1970s.

New notions of sexuality and gender identity resonated with television audiences overall. Two-thirds of viewers queried in a 1978 poll believed that the "sex-related material on television today accurately reflects what is happening," suggesting that realism as well as raciness drew them in. After decades of sitcom couples sleeping in twin beds, viewers welcomed the messiness of 1970s sex stories, even when they were salacious and simplistic. Still, television changed quickly, reacting to a broad range of issues, breaching the once-clearer lines between fact and fiction, no longer insular and inoffensive. The idea that "values are being formed, changed, manipulated, often subliminally," as *New York Times* critic John O'Connor observed, could be distressing. While there were plenty of studies addressing the impact of TV violence, only in 1977 did experts begin to ponder TV's sexual stories as a "potent and immediate means of affecting change."[40] Many Americans worried about TV. Most, however, continued to watch—to be entertained, educated, or outraged or to see some affirmation of their own modern lives.

For the outraged, stories about sexual minority characters constituted the most alarming element of the medium's new openness. Unlike other subjects explored by seventies TV, a majority of viewers had no firsthand experience with gay or lesbian sex or relationships. Television and film provided that majority with the opportunity to understand aspects of gays' lives, to see beyond the headlines. Overall, Americans welcomed TV's sexual frankness for providing "more understanding of others' life-styles," but only to a point. Viewers enjoyed watching stories about "premarital sex, scenes of couples embracing in bed, and women in revealing clothes," one study found, but were less comfortable with "homosexuality and mate-swapping," believing that the networks should "leave the evolution of new sexual patterns" to other institutions. As much as viewers flocked to watch TV's sexual revolution—one centered on the sex lives of single heterosexuals—many regarded as inappropriate subjects for television any sexual story that involved children or "directly challenge[d] the integrity of the family."[41]

Television's stories about sexual minorities celebrated the individual and supported new definitions of gender and sexual identity but fed conservatives' fears about the decline of the traditional nuclear family. For most of TV's brief history, conservatives saw images of families that matched their beliefs about gender. In this pristine TV universe, sex did not much exist and homosexuality did not exist at all. But the sexual revolution, the gay liberation movement, feminism, and the counterculture undermined even TV's fiction of this norm. Moral relativism not only prevailed, but it did so flamboyantly in front of children. Some Americans had trouble adjusting. Moreover, as Alice Echols has noted, liberation freed gays and lesbians to define their own cultural norms,[42] something late-1970s TV emphasized. As television began to project more freewheeling sexual attitudes, some viewers protested.

What disturbed them most was the challenge TV's depictions of sex posed to the values some viewers wanted to impart to their children. Protecting children from sexual and gender diversity was a central theme in the emerging social conservative crusade. Philip Jenkins calls 1977 "the year of the child," when "matters of sexuality [such] as sexual abuse and molestation appeared quite suddenly on the political agenda," placed there by conservatives. Gays and lesbians remained child exploiters in increasingly graphic TV stories. About a third of all episodes of 1970s dramas featuring gay or lesbian characters included teenagers or children rescued physically or psychologically from same-sex encounters, and two-thirds of TV movies that dealt with homosexuality involved young people. Those Americans most likely to see homosexuality as "more prevalent" in the 1970s (older, married, less educated, living in the Midwest or the South) were the most concerned "that children might be influenced to follow their [homosexuals'] way of life."[43] Those same categories of Americans were also the most likely to support a conservative or Christian movement opposed to renderings of sex on TV.

The range of organized groups opposing television violence was broad, including the national Parent-Teacher Association and the American Medical Association. Organized opponents of TV sex, by contrast, came primarily from evangelical churches. The key figure in the movement to rein in sexual representations and situations on television left his United Methodist congregation in Tupelo, Mississippi, to devote himself full time to, as *TV Guide* reported it, "make television repent its obsessive and excessive sex, vulgarity and profanity." Donald Wildmon became a vital part of a coalescing movement self-proclaimed as pro-family. Armed with a mimeograph machine and strong convictions, he founded the National Federation for Decency and the American Family Association. His followers monitored television content relentlessly for renderings that offended their sensibilities. He compiled his followers' notes and sent the results to sponsors, "threaten[ing] exposure or economic boycotts if commercials are not removed from unsuitable shows."[44] Wildmon objected to unmarried sex, jokes about drugs, or homosexuality, anything that he believed violated God's way. He was but the most visible organizer of a larger evangelical crusade that used customer boycotts to pressure producers to clean up television programming. Even though the target was broad, at the center of conservative objections was a particular variant of sexuality, gay sexuality.

Soap, a soap opera parody launched in the fall of 1977, served as "the opening wedge" in the battle over "sexually explicit material in prime time." The ABC series included many once-taboo sexual subjects, but the gay character, Jodie, played by Billy Crystal, attracted most critical attention. Long before the show aired, "the watchdogs of television morality" were already in "a lather," as one reporter wryly noted, based on published descriptions of the program's premise. Organized from a variety of church offices and family rooms, letter-writing campaigns targeted ABC and sponsors. Overall, members of what conservatives would come to call the liberal media dismissed the campaign, but sponsors and affiliates paid more attention. Despite relatively small protest numbers, ABC affiliates in Baltimore, Dallas, and West Virginia declined to air the series. Advertisers felt conservatives' pressure, and some pulled their ads from *Soap*. Others, however, likened the campaign to the "blacklist of the 1950s." The president of ABC Television called the protests hysterical and uninformed, "stimulated by hearsay." Even the American Civil Liberties Union waded into the controversy, with its executive director decrying the campaign as a "shameful" attempt to "control what's on the air." The battle against *Soap* largely failed, leaving its organizers feeling victimized by a media that regarded them as narrow-minded "vigilantes" or ignorant Southerners. The series aired and earned decent ratings and mixed reviews. Yet even the victors emerged from the fight afraid that they stood on the brink of a new era, one characterized by censorship. "ABC will long remember the sting of 'Soap' in its eyes," predicted Harry N. Hollis Jr., director of family and special moral concerns for the Southern Baptist Christian Life Commission.[45]

Indeed, conservatives accelerated their crusade against immoral "liberal chic." To Wildmon and others, the chicken-and-egg debate about whether television reshaped values or reflected back what had already been reshaped was no mystery. Television, they believed, undermined the traditional with its "soft-core, progressive statement about love, marriage, drugs, blacks, women, and gays" that depicted homosexuality "as natural and acceptable." "We watch adultery every night," Wildmon complained. "We laugh at homosexuality.... Where does it stop? Where do we draw the line?" Programming that presented gays and lesbians as ordinary people upended conservatives' belief that homosexuality was, as Southern Baptist conventions resolved, "deviant," with "devastating consequences for family life." In order to draw the line the culture seemed unwilling to draw, Wildmon suggested that committed members of congregations "speak out against this permissiveness of the new morality." Television, the place where the largest number of Americans encountered homosexuality in the 1970s, became one powerful center of campaigns against its depiction.[46]

Social conservatives like Wildmon often lived in insular communities. Their churches were at the centers of their social networks, and their institutions had media outlets. It did not really matter to them whether their values were majority values or not, as they believed theirs were God's values and the principles upon which American society had been founded. They understood the mainstreaming of 1960s ideals as a "values conspiracy" perpetrated by "a few hundred people" imposed on beleaguered families from outside. But social conservatives had absorbed many 1960s lessons, particularly how to express dissent and wield power against authority, in this case a new-style television establishment. Wildmon telegraphed governors and President Jimmy Carter soliciting their support, organized National Talk to Your TV Day and Turn Off Your TV Week in 1977, "gimmicks," he later conceded, that were necessary because his movement otherwise lacked visibility. He persisted anyway, taking aim at the TV industry's "pocket book," the sponsors.[47]

Sponsors were more sensitive to advocacy-group pressure than were the networks. Ratings determined the cost of an ad in a particular time slot, but that meant that the sponsors best able to pay for ads on highly rated programs were also often the most corporate ones—during an anti-Establishment era. They needed to appear principled. Conservatives promoted themselves as true Americans upholding tradition against liberal secularists, feminists, porn merchants, drug dealers, sexual deviants, and dubious celebrities of unclear sexuality eager to endorse a range of individual sexual practices. According to this scenario, media had "moral culpability" for supporting the 1960s' evil outcomes. Wildmon put the sponsors he thought glamorized TV's Sodom and Gomorrah on notice, warning them to consider their "company image[s]." He followed up with action, picketers with signs chanting outside Sears' Chicago headquarters. Soon Sears pulled its ads from *Three's Company* and *Charlie's Angels*, although representatives denied the boycott was the reason why. Wildmon next trained his sights on the Ford Motor Company, raising concerns among advertisers that the boycott "seemed to be spreading." In response, several of the most prolific TV advertisers hired consultants to help them choose inoffensive, family-friendly ways to spend their advertising dollars. They resented doing so, because they knew the larger segment of their audience liked the risqué programming, but the minority was vocal and volatile. Wildmon became less laughable over time, gaining more powerful allies, like influential Republican strategist-turned-radio-commentator Pat Buchanan, who commended the protest-and-boycott tactic borrowed from the Left as "a healthy development."[48]

Networks faced their own sorts of pressures. Cable television, able to show more sex, was making its first serious inroads on their audiences, and the best response they could imagine was to "pander to prurience in the most cheaply exploitative manner," as *Newsweek*'s TV reporter acerbically noted. Network executives had no respect for Wildmon and his followers and, under other circumstances, would have written them off as unimportant or unlikely viewers of their programs. *Mary Tyler Moore* executive producer Ed. Weinberger complained about "a few censors" imposing minority views on the public.[49] But as sponsors pulled their ads, networks' programming freedom seemed in jeopardy. Conservatives' pro-family crusade had an impact.

With interlocking mailing lists, syndicated television stations, and colorful spokespersons, conservatives were hardly the smug, small-minded fun-spoilers their opponents made them out to be. They were "on the political offensive," as scholars have noted, in the late 1970s, targeting the equal rights amendment, popular music, school curricula, and television.[50] Once Phyllis Schlafly got the anti-ERA bandwagon rolling, other activists followed. Anita Bryant picked up the conservative cudgel in 1977 with a campaign against a local gay rights ordinance in Dade County, one of a number passed by local communities in the years following Stonewall. Bryant, a onetime beauty queen, was a deeply Christian, Miami-based singer who believed that homosexuality was "an insidious attack on God" perpetrated by "militant homosexuals," whose agenda was to recruit a new generation of gays. She vowed a "crusade to stop it as this country has not seen before." Her Save Our Children group successfully orchestrated the repeal of the Dade County ordinance and sparked a national movement. Several other municipalities rescinded gay rights ordinances after Bryant's campaign, and California state senator John Briggs began a drive to place an initiative on the state ballot forbidding homosexuals from teaching in public schools. Bryant, meanwhile, announced that she intended to create a watchdog group "to identify and monitor TV shows that present gay life-styles as 'natural and normal.'"[51]

The conservative tactic "helped to redefine homosexuality as a civil rights issue," as media scholar Steven Capsuto has observed, legitimating its place within a discourse of diversity and broad-mindedness. The attacks galvanized the gay rights movement. San Francisco's 1977 Gay Pride Parade attracted more than twice as many marchers as the year before, which organizers attributed to Bryant's campaign. The *Los Angeles Times* commented on its retro look, "more like a protest march" than a celebration of sexualities. Protesters followed Bryant everywhere and made enough noise that the Singer Sewing Machine Company withdrew its offer to sponsor her syndicated TV show, citing her "controversial political opinions" as the reason why. Youth, the very people Bryant sought to protect, ranked her as destructive, along with Richard Nixon and Adolf Hitler. Ku Klux Klansmen showed up at one of her West Virginia public appearances to protect her from protesters, which did her image little good. While a majority of evangelical Christians supported Bryant's work, she also was a catalyst for gays and lesbians and their allies forming an effective political force.[52]

The Briggs initiative, which singled out California's gay and lesbian teachers, brought overt entertainment industry support for gay rights. Stories about homophobia, harassment, and discrimination against gays increased on television. Several programs took up the issue of gay schoolteachers, most notably ABC's drama *Family* and Norman Lear's syndicated show *The Baxters*. The latter's format was unusual, presenting an issue and then inviting audiences in cities where it aired to respond to the stories. The episode identified the plight of gay public schoolteachers as a "human rights" issue rather than a social threat. When a character challenged that notion, he sounded like Archie Bunker objecting to his son-in-law's friend: "What about our rights? I don't want homos teaching our nation's children." Matriarch Nancy Baxter, a continuing character, responded: "I don't want some uptight, narrow-minded, ill-informed parents bringing up our nation's children."[53] Critics applauded stories like *The Baxters* as sensitive and timely; but even as the wider public got a televised glimpse of the threats posed by anti-gay crusades, there were fewer stories to see.

As *TV Guide* noted in 1981, "Gays are featured much more rarely on weekly series these days." In 1976, the widely touted year of the TV gay, nearly twenty nighttime dramas or sitcoms offered either gay characters or plots. In 1977, there were sixteen; but the next year only three stories appeared. In 1976, there were five recurring gay characters on American television; by 1978, one remained. Gay villains scared conservative viewers, but gay victims disturbed their worldviews, just as anything other than sad, swishy gays upset their understandings of homosexuality. As the possible range of gay characters and gay story lines expanded, evangelicals and other conservatives upped their monitoring of programs and their boycotts. To avoid alienating interest groups, programmers fell back on the principle of the least objectionable programming, shows like *Little House on the Prairie* and *Donny and Marie* (Osmond).[54] Like other minorities, gays and lesbians had advocacy groups to defend them with the networks, but they were the only minority groups with advocacy groups to oppose them, which made them the subjects of the most controversial stories of all.

Negotiating the thicket of conflicting advocacy groups and gun-shy sponsors added an additional layer to the complicated late 1970s business of producing a show. In 1979, Danny Arnold, creator of *Barney Miller*, pitched a series based on the French film *La Cage aux Folles* to ABC, *Adam and Yves*. The network encouraged him to develop the project, but before he had a single script written, word leaked out about the projected series and American Christian Cause launched "Halt TV Smut" to oppose it. Form letters sent to a computerized mailing list warned of "militant homosexuals" who waged "war against the Christian family," providing postcards that could be sent to the Federal Communications Commission. Long before the series was in production, the FCC had logged more than 123,000 complaints against it.[55] Arnold abandoned the series idea, afraid that he could not fight conservatives, keep the network happy, satisfy gay activists, and still produce a quality show.

Like Arnold, the networks also struggled to find balance. In a more sexually open era, their Standards and Practices staffs, who once stood guard over television morality, became negotiators working out compromises between creative teams whose goal was to "mirror existing reality" in their shows and the minority of viewers "objecting to the depiction of changing moral values." The list of advocacy groups with opinions about program content grew. Norman Lear employed a full-time assistant just to deal with them. Everyone wanted to appear accepting of difference, but no one wanted to be perceived as kowtowing to extremists or allowing outsiders to dictate content. Not all interest groups carried equal weight within the industry. Some promoted what industry insiders perceived as "opening avenues and widening horizons," while others wanted "to write America's moral ticket," and it was the latter, conservatives, that most troubled the networks.[56]

Ronald Reagan's election in 1980 gave conservative media advocates greater scope without adding to the number of viewers they represented. Americans might have shifted rightward on economic and political matters, but, as Daniel Yankelovich predicted, "new rules" and a "new morality" prevailed. "More Americans are accepting the unconventional, progressive or liberal social behavior," the conservative American Enterprise Institute reported. In 1979, the Moral Majority brought together the family values crusaders into a single organization full of confidence and bluster; but it was not clear it could actually deliver the results its advocates threatened. Donald Wildmon backed away from a sponsor boycott in the fall of 1980, ostensibly "to give advertisers a second chance." Procter & Gamble, the nation's largest TV advertiser, dropped sponsorship of fifty shows without prodding. Other firms, though, quickly stepped in to claim the spots the company dropped. While "nervous," the networks renewed such sexually tinged series as *The Love Boat* and *Three's Company*.[57] Only one program seemed affected by conservative protests, NBC's new sitcom *Love, Sidney*, the story of an older gay man who had given up on life after his partner died until he took in a single mother and her daughter. Suddenly the network began to downplay the character's sexual identity in favor of the constructed-family theme. Series star Tony Randall chided NBC, urging its executives "to show a little more character,"[58] but when the series finally aired, there were no spoken references to the main character's sexuality. Just a picture on the mantelpiece reminded in-the-know viewers of Sidney Shorr's sexuality.

Although the controversy over *Love, Sidney* might suggest that a conservative minority of viewers drove representations of sexual minorities off the air in the early 1980s, the truth is considerably more complex. As TV's tales about sexual minorities shifted from simplistically preaching tolerance to playful or complex renderings of the experiences of LGBT characters, they facilitated a new visibility for sexual minorities that implicitly modeled acceptance and respect. Even as the number of stories about gays and lesbians declined, dialogue and smaller plot points suggested that many of the TV characters Americans had come to know and love were comfortable with a range of sexual practices and identities. News stories about the gay liberation movement, the battles in Dade County and California, and gay pride parades emphasized the rights angle so familiar to veterans of other battles, while TV dramas about gay teachers or students dramatized the human costs of sexual discrimination. By 1980, more Americans knew someone who was a self-identified sexual minority than a decade before; but much of what Americans knew about sexual minorities was still filtered through TV.

TV's sexual minorities seemed a lot more like familiar people in 1980 than they had in 1970, and it was not just the added subtlety and dimension of later representations either. The goal of gay liberation—to live freely and truthfully—was one widely shared by many members of the baby boom generation. Youth found common cause in their sexual rebellions and most especially in the notion that individuals constructed their own identities. The social conservative message did not strike the same note of familiarity. As singer-songwriter music helped to suggest, youth sexuality differed significantly from what had come before, with pleasure and desire rather than rules or marriage licenses distinguishing it, qualities equally relevant whatever one's sexual identity. Thus, once again, youth were forerunners in the process of 1960s mainstreaming. They counted for more as consumers of television than did social conservatives. By 1977, baby boomers were twice as likely as Americans over the age of fifty to believe that same-sex relations should be legal.[59] They helped to propagate ideas of sexual tolerance.

Even though modern social conservatives still describe their views as "family values," late 1970s television suggested otherwise. Programming often indicated that intolerance wrecked families, not sexual difference. Whether it was Sidney's ersatz family or *Soap*'s Jodie's biological one, TV families embraced their gay members, often with love. Stories of family reconciliation rested on understandings of minority sexualities as variants of human behavior, not perversions or threats. Although not all Americans believed that sexual identity existed in many varieties, the shift from gay sex as psychological disorder to simply different sex occurred very quickly in the 1970s, and media played a significant role in disseminating the change. As Vice President Joe Biden noted about more recent television programing, "*Will & Grace* probably did more to educate the American public than almost anything anybody's ever done so far." What *Will & Grace* showed, like previous gay-themed programming, was that sexual identity is "something a person is born with,"[60] an idea refreshed by sitcoms, dramas, documentaries, and TV movies.

The more recent quick public turnaround on gay marriage or the public response to Caitlyn Jenner suggests how important the 1970s were for setting a tone on gay, lesbian, bisexual, and transgender rights. Those who were young in the 1970s are not so young anymore; but they are more likely to support gay marriage than those who were born before the baby boom, and their children and grandchildren are even more nonchalant about the once-radical idea that human sexuality is very individual.[61] In the 1970s, understandings of homosexuality quickly transformed from a psychological illness to another version of sexuality and from learned behavior to biologically determined behavior. Television played a part in this transformation, shifting from the preachy clinical tone of the documentary to the freer, more playful sitcom mistaken-identity plot, and then, as conservatives began to challenge that transformation, TV documented the impact of those actions on people who seemed just like us. This transformation was hardly the conspiracy Donald Wildmon or Anita Bryant imagined it was. Instead, it revealed a medium trying to reinvent itself in order to cater to an audience that had grown up believing in difference, tolerance, or, at the very least, the power of the people to change what they did not like. Not all Americans embraced newer ideas about sexuality and gender, but substantial numbers of Americans had, thanks in part to television.

Representations of sexual minorities on television were but one expression of the sixties. The women's movement, the sexual revolution, and the gay liberation movement challenged stereotypical notions of gender and sexuality, masculine and feminine, male and female. Sociologists first distinguished between gender and sexuality in 1978.[62] Series television expressed the same thought more idiomatically. Growing from its tentative early 1970s pictures of inoffensive gay men, television became bold in its rendering of gays, lesbians, and transgender individuals, about whom many Americans have learned, thanks to programming like *Transparent* and *Orange Is the New Black*. Alongside the television portrayals, tolerance for minority sexualities grows. And, contrary to what "family values" conservatives warned, gays and lesbians have not threatened families but instead have provided a foundation on which to construct—to borrow the title of one of the nation's most popular sitcoms, which includes a married gay couple with a daughter—modern families.

6 : Don't Drink the Kool-Aid

The Jonestown Tragedy, the Press, and the New American Sensibility

On Thanksgiving Day 1978, my parents hosted dinner at their home in the San Francisco Bay Area. What everyone expected to be an ordinary multigenerational family gathering turned into a wake of sorts when, several days before, the story of the mass death of Peoples Temple members first appeared in the press. My father's favorite cousin, his cousin's wife, and the son Temple leader Jim Jones had persuaded them to foster were all residents of the Temple's jungle commune, Jonestown, in Guyana. Although the details were still emerging, our relative's name had already appeared on the earliest lists of Jonestown dead. We compulsively watched TV news reports through our dinner, mourning our relations while indulging in turkey and pumpkin pie. I also harbored a secret as I sat at the table, one I did not want to bother my rattled parents with. A reporter had contacted me, finding my unusual family name in the phonebook. The encounter unnerved me a little, too, as Temple defectors warned of "avenging angels" harassing relatives. Not long after that odd Thanksgiving, one of my Berkeley housemates came home from an end-of-the-term party that, he reported with great mirth, featured a vat of alcohol and Kool-Aid, "jungle juice," he called it, a reference to the tub of cyanide and flavored drink mix that killed the more than 900 members of the Jonestown commune.

While most Americans did not know anyone affiliated with the Peoples Temple, my encounters with the deaths in Jonestown were otherwise typical. The nation received the news with sadness, confusion, paranoia, anger, disbelief, and, sometimes, black humor. Not surprising, a story that big provoked "a compulsive searching for explanation, whether cosmic, social, political or psychological," a commentator noted. The public interpretation of Jonestown went through many phases but ultimately came to be symbolized by a warning phrase, "don't drink the Kool-Aid," meaning, "don't fall for a charlatan, a too-good-to-be-true promise, or a lie." Lost since the sixties was any "broad faith"[1] in American institutions to protect ordinary people, their needs, and their interests. In response, a new personal ideal emerged as the seventies ended, one that was independent, resilient, and resourceful—a survivor. In the case of Jonestown, Americans practiced their skepticism and self-preservation skills against many different kinds of establishments, some old and some new. Helping them to make sense of the senseless was a press likewise determined to stay relevant and be anti-Establishment.

For years, "nobody was paying attention" to Jones or his jungle compound in Guyana. After more American civilians died in a single day than had ever died before—only the 9/11 attacks would surpass it in scope—"the amount of attention [the press] devoted transformed it into a major event."[2] Tragedy got peoples' attention. Gallup polls taken after the event indicated that 98 percent of Americans were familiar with Jonestown and the Peoples Temple. People ranked its significance with Pearl Harbor, the dropping of an atomic bomb on Hiroshima, and the assassination of President John Kennedy. Yet unlike those events, the Jonestown deaths did not directly affect most Americans. What made the story so compelling anyway, according to a British pundit, was its considerable similarity "to the modern imagination of disaster." Historian William Graebner notes that Americans developed a revealing fondness for disaster movies in the late 1970s, a taste encouraged by the decade's supposed "existential despair." The "collapse of [traditional] meaning and values" in the sixties, he argues, left people feeling vulnerable. Negotiating modern life required less conformity and more choices, along with the ability to improvise, resist authority, and persist, despite the many evils the world contained. Graebner sees disaster movies as a metaphor for 1970s life, a set of challenges Americans met by "defining themselves . . . as survivors." Stories of "catastrophe" vicariously tested people, providing "a curiously pleasurable space—a space of emotion, of decision, of action, of caring, of sacrificing, of agency." As interpreted by the press, the story of Jonestown, like disaster films, countered "feel[ings of having] . . . no leverage."[3] Just as the survivors of movies like *The Poseidon Adventure* (1972) or *Earthquake* (1974) fought back against overwhelming danger, so too did accounts of what happened at Jonestown acknowledge that in the modern world, individuals might have to take more responsibility for their own welfare.

The press delivered to the public a Jonestown story replete with the hallmarks of a disaster film. There was a seemingly indifferent Establishment, maverick heroes, hints of conspiracy, sex and violence, and the perceived presence of evil. Since the deaths occurred outside the country and the U.S. government's longtime response to Jones had been very hands off, media had unusual power to shape the Jonestown narrative. In their version, disaster occurred because individuals, like their government, disavowed responsibility for their own well-being, ceding power to a madman. Although the vast majority of Jonestown residents died, some survived, and they did so by resisting Jones, even at the last moment. The narrative created by the press and embellished by experts encouraged people to identify with the heroes of Jonestown rather than its victims, teaching them to recognize and embrace the differences between themselves and those who drank the Kool-Aid. It was a message many would carry into the 1980s and beyond.

Until its very end, the Peoples Temple flew below the national radar, even in an era when oddities tended to attract a lot of media attention. Its seeming lack of newsworthiness, though, was to a degree contrived. Like my family, West Coasters might have known someone who belonged to the Peoples Temple, listening politely to their recruitment efforts and then moving on. Politically liberal San Franciscans might find Temple members robotic and Jones a little too fond of adulation, but "the Reverend Jones could also turn out a crowd for election day," so they did not look a gift horse in the mouth. Compared to other religious or pseudo-religious groups, the group appeared benign since its roots were Christian and its membership diverse. Its press was sparse but generally favorable. Local papers depicted it as "an alternative religious sect involved with timely and important social issues," not a cult. Once the press did start to question, even a little bit, Jones moved the group to the commune it was already building in the Guyanese jungle. Once there, he controlled the story, preferring no news at all to trying to generate propaganda for the consumption of outsiders. As the archivist of the group noted, nobody really seemed to care "how they [Temple members] lived; but we all remember how they died."[4]

Consequently, when Bay Area congressman Leo Ryan decided to visit the Temple, it was not a media event. Ryan could not induce colleagues to make his investigation an official congressional enterprise. Instead, he put his faith in the press to "act as a lever to force open the doors of the Jonestown jungle settlement," even though he could entice mostly local press to journey with him. Only NBC's *Today Show* and the *Washington Post* sent crews, and the *Post* reporter was not happy about

Congressman Leo Ryan interviewed Jim Jones in Jonestown just hours before Ryan died. Left to right: *Ryan, his aide Jackie Speier, Jones, his attorney Charles Garry, and the U.S. attaché to the American embassy in Guyana, Richard Dwyer. Dwyer and Speier survived the airfield attack. Photo courtesy of* San Francisco Examiner *Archives, Bancroft Library, University of California, Berkeley.*

having to cover "a zany story about a congressman wanting to investigate a freaky religious commune" instead of having Thanksgiving with his family.[5] Virtually everyone else accompanying Ryan had a family member in Jonestown, representatives of a group known as the Concerned Relatives, which had had no success inducing the federal government to intervene in Peoples Temple affairs. The party had a mostly positive visit and were impressed by the colony, but not by Jones. It was only at the end when some residents asked to leave that the encounter grew tense. An assailant pulled a knife on Ryan, bloodying him a bit, but the party regrouped and got ready to depart. As they reached the local airfield, the reporters were mentally planning their stories, and Ryan likely thought the worst was over. Out of nowhere came Temple gunmen, who killed five members of the group, including Ryan, and wounded more. The story that would consume the country, though, was about to start a few miles away, as Jones called his people around him and had his lieutenants bring forth vats of cyanide and flavored drink mix in order to commit suicide as a revolutionary act. Only then did the story become national in scope. Only then did the press, politicians, and most people pay attention.

The press explained its previous disinterest in the Peoples Temple as accidental, a "'missed' news story." That claim was disingenuous at best. Jim Jones wooed editors, riding an anti-Establishment tidal wave by providing cash awards to newspapers for preserving free speech. Simultaneously, and less visibly, he also intimidated those questioning the group's carefully crafted veneer. *San Francisco Examiner* religion reporter Lester Kinsolver published only half of his 1972 series on the group before Temple members picketed the paper's offices and his editor ended it. *San Francisco Chronicle* reporter Marshall Kilduff was "put on notice very quietly that Jones was a friend of my superior's," a point reinforced when he spotted him at a Peoples Temple service. Despite securing interviews with a number of Temple defectors who told of "the Spartan regimentation, fear and self-imposed humiliation," along with the discipline, physical punishments, and psychological pressures Jones exerted on church members, Kilduff had to publish in a smaller venue, *New West* magazine. *New West*, in turn, had its offices burglarized by Temple members. "The story of Jim Jones and his Peoples Temple is not over," Kilduff and his *New West* coauthor, Phil Tracy, predicted. Indeed, the details were damning enough to send Jones and his followers prematurely to Jonestown. But neither *New West* nor any other news outlet followed up. While the *Post*'s Charles Krause believed that "it was the press . . . which finally began to pierce the veil and reveal the truth about the Peoples Temple," those endeavors only happened after the fact because journalists often "shar[ed] the same perceptions" as the liberal Jones or were afraid to challenge him.[6]

The press's failures to investigate the Peoples Temple stand out particularly because of its commitment to exposure, which earned it respect in 1970s America. Few mainstream institutions survived the sixties as successfully as did the press. Its reputation, moreover, rested on its willingness to take on sacred cows and authority figures. The contemporary press featured "reporters for the public—not for the politicians," according to famed journalist Theodore H. White. Investigative journalism, which was supposed to reveal hypocrisy and lies, was in vogue. Launched in 1968, *Sixty Minutes* documented scandals, often with reporters confronting the guilty on camera. The *New York Times* published the famous leaked documents revealing governmental deceit over the war in Vietnam, the Pentagon Papers. Reporter Seymour

Hersh's investigations into the My Lai massacre prompted public outrage and forced the military to react. The Watergate scandal marked the apex of the "heroic-journalist" and the nadir of public trust in government. By 1976, only 11 percent of Americans had faith in their government (down from 44 percent a decade before), but the two *Washington Post* journalists who stayed doggedly on the Watergate story, Bob Woodward and Carl Bernstein, ranked at the top of youth's list of heroes.[7] The public had high expectations for the press about to cover the end of the Peoples Temple community. But the distance, the terrain, the fierce Guyanese government, editorial hesitation, and previous public disinterest had already worked against exposés of the Peoples Temple.

Other journalistic trends pushed the story toward the disaster genre. Although investigative journalism was the professional ideal, audience, costs, and competition often undermined its rigor. Like so many other parts of 1970s culture, the news media was fragmented, reflecting a shift from a single mainstream media to one with more outlets and more voices. Sometimes it just was not clear what constituted the Establishment's media and who its challengers were. So much competition sometimes put greater value on getting the story first rather than the accuracy and completeness of the reportage. Ambitious young reporters like Geraldo Rivera parlayed local stories into independent careers. Visuals competed with analysis, a means of allowing members of a fractious public at least the illusion of deciding for themselves what events actually meant. Local TV news producers, as Mary Richards and her fictional WJM news team discovered, wanted human interest stories. Supermarket tabloids paid for firsthand accounts, undermining professional ethics. Personality mattered on the air. Print reporters created personal style through New Journalism, a journalistic method pioneered in the 1960s by writers like Tom Wolfe and Truman Capote. New Journalism featured "colorful style, extensive description, experimental use of language and punctuation, changing points of view, [and] personal commentary from the writer." Like the era that nurtured it or the "faction" and docudramas spawned by *Roots*, New Journalism was also subjective. As television stopped self censoring, newscasts began to include graphic coverage of sex and violence. "The commercial value of blood and gore," a contemporary scholar studying media responses to Jonestown noted, heightened interest in the tale. Indeed, a Temple representative in San Francisco recalled that what the press wanted from her was "the most gruesome details."[8]

The journalists accompanying Ryan saw themselves as mavericks and individuals rather than as Establishment voices, even though they represented "institutions of great 'power.'" Reporters expected to fight their editors, pressed to see parts of Jonestown their hosts preferred not to show them, and tried to trip up Jim Jones when they interviewed him. On the way to the Port Kaituma airstrip, where he would be wounded by Temple gunmen, Charles Krause already anticipated a conflict between the "scoop" he assumed his editor wanted and the "long and thoughtful piece" he wanted to write. Yet his work was also opinionated and at times cynical. Until the end, he "rather admired Jim Jones's goals" and did not believe the Temple was a "crazy fringe cult." His eyewitness status afforded him popular credibility, which the *Washington Post* parlayed into greater exposure. The *Post* arranged his reports into a "quickie" book released two weeks after Ryan's death, the rights for which Krause sold to CBS in a development deal.[9] Many Jonestown journalists approached their topic as Krause did, believing their professional responsibilities were anti-Establishment.

Congressman Leo Ryan was a politician made for the changing world of journalism. He too was a crusader. He spent a week as an ordinary inmate at Folsom Prison studying conditions there and boasted that he was the only American congressman ever to chain himself to a baby seal to prevent its slaughter. When several reputable constituents told him that they suspected their relatives were being held in Jonestown against their wills and the son of an old friend, and Temple defector, turned up dead, he decided to investigate. Since no other member of Congress joined the venture, Ryan decided to go it alone, bringing the press and family members to try to expose what the American government seemed disinclined to examine. State Department representatives and diplomats on the ground in Georgetown were polite, skeptical of Ryan's entourage, and not especially helpful. Most of what he learned about Jonestown came from alternative sources, particularly the Concerned Relatives organization. Ryan seemed undaunted by the makeshift status of his investigation, trusting that so long as he had the press along to document the truth, nothing bad could happen to him.

The drawbacks of Ryan's strategy became clear only after the fact. On the Port Kaituma airstrip, Temple assailants targeted those with visible tools of the journalistic trade, cameramen. As eager to use Ryan as he was to use them, the reporters accompanying him disregarded State Department warnings that they might "anger the cultists." They felt confident they could handle "the public relations–conscious Temple." When there was only limited seating on Ryan's plane into the jungle, they successfully lobbied for seats over communards' family members, arguing that publicity was a useful thing. They assumed that, unlike previous journalists, they would be able to see past Jones's "obvious, naïve, and unsophisticated" methods. Members of Ryan's press entourage were cocky and, as it turned out, themselves naive. Charles Krause thought nothing of the Temple leaders who watched their arrival at the airport in Georgetown and the press visas that had to be renewed every twenty-four hours and assumed it was an "irritating" coincidence when the hotel where members of the press had reservations had no room for them. Eventually, he realized that Jones "could stop us by having us killed. The thought that he might try never crossed my mind." A *Los Angeles Times* reporter finally concluded that bringing the press to Guyana "probably led to his own death [Ryan's] and the deaths of three news media persons with him."[10]

That possibility did not put a damper on press coverage. Perhaps given the danger, the remoteness, or the proximity to the Thanksgiving holiday, many of those assigned to cover the unfolding news were of Krause's generation, including NBC's Andrea Mitchell and Meredith Vieira. They were young, ambitious, and intrusive. In Guyana, they swarmed all over witnesses, including people who had just seen family members die. In San Francisco, they thrust microphones in front of visibly upset relatives of Jonestown casualties and pushed on barricades, in some cases following people home. Local reporters called bewildered people like me, hungry for any added drama they could put in a story. Krause's book was one of three to appear within six weeks of the mass death, "like vultures picking over the remains," a *New York Times* reviewer opined. *Roots*' success at dramatizing unpleasant history practically guaranteed a Jonestown docudrama. Within days of the tragedy, pitches were "pouring into ABC," and a cartoon in the *Chicago Tribune* suggested that the story was so "disgusting, repulsive, and nauseating . . . [that it] ought to make millions." A Mexican-made movie starring American actors appeared less than a year later, "superficial" and inaccurate, at least according to the CBS television team making *The Mad Messiah*, later renamed *The Guyana Tragedy*, based on Krause's book. Although the books did poorly, the American TV film earned high ratings and an Emmy for its lead. Several months after the deaths, it was possible to buy a tape of the commune's last hours, with wailing

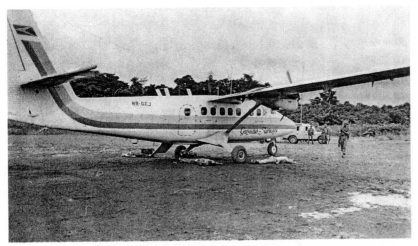

San Francisco Examiner *reporter Tim Reiterman used slain cameraman Greg Robinson's camera to document the dead bodies on the airstrip at Port Kaituma, Guyana, before being flown out of the jungle the day after Congressman Leo Ryan, Robinson, and three others died there, killed by Peoples Temple gunmen. Photo courtesy of* San Francisco Examiner *Archives, Bancroft Library, University of California, Berkeley.*

babies and Jones demanding, "For God's sake, let's get on with it," as some seemed reluctant to drink the potion.[11] Americans sometimes decried the media's excesses but craved the vicarious experience of disaster, counting on the press to put them straight into, as more than one journalist quoted Joseph Conrad, the "heart of darkness."

Rather than being perceived as the catalysts for disaster, journalists became the first heroes of Jonestown. Three died with Ryan, several others were wounded, and all were stranded overnight in the jungle, awaiting transportation out of the crime scene while hoping that Jones's henchmen did not return. "Lying in a hospital bed with one arm immobilized and the other carrying an intravenous tube, reporter Tim Reiterman early today dictated this story," read the editorial note before one *San Francisco Examiner* report. NBC *Nightly News* filmed Los Angeles-affiliate cameraman Steven Sung in similar condition: heavily bandaged arm, IV bag, and a phalanx of microphones. Colleagues lauded *Examiner* photographer Greg Robinson and Bob Brown, a Los Angeles NBC-affiliate cameraman, both killed by Temple gunmen, for their courage and professionalism. "Sure he was worried," speculated one of Robinson's colleagues, "he was worried about the humidity in his camera. He was worried about getting the pictures out and about having his camera taken away from him." Brown served as the model for actor Michael Douglas's character in the 1978 film *The China Syndrome*. Douglas had shadowed him for the role and memorialized him thereafter as the man who "kept his finger on the button of his camera even while he was dying." Television viewers could read the jeans or safari jackets worn by the journalists accompanying Ryan just as easily as could one of the Concerned Relatives, a college student who thought the journalists "kind of 'hard core'" and Brown, in particular, "real macho." Ryan's press phalanx looked, talked, and acted like countercultural, anti-Establishment activists.[12]

As reporters, however, they were at the mercy of the situational realities of Guyana, excluded from the Jonestown commune by Guyanese authorities they did not respect or trust. On 20 November 1978, NBC news anchor David Brinkley reported that more than 300 "cultists," as he called them, were dead. For the next few days, journalists tried to piece together the "grisly mathematical puzzle" of Jonestown by reconciling the number of the dead that Guyanese soldiers had removed with the number of followers Jones boasted he had, which left 800 people missing. Nobody in authority offered a convincing explanation for the missing, leading the normally sober *Los Angeles Times* to improvise that they "ran, screaming, into the jungle" before they could be "mowed down" by "grinning executioners, loyal to 'Bishop' Jones until the end." By Thanksgiving Day, 23 November, military forces, American and Guyanese, counted beds at the commune and lowered the number of missing to several hundred. A day later, U.S. military personnel removed the first layer of bodies closest to Jones and found more lying beneath them, just over 900 in all. "Day by day," the *Chicago Tribune* noted, a "new stunning horror" unfolded. The unlikeliness of what authorities told them made reporters suspicious that crucial pieces of the story had been withheld or misrepresented.[13]

In Guyana and back home, competition was fierce for a story that was unprecedented, bizarre, and utterly opaque. As CBS newsman Roger Mudd noted, Jones's group was "little known outside of northern California." Those most willing to be interviewed in the early days had strong opinions about the Temple, either pro or con, which skewed coverage and spurred reporters to press harder for details. Temple defectors predicted revenge by Jones loyalists, adding emotionalism to an already emotional story. Guyanese natives told ABC and CBS crews that

Jones had a body double, leading to rumors that the double had died in his place. Three members of the Temple inner circle materialized outside the compound carrying guns and a suitcase full of money. Had they really been dispatched by Jones's mistress to bring the money to the Soviet embassy (their story), or were they, as most Temple defectors told reporters, part of a hit squad to kill Jones's enemies? Early reportage emphasized uncertainty, anxiety, and panic, the same sense of "what next?" that Americans felt after 9/11, the same adrenalin-pumping qualities that prevailed in disaster movies like *Jaws* or *The Exorcist*.[14]

As more journalists arrived in Guyana to cover the story—"literally hundreds," according to *Rolling Stone*'s Tim Cahill—a sense of barely controlled chaos prevailed. For several days, reporters had to bide their time, limited by changing Guyanese and U.S. military policies, "endlessly [describing] the logistics of body removal." When the governments finally granted "about fifty news ghouls" access to Jonestown, they fought for seats on helicopters and planes, "like a Tokyo subway at rush hour." Finally in Jonestown, "everything was ironic," Cahill thought. He saw "bits and pieces" that had fallen off human bodies plowed under by Guyanese workers using tractors once used to work commune crops. At Jones's cottage, there were "books and magazines . . . about conspiracies . . . hundreds of Valium tablets . . . a pile of blank Guyanese power-of-attorney forms," and a series of confessions addressed "to Dad." "No one," Cahill noted, "admitted to being happy and well adjusted." He saw a guard tower painted with "bright seascapes" and outfitted with a slide, a "denial of the tower's function" he likened to the Newspeak in George Orwell's dystopian novel *1984*. Looking up, he spied a double rainbow "encompassing the whole of Jonestown." Cahill seemed particularly taken by the juxtaposition of evidence of gruesome death with ordinary life, a commentary that to him represented the senselessness of it all. Seeing Jonestown, even with the bodies removed, confirmed that evil had been perpetrated there.[15]

Photographs captured what the reporters saw. Out of necessity, early stories had to be visual, since most journalists were denied access to the commune. Enterprising news teams chartered planes and flew over the compound to secure images from the air. The "crazy quilt" of bodies below defied interpretation but interrupted many a viewer's dinner, much as Vietnam's television war had interrupted meals half a dozen years before. Later, with access to the compound, photographers snapped pictures of "the instruments of death," paper cups and hypo-

Photographs like this one both startled and fascinated an American public grown used to visual representations of death yet not prepared for the shocking deaths of so many "ordinary" people. Photo courtesy of San Francisco Examiner *Archives, Bancroft Library, University of California, Berkeley.*

dermic needles and the "vat of cyanide-laced ade." But the most gruesome images preceded the removal of the bodies. Guyanese authorities gave the first journalists on the scene early access to the compound. They sent home to American news outlets photos of "the incredible carpet of bodies" and Jim Jones's corpse, "so swollen" his torso had "burst through his red shirt," his "once-handsome features . . . barely recognizable."[16] *Time, Newsweek,* and most daily papers included panoramas of dead bodies in their Jonestown coverage, requiring editors to make on-the-spot decisions about what was and was not appropriate for public consumption. The photos put Americans face-to-face with ordinary people who died horrible and unnecessary deaths.

Like history textbooks, American journalism became more visual in the 1970s. Satellite feeds made distant images instantly accessible, and newsmagazines added color to their photographs. While baby boomers were raised on puffy photojournalistic pieces about astronauts' families or Kennedy offspring, the war in Vietnam normalized the idea of the photo exposé, whether it was the teenager hovering over a dead body at Kent State or a naked Vietnamese girl running from napalm. Jonestown pictures were both ubiquitous and unsettling. They "wouldn't go away," the parent of victims recalled. No longer protected by a family-friendly culture, children saw them too. The "stacks of bodies," columnist Colman McCarthy noted, became schoolyard conversation, a disturbing new-age "initiation rite . . . into adulthood." "Can a society take bloated bodies and trailer-loads of shiny corpse containers with its evening meals and be unchanged?," a *Washington Post* editorial wondered.[17] A few readers or viewers complained; most, however, just looked.

Once the body counts were accurate and the bodies were removed, the press, experts, and the public turned their attention to making sense of Jones and his movement. Was he "the product of a peculiar lunacy, or does it reflect on us all?" Commentators usually suggested that it was some of both, that Jones was a fraud who effectively cultivated followers through manipulation. Journalists retroactively put the Peoples Temple into a category they had resisted before—the cult. "In this bewildering era," as *People* magazine put it, the average American already knew a lot about cults, including the "Moonies [Sun Myung Moon's Unification Church], Children of God, Hare Krishnas, Synanon [a California-based group for recovering addicts] and Scientology." Citizens encountered their members in airports and on street corners, read about them in *Time* and *Newsweek*, and, if they lived in the college towns where so many of the groups recruited, likely warded off their solicitations or invitations on a regular basis. *Newsweek* reported that there were 3,000 different cults, and *Time* noted that they "come roughly in 50-year cycles," especially during "times of great social change." "People under the age of 30" were said to be particularly vulnerable, as they were "searching for meaning" in uncertain post-1960s times. Cults offered "the attractions of living within a single closed system of life and beliefs," columnist Ellen Goodman explained, providing "relief" and "retreat" from a complex world, one where individuals longed for "a sense of meaning and place."[18] Cults served, most news outlets suggested, those rendered desperate or confused by sixties changes.

Cults flourished because of the times; but many Americans also blamed the federal government for enabling them. Some felt President Jimmy Carter facilitated their spread by "just managing" rather than "leading the nation." For others, however, the government's disinclination to regulate or monitor cults revealed what mocking leftists already called "political correctness" when describing their colleagues' overzealous and inflexible application of sixties values. By the second half of the decade, one political establishment seemed to have replaced another. In this new one, dogmatism shaped by equal justice prevailed to an extreme and illogical degree. Political correctness, in this instance the government's too-careful recognition of "rights of individuals" and respect for diversity, meant that federal authorities trod carefully around cults, creating a kind of authority vacuum that gave unscrupulous leaders great scope. Many a family member with a relative in the Hare Krishnas or the Church of Scientology turned first to the federal government, only to discover a legal wall of protections for cults. Between 1975 and 1978, the Justice Department received from 400 to 500 complaints about them and prosecuted only one case, and lost it. A new profession, that of deprogrammer, emerged in the 1970s, an individual who could be paid to kidnap an adult from a cult and, using many of the same techniques cults were said to use, undo any brainwashing. An American Civil Liberties Union spokesperson described deprogrammers as "hired thugs," but parents felt they had few other alternatives since the government failed to advocate for their children. After the fact, the State Department's investigation into the Jonestown matter concluded that "officials were hampered by constitutional and legal restraints, which guarantee freedom of religion and assembly."[19]

Jonestown invigorated and focused the ongoing public debate about cults' powers, with most public voices scapegoating the American government for its failure to regulate or scrutinize cults that exposed the vulnerable to exploitation. "When is our society going to come to its senses," one woman wondered in an outraged letter to the editor, "and make a distinction between sober, legitimate religious belief and sanctified insanity?" Blaming the Establishment was almost a reflex by 1978, but it was hard for those with family or friends in cults to draw the line between tolerance and diversity on the one hand and what seemed like reckless political correctness on the other. Conservatives faulted the "liberal establishment" for giving Jim Jones "a free ride," extending First Amendment freedoms to his church that really was not a church. Of course, many conservative evangelical churches also counted on those same privileges as did Jones. Peoples Temple survivors in California continued to assert their rights as the body count rose in Guyana, insisting theirs was "an ongoing church" and, therefore, not "subject to government interference." Carter finally weighed in at a press conference, where he cautioned against using the deaths as an excuse for giving the federal government license "to control people's religious beliefs." Yet for many Americans, it was government's responsibility to protect its citizens against the dangers posed by cults. Polls taken one year later found that nearly four out of five Americans thought some religious groups were dangerous and more than three-fourths believed the government should investigate any cult with complaints against it.[20] The Jonestown tragedy reinforced what a lot of Americans already believed, that the American government lacked the wherewithal to protect its citizens against the many dangers of life.

In many public forums, lawyers became symbols of political correctness, the for-hire enforcers of individual freedom who kept the feckless federal government at bay. A lot of Americans bemoaned the growing litigiousness of the nation, which they assumed grew out of some version of political correctness, including civil rights complaints, environmental impact statements, affirmative action, and consumer protection laws. "The public is not pleased with lawyers," conceded American Bar Association president William B. Spann Jr. Surveys found that a majority of citizens believed the legal system favored the rich and powerful, and a substantial minority thought an attorney would act unethically if it helped his or her client. By the late 1970s, Americans were chuckling over a cycle of lawyer jokes that lampooned a once-sterling profession as "morally deficient." "Send lawyers, guns and money," urged rocker Warren Zevon in a contemporary song, because "the shit has hit the fan."[21]

Jim Jones employed two of the "radical brand of inkeater[s] [lawyers]" skilled at manipulating political correctness to defend sixties radicals. These "seamy characters" effectively fought the government but also made it impossible for family members to rescue or even contact Temple members. Both became villains in the Peoples Temple story. "To an ordinary person," one commentator noted, they "might seem . . . guilty of a terrible crime for which they are not being prosecuted." The first, Charles Garry, *People* magazine explained, "had been a rebel with one cause or another" all his life, defending Black Panther leaders with "flair." Garry knew how to manipulate the system. He filed an individual Freedom of Information Act claim for every person in the Peoples Temple, seeking evidence of government harassment, the sheer volume of which hamstrung personnel at the American embassy in Guyana and kept individual employees' gut opinions about Jonestown out of any official logs or transmissions. Garry "practically forced" Jones to grant the Ryan party entrance to his community and helped to show the Ryan party around but did not stick around when the poison appeared. Rather, he and Jones's other attorney, with whom he was not speaking, forged a temporary truce to get out alive. His confession that he was partly "responsible" for what occurred led to no consequences, just a bill sent to the few remaining Temple members. To a frustrated public, he symbolized the abuse of legal power by cunning leftwing attorneys.[22]

Jones's other lawyer, Mark Lane, also accepted no responsibility for Jones or Jonestown but seemed even "more deserving" of blame. While Garry perfected an assertive legal strategy to keep the U.S. government from probing into Temple affairs, Lane's forte was conspiratorial plots. He believed the CIA was responsible for both John F. Kennedy's and Martin Luther King's deaths. Lane fed Jones's paranoia, helping to convince the Jonestown communards that the CIA surrounded their compound. Garry feared the more flamboyant Lane was squeezing him out of a job, although he benefited when Lane's quick wit and smooth talk got the two past a Temple guard and into the jungle as the deaths began. Once outside, Lane warned of more horrible acts to come, that is, political assassinations and "death squads" poised to attack public figures, but accepted no responsibility for failing to alert authorities about the danger he believed Jones posed. Soon he capitalized on Jonestown notoriety with paid public talks and a book, *The Strongest Poison*. Lane epitomized a legal profession influenced by the theatricality of legal proceedings against radicals. This "vulture named Mark Lane," a *Chicago Tribune* headline read, "circles over Guyana's dead."[23]

That the self-promoting and exploitative Lane did nothing about Jones surprised few; the State Department's hands-off stance, by contrast, infuriated journalists and citizens alike. Congressman Ryan's staff assessed their boss as a victim of the agency's "indifference and hostility." State Department personnel assured Ryan that Jonestown "was benign and reasonable despite (contrary) information." An editorial in the Temple's hometown Ukiah, California, paper declared that State Department personnel "sat on their broad butts just as though the Peoples Temple commune was not a bomb just ticking away." The idea that the State Department might look the other way rather than wrestle with diplomatic complexities or a litigious Mark Lane infuriated a public exasperated by its public servants. A State Department spokesperson argued otherwise, but the coda to his comments confirmed the sort of careful legal tolerance Garry and Lane exploited, the political correctness that made so many Americans angry. His people and the embassy staff in Georgetown, he explained, had "discharged their responsibilities fully and conscientiously *within the limits placed upon them by law and basic constitutional guarantees of the right to privacy.*" Indeed, when quizzed at a press conference, President Carter refused to engage in any after-the-fact hand-wringing about deaths that "did not take place in our own country" within a group that had broken no federal laws. The federal government's handling of the Ryan visit to Jonestown, like its oh-so-carefully calibrated policies toward the Peoples Temple more generally, fit 1970s Americans' belief in a growing social lawlessness borne of the government's weakness and indifference for the general welfare.[24]

Journalists retrospectively noted Jones's skills at exploiting political correctness, beginning in his home state of Indiana, and next in the small town of Ukiah, where he resettled his followers, and then in San Francisco. He expected—and got—favors in return for political work. He served as the head of San Francisco's Housing Commission, and the Temple's legal adviser before Garry or Lane, Tim Stoen, secured a job in the San Francisco District Attorney's Office. Jones's choice of Guyana as a place to build a new community was deliberate, stories indicated; Guyana's government was Marxist, black, and intimidating to American politicians. U.S. law did not apply and there was no extradition treaty between the two nations, and by throwing around some "precious U.S. currency," Jones bought privacy and protection. A "strange deal [existed] between Guyana and Peoples Temple," the *San Francisco Chronicle* concluded, cemented by money and racial politics, including a batch of young white women sent "to seduce officials." All this friendliness, articles noted, resulted in customs inspectors willing to look the other way as crates of guns and drugs passed through their offices on their way to Jonestown. Ryan's press entourage quickly realized the sinister dimensions of what U.S. diplomats warned them about, that Jones "seemed to have a lot of clout with the Guyanese government."[25]

Wily attorneys and a seemingly ineffectual federal government merited journalists' attention, but what the public really wanted to read were stories about the Temple's underside and the details that demonstrated that Jones was "totally and completely mad." A note left behind in Jonestown urged Americans to "see what we have tried to do" and to understand that the community "was a monument to life, to the [re]newal of the human spirit . . . built by a beleaguered people." The public, though, was not interested in the ideals that initially shaped the community nearly as much as in Jones's "dark, private side," including "the pornography of Jonestown . . . lurid details of beatings, sexual humiliations, and public acts of perversion" that he used to maintain his power, the "kooky stuff about his sex life," and the cruel punishments inflicted on disobedient Temple members. Reporters uncovered an old arrest of the preacher for soliciting sex in a public restroom in Los Angeles. Jones's "fascination with death," dating back to his childhood days performing pet funerals, also became grist for the journalistic mill. Such details disturbed, alarmed, titillated, but finally fit into the narrative of disaster, featuring the same sort of psycho-killers, child molesters, and gay predators featured on TV dramas.[26]

Compelling firsthand accounts of the Temple's last six months supported a narrative of sixties-dreams-crushed-by-Jones's-paranoias, as survivors offered justifications for joining the movement, details of their disillusionments, and the unlikelihood of escape. "The heroic effort of carving the settlement out of a wild jungle had been all but abandoned," one explained. The new sawmill sat unused and promised farm animals never materialized, suggesting that Jones had simply given up trying to make his utopia functional. He stopped leaving the compound, imposing a pervasive gloom over the community that bore his name. He worried obsessively that the U.S. government would make good on court orders it had issued to return John Victor Stoen to his parents. Jones insisted the boy was his child; a birth certificate suggested otherwise. One of the women who tended to Jones and Temple business, Deborah Layton, defected, appalled by what the movement had become. She told the American consul to Guyana that Jones believed CIA or FBI agents surrounded the camp or that the Guyanese Defense Force stood ready to invade it. Survivors noted that the "white nights," suicide drills, began that summer, ways of slowly normalizing mass suicide into what Jones assured them was a revolutionary act. So too did Russian language and education classes begin, engaging the colony in the distraction of relocation, even though Jones had barely made contact with the Soviet embassy in Georgetown. The drills, the classes, and the prolonged nightly harangues exhausted even the Temple faithful, although accounts tended to divide over whether most of Jones's remaining followers were disgruntled but trapped or still believers near the community's end. In the fall of 1978, Jones sent a subordinate to California to spy on defectors. This spy informed Jones of Ryan's intended visit, prompting a massive shipment of cyanide into the jungle. Former movement people confirmed that Jones claimed to be the re-incarnation of Jesus or Lenin. His use of drugs escalated, they observed. "White bags filled with pills and medication—mostly Percodan and Valium," *People* magazine reported, were "with him all the time." *Time* magazine explained that by the penultimate stage of Jonestown life, its authoritarian leader was beyond rescue, enveloped by a "progressively suicidal depression."[27]

Historian Philip Jenkins contends that in the second half of the seventies "many Americans adopted a more pessimistic, more threatening interpretation of human behavior," an analysis consistent with William Graebner's observations about the popularity of catastrophe narratives. During the era, Jenkins tells us, "the worst criminals were seen as irrational monsters driven by uncontrollable violence and lust." Such behavior could not be predicted or controlled by traditional authorities, especially not those trying to observe the spirit and letter of the law. What we today regard as terroristic actions seemed to escalate in the seventies—assassination attempts, serial killers, seemingly random bombings, political kidnappings. Urban crime rates climbed in the 1970s, but scarier were the demented killers, like Charles Manson or New York City's Son of Sam, who terrorized communities because they were angry, frustrated, or thwarted. Phil Zimbardo's Stanford prison experiment (1971) demonstrated that anyone, when given power over others, had the capacity for cruelty. "Since the three terrible assassinations of the 1960s, most Americans seem to have become believers in conspiracy," political analyst Anthony Lewis noted.[28] Many kinds of emotional and irrational frames of reference affected how journalists reported and Americans understood the Jonestown deaths.

Consequently, conspiracy explanations for what happened in Jonestown became "no more far-fetched" than any other to some. Black activist Dick Gregory believed that the CIA and FBI killed everyone in Jonestown, and conspiracy-fancier Peter Beter announced that the U.S. government staged Jonestown to cover up its destruction of a Soviet missile base in Guyana. The anticult activists at the Berkeley-based Human Freedom Center assumed that the U.S. government had managed "a cover-up" in Jonestown, although different people believed in different cover-ups. Some hypothesized that on the final night, part of the community escaped into the jungle but were driven back into the compound "by agents of somebody" and gassed. Others speculated that the deaths were not self-inflicted but a "horrible government experiment" "to exterminate blacks."[29] Those who advanced the theories were generally outside the mainstream, but nevertheless the press reported them without commentary. Conspiratorial explanations of Jonestown's end spoke to some individuals' feelings of utter helplessness.

Even the U.S. government itself seemed to credit some of the conspiracy theories about Jonestown, conceding its inability to protect the communards. The FBI investigated warnings about death squads and hit lists, and a Berkeley Police Department SWAT team surrounded the Human Freedom Center in case of reprisals. Officials worked to squelch rumors that a "Temple security officer known to look like [Jones] . . . may have been murdered in his place," checking dental records. FBI "fingerprint specialists" confirmed that it was Jones, but "there were a lot of people who thought that Jones did not die in Jonestown and would surface someplace else," remembered Tony Tamburello, the court-appointed attorney for Congressman Ryan's alleged shooter. The idea seemed plausible enough that novelist Armistead Maupin built his 1982 book, *Further Tales of the City*, around it. While none of the rumors about look-alike Joneses or "avenging angels" turned out to be true, their wide circulation further undermined general confidence that the full Jonestown story had been told. Six months later, a congressional investigation conceded that only "time may diminish" what many still regarded as a possibility, "that a Peoples Temple death squad" was prepared "to carry out the last wishes of the Rev. Jim Jones." A year later, a defector assured NBC *Nightly News* that a "hit squad" was just biding its time before coming after people like her.[30]

In a situation where authorities either would not or could not act, survivors became the heroes, celebrated for their willingness to defy the powerful. In some cases, they almost literally avoided drinking the Kool-Aid. The public celebrated Leo Ryan and the journalists killed alongside him as brave and dedicated, but what really sold newspapers and magazines were the stories of ordinary people who joined the movement, became disillusioned, and escaped it. Their examples provided inspiring tales of, as one reader said, "individual courage and intelligence." Such stories emphasized the same qualities that made Alex Haley's ancestors so popular—resistance, determination, powerful senses of identity, and resilience. Virtually every survivor's story began with a "dream of social equality," which finally collided with the reality of Jones and Jonestown, prompting escape plots and plans. Survivors and defectors emphasized the many obstacles they faced: the guards along the commune's perimeter, the possibility that a family member might report even mildly critical complaints about the community, the dangerous jungle surrounding the compound, and the horrifying punishments should you be caught. "How do we get out of Jonestown?," wondered Richard Clark, who used the opportunity of a "day off" during Congressman Ryan's visit to pretend to go on a picnic, carving a path into the jungle that enabled eleven people to escape just before the deaths began. The Parks family planned their escape together for two months, setting aside food and water and scouting an escape route. When the Ryan mission arrived, they asked to leave. Even then, "I never expected to get out alive," one remembered. Patricia Parks, mother of three, was killed while boarding a plane out of Jonestown, but her "children had had the presence of mind to pull up the gangway and lock the door" to protect themselves. Young Tom Bogue asked local Amerindians "to teach him ways to live in the forest." His first escape attempt failed, but what he learned served him well when he and his family left with Ryan. He was wounded during the airstrip shooting but took "flight into the jungle," leading other Jonestown young people safely through the underbrush. These stories were "like thrillers," psychologist Phil Zimbardo noted, but also "hopeful" in that they proved "that people can reject an evil system once they recognize that it is evil."[31]

The Concerned Relatives, who had been invisible before the white night, gained public traction after the fact for their efforts to secure their family members' freedom from Jones. Once written off as "paranoid and crazy" to the few people who had noticed them, they became some of the most compelling experts on Jones's sinister plots. The group, led by Greek-Orthodox-priest-turned-psychologist Steven Katsaris and Tim Stoen, former Temple attorney, had tried both legal and extralegal means to extricate their family members from Jonestown, none of which had interested the press. Katsaris and Stoen traveled to Guyana with Ryan, but not to Jonestown, knowing that Jones would use their presence to deny entrance to the group. Katsaris sent his son in to reason with his sister Maria, one of Jones's much-younger mistresses. Charles Krause found deep humanity in Katsaris's actions, a sort of positive emotionality that contrasted sharply with Jones's paranoia. He "simply wanted Maria to come home," demonstrating the unconditional love of a father for his daughter. Yet Krause also believed that Maria was "old enough to make her own decisions," a pronouncement that summarized the dilemma of political correctness, tolerance over paternalism and protection. Maria Katsaris died at Jonestown after helping to distribute the poison and dispatching armed men with a suitcase full of money from the compound, no ordinary victim, but an accomplice of sorts. Concerned Relatives fought a Quixote-like battle against Jones that, like slave resistances or conservatives' attempts to halt the gay liberation movement, was noteworthy but unlikely to succeed. In any case, the organization's persistence serves as further evidence of the ongoing strength of family in the 1970s.[32]

Speaking up for the victims of Jonestown fell, as it did to Katsaris, to their family members. They might be critical of the government, of Jones's attorneys, and of Jones himself, but they had Katsaris's deep unconditional love for their relatives. Their advocacy took the form of insisting that their relations had not committed suicide but instead had been murdered. The press and the public initially described what happened at Jonestown as a mass suicide. The "sect lined up to get poison," the *Los Angeles Times* reported, while the *Chicago Tribune* declared that "religious zealots obediently joined self-proclaimed messiah Jim Jones in a mass ritual of suicide." Almost immediately, however, eyewitnesses challenged the idea that many of the communards drank the Kool-Aid so willingly, and family members of the dead demanded "that the death certificates of the Jonestown tragedy . . . not be written off as suicides/ mass suicides . . . only homicide." "Jones ordered cultists to drink cyanide potion," the *Los Angeles Times* later told its readers, while "gunmen prevented escapes." Defectors remembered people arguing against death during suicide drills. "Is it too late for Russia?," a woman asks on a tape of the commune's final hours. She was later found dead with syringe marks on her neck. The few eyewitnesses to the commune's end noted that Jones's henchmen forced the poison down some throats, and journalists who saw bodies said that some had syringes jabbed into them. Nearly everyone pointed out that children could not make informed decisions about suicide. Describing what occurred as murder rather than as suicide gave family members and friends of Jonestown victims at least the consolation that, at the very end, their loved ones were not also fanatics willingly going to their graves on Jones's instruction.[33]

Soon the acceptable phrase to describe what occurred in Jonestown was "murder and suicide," a politically correct term that accommodated both agency and Jones's overweening power. Commentators explained how Jones cunningly gained control over his followers. "In San Francisco, they'd have run," a psychiatrist explained, "but where the hell were they going to run in Guyana?" Isolation became crucial to any explanation of how Jones stole individual identities. Journalist after journalist used the phrase "concentration camp" to describe Jonestown, implying a set of power dynamics that rendered individuals helpless and without hope. In Jonestown, *Newsweek* said, "every aspect of life" was regulated and controlled. Food became scarce, with residents surviving on "rice and gravy," which kept them weak. Jonestown was hot, but most people were expected to work in the fields with little rest. "The workday," *Newsweek* noted, "increased from eight hours to eleven." In the evenings, Jones made everyone attend meetings, "railing against everything from the white man's sins in Africa to the venality of some communards who balked at giving him their wristwatches." There was never time to sleep, to think, to be alone, themes that exposés of the Hare Krishnas or the Unification Church had already introduced to the American public. Communication with the outside world, survivors reported, was impossible. Anyone breaking the rules would be publicly humiliated or privately drugged. Finally, *Newsweek* explained, Jones brought everyone together for "a three-day period of brainwashing and intimidation," a pilot white night that proved to Jones he could induce people to die for him. Jonestown was supposed to be a utopian colony for Americans disgruntled by their own society. It ended up, virtually everyone agreed, as an extremely dysfunctional and authoritarian community Jones deliberately manipulated to his advantage.[34]

Altering the mind — brainwashing — became crucial to understanding that tenuous line between suicide and murder, survivors and victims. Survivors, defectors, journalists, even the president, used the word "brainwashing" to describe how Jones took away people's agency. The American conversation about brainwashing began with the Korean War but reached a pitch in the mid-1970s as an explanation for cults, conspiracies, and "programmed assassins," like Lynette "Squeaky" Fromme, the follower of Charles Manson who attempted to kill Gerald Ford in 1975. It was a common way parents talked to the press about their grown children's fascinations with extreme movements, and it became family members' go-to understanding of why their relatives might take poison. One mother of a Temple member who perished described her daughter as "a normal person" before she met Jones, but "like a machine" under his influence. Charles Krause recalled that Congressman

Ryan pointed out a Temple member "almost in a trance. . . . It was an observation I wouldn't forget." "He was a robot," declared the father of Larry Layton, the Temple member charged with Leo Ryan's murder. Katsaris used the phrase "mind-programmed" to describe his daughter.[35] Brainwashing helped relatives of the dead understand why their loved ones might have drunk poison if Jones asked them to, balking perhaps only at that final moment when the full realization of what they were about to do hit them.

The transformation of heiress and college student Patricia Hearst into the self-proclaimed revolutionary Tanya and back again shaped the public discourse about what paralyzed even doubting Temple members, keeping them under Jones's control. Hearst's 1974 kidnapping, followed by her participation in Symbionese Liberation Army crimes, her capture, and her trial, dominated the press for years before Jonestown. Stockholm Syndrome, which posited that kidnapped victims eventually accepted their capturers' beliefs, often was used to explain Hearst's radical switch. So too might it explain why Temple members believed Jones's claims about CIA assassins lurking in the bush outside the compound. As William Graebner has noted, "The discussion about whether and how Patty had changed—had she been brainwashed, converted, coerced, persuaded? Had she 'seen the light'?—took place within the context of a larger, and no less intense, discussion about the nature of human beings, about the self." Graebner argues that Hearst's often-unfathomable saga illustrated the idea of the "fragile self" that could be self-actualized for the better or traumatized and brainwashed for the worse. The idea of a constructed self was very much a sixties phenomenon, undergirded by confidence that individuals determined their own paths in life independent of their gender, race, class, or sexual identity. Jim Jones lauded Hearst's revolutionary transformation, which landed him on a Los Angeles terrorist list. Leo Ryan, who served Hearst's parents' district in Congress, by contrast, believed Hearst had been brainwashed and was lobbying Jimmy Carter to commute her prison sentence when he died. "I wept every time I read about Patty Hearst," the father of Ryan's killer told a *San Francisco Chronicle* reporter, "and then it all happened to me."[36]

Brainwashing explained, but did not necessarily excuse, what happened to the Jonestown dead. The idea that one could fashion one's own identity meant that one could make bad choices as well as good ones, and believing Jones's increasingly crazy claims was a bad choice, despite the extenuating circumstances, including isolation and brainwashing. Survivors got themselves out of Jonestown alive; victims' bodies had to be transported out, with somebody bearing the cost. A political backlash set in, turning victims into, an angry family member complained, "so many pieces of meat." The Guyanese military began the task of identifying bodies, which were to be buried on-site. But the jungle heat forced a speedup the Guyanese could not handle, and once the U.S. military arrived to assist with counting bodies, the plan changed. Military transport brought bodies to a mortuary in Dover, Delaware, for identification. The choice, according to the government, owed to the location of resources. Family members thought otherwise; they suggested that depositing bodies on the East Coast was cheaper than transporting them to California and also reduced the "chances of families crowding the scene," as the NBC *Nightly News* reported. Family members of the dead were a decided minority bucking politicians eager to rein in the growing cost of getting Jones's victims home to their families. In Dover, the once-solemn process of removing the dead devolved into a political battle. "Who must pay the costs?," wondered the *Chicago Tribune*, of removing and burying the dead, estimated to cost millions of dollars.[37]

Conservative politicians used the issue to score points with their constituencies about the overreach of government. Senator William Roth of Delaware contacted the secretary of defense and the secretary of state, angry at the prospect that his home state would have to suffer the consequences of "the final chapter of this bizarre tragedy." The state legislature finally passed a bill prohibiting any cremation or burial of a Jonestown body on Delaware soil. The press helped to stir up outrage over "the reported $10 million cost to the US taxpayers" to bring the bodies home, identify them, and transport them to family members. The Peoples Temple had assets, but San Francisco courts took four years to locate all of them, retrieve them from foreign accounts, and pay out money, much of it to the families of the five victims of the airstrip shootings. Family members failed to step forward because they feared the government would bill them or garnish their wages if they claimed a body. Finally, an interfaith group of clergy arranged for transport to California of the bodies that remained. Cost was not the only reason Americans balked at helping victims' families. Many feared that "kooks coming from out of state to worship these people that killed themselves" would spread the Jonestown craziness like a disease. Better to, as one caller to a Dover radio program suggested, "let this be California's problem." California cemeteries, however, also did not want the unclaimed bodies. "No way. No Jonestown," one spray-painted sign on the wall of a Marin County cemetery declared. Evergreen Cemetery in Oakland took the unclaimed bodies and buried them in a mass grave with a discreet marker. The prolonged debate dehumanized the dead and turned the burial arrangements into a political circus, although it accurately reflected the distance many individuals wanted to put between themselves and Jones's victims.[38]

Literal distance became one common way Americans put psychic distance between themselves and the "California crazies" who were more likely to drink the Kool-Aid. Blaming "Cultofornia" explained Jones and what happened at Jonestown, differentiating between ordinary people and the denizens of a state many regarded as anything but ordinary. California had long been an Eden for the discontented. The sixties brought both seekers and people eager to exploit them to California, particularly to the Bay Area, commentators explained. *Time* opined that while San Francisco had once been the "very citadel of culture in California," it had "been scarred repeatedly in recent years by outbreaks of violence and turmoil." In the 1970s, California seemed the place for hedonists, rule breakers, and crazies, the "wonderland of cults." "I Want It All Now" was the title of an NBC news' 1978 story about suburban Marin County, just across the Golden Gate Bridge from San Francisco, suggesting that in the Golden State, narcissism ruled. California represented the "other" in Peoples Temple discourse, that strange place where living was too easy, a "mecca for restless dreamers." "California," *Time* concluded, "has long been fertile ground for cults."[39]

Cementing San Francisco's reputation as a place of craziness, senseless violence, and evil were the deaths of San Francisco mayor George Moscone and city supervisor Harvey Milk barely a week after Congressman Ryan's death. Some political analysts had credited Jim Jones for providing the margin of victory for Moscone, which Moscone rewarded by appointing Jones to a city position. Both Moscone and Milk owed their political successes to the sixties, while their assassin, former city supervisor Dan White, had been the lone conservative on the San Francisco Board of Supervisors. White resigned and then tried to take back his resignation. When the mayor indicated that he intended to appoint someone else to serve out White's term, White grabbed a gun and went after two people whom he perceived as enemies. He later claimed in court that too much junk food had rendered him temporarily insane, instantly dubbed by journalists the "Twinkie defense." The story was so unexpected and bizarre that it, like the death of more than 900 followers of a weird fake religious cult that was also associated with San Francisco, could be explained as peculiar to a "sick city cut off from the reality of the rest of the world."[40]

Psychic distance between oneself and Jones's victims could also be achieved by stereotyping the Jonestown dead as nonwhite, poor, and uneducated, "simple people with only a rare high school graduate among them," have-nots "for whom the American promise is ashes," the "dregs of society." Reports emphasized the credulous and naive views of Jones's victims, their belief that he cured their diseases, and their willingness to hand over their Social Security checks or the deeds to their houses. Journalists maintained an "arm's-length" attitude that turned the dead into "those others" too weak to resist Jones. Defectors, by contrast, always seemed to have college degrees or, in the case of former Temple attorney Tim Stoen, freedom from the daily drudge of Temple work. Their status made it more possible to resist Jones, and their education made them more likely to see through him. Once the group relocated to Jonestown, some stories noted, the wily Jones shifted governance models, replacing the college-educated males who initially served as his lieutenants with young females he had seduced, women reportedly very willing to cater to his needs. Temple defector Deborah Layton later observed that "nobody joins a cult. Nobody joins something they think is going to hurt them." But Americans wanted desperately to find differences between cult members and what one reporter called "normal people like us."[41]

Looking at government inquiries into the Jonestown tragedy suggests that the victims of Jonestown were not important enough to matter. Each passed the buck to some other part of the government, an outcome many citizens expected. The House Committee on Foreign Relations blamed Jones, the Guyanese government, U.S. Customs for allowing the Temple to ship guns, and the U.S. embassy in Guyana for lacking "common sense." The public portion of the FBI report "contain[ed] neither recommendations nor conclusions," just a quick and sometimes inaccurate examination of the facts. A 110-page State Department report criticized U.S. embassy personnel in Guyana for "errors and lapses" and conceded that legal restraints hampered any efforts to challenge Jones but never quite indicated whether improved policies would have made any difference. "There are some things the government can't do for us, and shouldn't even try," concluded syndicated columnist William Raspberry. After Jonestown, Americans with loved ones in other cults hoped there would be more vigilance and regulation, but nothing changed.[42] A blame-the-victims mentality was beginning to emerge.

Writing from the distance of six months, Diane Johnson noted that the "dismay and pity" the public initially felt for both the dead and the living members of the Peoples Temple gave way to "unspoken anger." The ongoing saga of body removal and burial had something to do with the changing mood, as did the government's unwillingness to acknowledge that it might have exercised more control over the Peoples Temple. Mostly, though, it was "distancing or outrage, even blame," taking place as Americans looked for explanations that reassured that they themselves would never fall under the sway of a "mad Svengali" like Jones. "The push-them-away answer" took many forms, each designed to help establish that the "ugly thing that happened in Guyana" would not happen to reasonable people.[43] Such a claim, of course, required that there be something fundamentally different about those who drank the Kool-Aid.

As sympathy gave way to anger and distancing, a common—and very modern—response to the tragedy was humor. Rebecca Moore's two sisters had not yet been identified among the Jonestown dead when, at their Thanksgiving dinner, "half the people were watery-eyed," she noted in her diary, and "the other half made jokes." What a more recent commentator calls the "unfunny joke" became a defense mechanism invoked by people in response to Jonestown, an increasingly familiar cultural trope. Many a disaster movie had its moments of humor, including the 1980 spoof of disaster movies, *Airplane*. Dark humor "changes your perception of the world, and of the official picture of the world," a statement of fearlessness and power. Such humor littered the Jonestown reportage and enhanced journalists' reputations as jaded and professional. Tim Cahill of *Rolling Stone* responded to a persistent rumor "that the Guyanese had considered making Jonestown a tourist attraction" with the question, "What would they call it? Club Dead?" When he first arrived in Guyana to accompany Congressman Ryan to Jonestown, Charles Krause had imagined the tone of what he would write as "farce." Even as the story changed significantly, in some ways Krause's tone did not. Commentators responded with "almost stylized ritual," paying "pro forma lip service" to victims they did not particularly respect. When one reporter talked to his editor in New York about how much money he was authorized to offer a survivor for an exclusive story, he recorded his editor's reply: "Offer him a glass of Kool-Aid."[44]

Dark humor did not originate in the sixties, but it certainly flourished in the guerrilla theater of antiwar protests and the counterculture's irreverence. In the 1970s, it expressed anti-Establishment feelings and a new freedom to be offensive. One of the most lauded episodes of *The Mary Tyler Moore Show* told the story of the death and funeral of a television clown who was killed during a parade by a rogue elephant because he was dressed as a giant peanut. On a television program borne of dark humor, *Saturday Night Live*, cast member Chevy Chase taunted host Richard Pryor with a series of racial epithets. On the University of California's Berkeley campus, undergraduates collected dead baby and Helen Keller jokes for folklorist Alan Dundes. Kurt Vonnegut's novels used environmental tragedies and the World War II bombing of Dresden as settings for humor. Dark humor was brazen and audacious and disrespectful of tradition and authority. It simultaneously demarcated an individual as unique and created a small community of like-minded souls, insiders together thumbing their noses at respectability. Like wearing Birkenstocks before they were mainstream or being the first to discover a new musical group, laughing at potentially offensive jokes helped to establish a person as hip or cool, a trendsetter rather than a follower. Dark humor was a facet of the new post-1960s American. So too was it an expression of independence, acknowledging the contradictions of the world, expressing cynicism, and demonstrating that one was a survivor. It was proof a person was too hard-bitten to drink the Kool-Aid.

References to Kool-Aid took the Jonestown story from the realm of the all-too-real into the absurd, a form of dark humor that, one survivor noted, "trivialize[d] such a horrific event." Kool-Aid represented something artificial, something from baby boomers' childhoods, something banal. People fixated on the Kool-Aid, even though pedants pointed out that what the colony drank was a local variety of the instant drink mix, Flavor-Ade. Several journalists confessed to having taken empty packets as souvenirs. Publicity hound Mark Lane claimed he found four Kool-Aid packets on his front steps when he returned home from Guyana. The *Hollywood Reporter* published an item about a "variety special 'Kool-Aid Presents Fifty Ways to Leave Your Lover,'" a "sick joke" snuck in by a disgruntled employee. A cartoon featuring Jones sitting with

Adolf Hitler in what was clearly Hell had Hitler saying, "Kool-Aid! Why didn't I think of that?" My housemate was not the only college student attending a party with a vat of "jungle juice." Jungle juice, in fact, is a staple at fraternity and sorority parties even today. Making light of the poison that killed so many, a reporter recently noted, allows for "cultural disassociation and amnesia."[45]

Tim Cahill, reporting for *Rolling Stone*, began his long Jonestown piece on a darkly humorous note, describing an encounter between himself and someone who drank a different kind of Kool-Aid, a member of the Hare Krishnas he met on his way to Guyana in the Miami airport. "A smiling woman with large, syrupy eyes" asked if he would "like to cough up a donation." Cahill began taunting her with grotesque images of what was just emerging from the jungle, telling her, "They killed the babies first," and that human beings had become "thirty or forty tons of rotting meat" "until she ran from me." While he felt "ashamed," he was also "full of fierce, brutal joy" that the Krishnas "fled like rats." The opening defined for his readers how the reporter wanted to be seen, as an outsider, someone way too cynical to ever be caught out by a charlatan like Jones. His presentation likewise suggested to his readers that they might remain detached enough from the tragedy to appreciate its more macabre elements. Some Americans wanted to be "too jaded" to reveal vulnerability. *Saturday Night Live*'s satiric newscast, "Weekend Update," featured a joke about Jonestown, likening Jim Jones to the host of an absurd television program on which contestants with ridiculous talents could be gonged off the set by celebrity judges. A few members of the studio audience groaned, but most laughed, and they laughed again about a fake news report of the Moscone and Milk shootings. The late 1970s comedic sensibility of sick humor, parody, and satire, even the "anti-comedy" of Andy Kaufman on occasion, provided insulation against some of the shock of 1970s events.[46] It was a coping mechanism employed by people who valued toughness, agency, and independent thought, people who had been liberated from convention by the sixties. Americans were moving toward a new type of persona, one for whom irony was a central personality trait.

Two years after the Jonestown deaths, a renewed spate of books and survivor accounts began to appear. Reviewing them for the *New York Review of Books*, Diane Johnson found their collective tone "finally blackly comic."[47] Even today, the defiant, I-wouldn't-drink-the-Kool-Aid attitude continues, expressed by bands like the Brian Jonestown Massacre, a blog called "Odd Things I've Seen," which includes a visit to Evergreen Cemetery, or photos of Jonestown dead on the "Best Gore" website. The Temple's San Francisco church is now a branch of the U.S. Post Office; locals boast proudly of its previous incarnation. The mass gravesite at Evergreen draws occasional curiosity seekers but none of the fanatics the good citizens of Delaware feared it would. A few years ago, several sets of Jonestown remains surfaced at a mortuary in Delaware, which the press found somehow symbolic of the government's lack of respect for the Temple dead. Our attitudes toward Jonestown have not really changed. We continue to approach human tragedy with a mixture of panic, curiosity, cynicism, and, finally, often-amused detachment, as though we are still trying to demonstrate that what happened to the more than 900 communards of Jonestown could never happen to us.

Public reportage of the Jonestown tragedy reflected many contemporary themes, including anti-Establishment feelings, general anti-Establishment attitudes, suspicion of lawyers, a shift toward less-rational ways of thinking, and the reemergence of evil as a potent social belief, already embodied by mass murderers and cult leaders and soon to be identified with America's cold war enemy, the Soviet Union. But the warning "Don't drink the Kool-Aid" and its opposite, "He/she drank the Kool-Aid," emphasize a very 1970s lesson: that people ought to think for themselves. Being susceptible to drinking the Kool-Aid—any Kool-Aid—made people vulnerable and easily exploited. Having the wherewithal to stand apart from a situation and assess it for what it truly was, to defy authority figures, be they presidents, bosses, teachers, or cult leaders, was necessary for survival. Tim Cahill started his piece on Jonestown with cynicism and dark humor but ended it on a more affirmative note, celebrating "the resilience of the human spirit." What gave him hope were not all those bodies rotting in the jungle but the stories of the survivors, the people who resisted Jones, fought back, and came out of the experience with their identities intact, despite the many horrors visited upon them.[48] The themes of resistance and resilience run throughout the Jonestown story, whether you focus on the anti-Establishment reporters chasing the scoop, the relatives who battled cults and demanded dignity for their lost family members, or the survivors of the tragedy themselves. This independent-thinking, assertive, ideal human being stands in stark contrast to pre-sixties' America.

Yet, paradoxically, the Jonestown story is also an affirmation of community. It warned of the dangers of too-powerful leaders when individuals cede control over their destinies. It passed judgment on community dysfunction and revealed the dynamics of healthy ones. It celebrated the families who got out of Jonestown, the professional community of reporters who tended one another on the airstrip in the jungle, and the families and friends who advocated for the victims and helped one another cope with a horrible event. Even Jones's attorneys put aside their machinations long enough to work together to escape Jonestown. The post-sixties American ideal was both independent and communal, bound to a country from which many wanted distance but also nurture and protection. Many of the Jonestown communities were constructed or imagined ones, professional organizations or groups like the Concerned Relatives, whose members shared little beyond rather personal and private concerns. Some were even extreme communities, cults. Like constructed families, seventies communities emphasized diversity, tolerance, and individual strength. Whether or not they were successful at this task, their purpose was to provide both protection and support as individuals moved from their old lives into their new ones.

Conclusions

Free to Be, You and Me

For much of our history, Americans believed in the unique greatness of our country, its inevitable progress, and its democratic institutions. Our government made us strong; our technological inventiveness made us rich; and our willingness to serve made us successful. Destiny, thus, ensured our triumphs, although sacrifice and hard work urged us along. This powerful set of assumptions about American society culminated in the Greatest Generation, which flourished despite a depression and a world war, making the country better than it ever had been before. The personal qualities that made the Greatest Generation so great included the wholehearted embrace of responsibility and duty. The foundation of that reality was hierarchy. Gender, race, class, sexual identity, and age determined precisely a person's duties and responsibilities, a system buttressed by law, custom, and religion. Well into the 1960s, we remained committed to the idea that everyone toiled in his or her own socially determined way for the benefit of us all. "We're all in our places, with bright, shiny faces," millions of American children sang in their 1950s classrooms, a new generation being trained to fit in and get along.

But then, all hell broke loose. A host of rights and liberation movements challenged the privilege of those at the top of the hierarchy and demonstrated that everyone else enjoyed fewer rewards. Our leaders demonstrated just how fallible, selfish, and deluded they could be. The war in Vietnam undermined faith in our nation's progress, honesty, and idealism. The counterculture urged us to "let the sunshine in," to embrace the transient, the pleasurable, and the unexplainable, to privilege joy over duty or responsibility. Americans got liberated from old ideas, traditions, and the downsides of being "all in our places." In the 1970s, another children's song, the title track of a larger enterprise funded by the *Ms.* Foundation in 1972, better represented how Americans started to imagine themselves. Its title? "Free to Be, You and Me." Its message was that people should live their lives apart from the sacrifices, hierarchies, responsibilities, and conformities that to their parents described how things were supposed to be. "Free to Be" promised that people were not so much destined to live certain lives (and to be punished for failing to fit in) as they were able to define themselves, and by the same token, people should respect and tolerate how others chose to define themselves. From the perspective of 1981, Daniel Yankelovich assessed what had occurred as "nothing less than the search for a new American philosophy of life."[1]

The younger generation might have been groomed to fit in, but it played a pivotal role in rejecting the old and embracing this newer, freer version of what it meant to be American. Forerunners, not all of them the privileged, white middle-class baby boomers Yankelovich observed in his polling work, had little attachment to the status quo. They experienced more of the problems of fifties conventionality and fewer of the affirmative qualities that made the Greatest Generation great, often finding a cultural chasm between ideals and reality. Rejecting the idea that everybody had a socially/economically/religiously assigned place drove many movements, protests, and rebellions in the 1960s and 1970s. The sheer size of the baby boom gave its members numerical power over everything from the economy to the culture. Their elders had little choice but to, as Bob Dylan said, "get out of the road if you can't lend a hand, for the times they are a-changin'." Pleasure replaced service or sacrifice as an individual goal. Assertiveness and rebelliousness challenged conformity and obedience as social norms. People felt less responsibility to others and more to themselves.

Many Americans embraced new ideas about equality, diversity, and tolerance as ideals and worked, often against social conditioning, to infuse them into their lives. TV, movies, music, record jackets, reportage, and advertisements showed people raised with one set of expectations how to live in a modern world. Shifting from hierarchy to more freedom required new personal traits: independence, confidence, adventurousness, and resilience. Too much respect for authority and unwillingness to think for oneself potentially made one a victim. Too much sacrifice on behalf of others thwarted the full development of the individual spirit. Americans raised to conform learned to take risks, whether the outcome was as simple as longer sideburns or as profound as coming out publicly. Even conservatives reinvented in the 1970s.

Inspired by the ideas of the sixties, Americans lived the rituals of their lives differently in the seventies, rewriting norms in ways that are familiar today. They practiced more serial monogamy and less marriage-for-life. They expanded what it meant to be a family, recognizing its contingent nature while extending its bonds beyond biology. They learned to exercise their freedom of choice. They shopped with more intentionality, seeking vendors who shared their values and, on occasion, boycotting those who did not. Suspicious of authority, they sought out alternative venues for their news, their information, and their entertainment. They tried to be true to who they believed they were, even when that meant confronting others. They rejected — at least officially — the passivity they associated with 1950s duty, valuing assertiveness in all arenas of their lives. Agency was a key trait teased out by the sixties. Like Rosa Parks refusing to give up her seat on a segregated bus, sixties activists emphasized the importance of standing up for oneself, fighting back, or resisting. The less-optimistic seventies laced that agency with resilience. "I Will Survive," declared one of the most popular songs of 1979.

Survival spoke to the contingencies of modern life when romances could end for no reason, good employees could get fired, and race, gender, and sexual identity still limited life's possibilities. Survival required a healthy dose of cynicism and skepticism, qualities less typical of the Greatest Generation, as well as a certain amount of comfort with moral ambiguity. Like Mary Richards, who was loyal to her workplace family but not to the corporate types who ran the television station that employed her, most Americans learned to live with the tensions of being only halfway committed to things. Muted rebellion became a way of life, expressed in our past as well as our present. We found resistance in stories of the enslaved and in songs by female singers. Our clothing was rebellious; our religious preferences were often unorthodox; our favorite TV shows lampooned those with traditional values as leading unexamined lives. By decade's end, we fought multiple establishments, including some anti-Establishments. But nobody wanted to be a victim.

Yet, there are significant differences between those who partook of 1970s changes and those who fought the changes. Conservatives mounted a counteroffensive in the 1970s, zeroing in on what they found most troubling about the sixties, the individual liberation it encouraged. They fought hard to keep Americans in their places, even resorting to using the government to privilege a particular model of family. Certainly they had some successes. The more effective path forward for conservatives, however, involved reversing the economic choices the 1960s Establishment had made, reasserting American greatness, and challenging political correctness. Ronald Reagan's administration improved the economy, giving corporate authority new status in the 1980s. His aggressive foreign policy at least hastened the collapse of communism in Eastern Europe and Russia. But he was much less able to foster a return to the social norms even his own family did not manifest. Social conservatives continued to wage war against the sixties, without significant success.

One reason is that the Establishment learned to harness anti-Establishment thinking. Marketers and businesses commodified rebellion, and advertisers sold it. While that might be an inescapable truth, it is also more complicated than it initially appears. At a time when any emissaries of the Establishment were suspect, economic and cultural establishments could not be the authorities they once were, becoming, instead, partners in the project of self-fulfillment so many Americans lived in the seventies. Baby boomers were not just some of the decade's biggest consumers; they were also many of its producers. They incorporated their anti-Establishment values into the mainstream, encouraging choices. They brought realism and authenticity to television, movies, and popular music. They encouraged cultural dissonance, modeling independence of thought. One of the most famous commercials of the era, for Life cereal, featured two little boys testing out their breakfast on their little brother, who "hates everything" but liked Life, confirming that even the very young could make choices and march to their own drummers. That same attitude extended beyond Life cereal to life. Nonconformists and rebels became cultural heroes, although they too made their compromises with real life. People had some control over their destinies, but sometimes they had to "rise with the tide and go with the flow," to quote a song James Taylor and Carly Simon popularized.[2]

Although baby boomers represented many of the catalysts that helped move America toward a value system predicated on equality, diversity, and self-assertion, many boomers today are nervous that their version of "normal" will inevitably give way to that of an even-larger generation, the Millennials, born between 1980 and 2000. In millions of American workplaces, boomer bosses scratch their heads over new workers, who might manifest some familiar attitudes but have other expectations about how their work lives will unfold. On college campuses across the country, professors debate whether to accommodate to the millennial style or force students to put away their cell phones and stop using the classroom as another opportunity for multitasking. There is a national conversation about the shift away from a college experience shaped by the free speech movement to that shaped by trigger warnings, a shift that instructors worry impedes *their* free speech. Parents might understand their children's reticence to marry, but their tendency to live at home longer "violates our cultural sense of how young adults should live their lives," notes sociologist Andrew J. Cherlin.[3] Dating apps and the so-called hooking-up culture make it impossible for elders to understand modern romance. Politicians strategize to figure out new ways to connect to younger voters, who, overall, manifest less interest in the political process. Technology, in particular, gives youth different frames of reference. Although boomers helped to lead the charge against conformity, as the elders in a world with ever-changing norms, they are, at best, ambivalent about some of what replaces the once-radical sixties ideas they helped to mainstream. Yes, it is ironic, but so too is it not surprising that, having lived their lives as the center of everything, they have trouble imagining something different.

Notes

INTRODUCTION

1 From "Cactus Tree," written by Joni Mitchell.

2 Yankelovich, *New Morality*, vi, 9; Lassiter, "Inventing Family Values," 13–28.

3 Yankelovich, *New Morality*, v.

4 Wolfe, "The 'Me' Decade and the Third Great Awakening"; Lasch, *The Culture of Narcissism*.

5 Foley, *Front Porch Politics*, 3.

6 Carroll, *It Seemed Like Nothing Happened*; Schulman and Zelizer, introduction, *Rightward Bound*, 5.

7 Quotations are from Cowie, *Stayin' Alive*, 364; Perlstein, *Nixonland*, xii; Perlstein, *Invisible Bridge* (both quotations from the preface); and Jenkins, *Decade of Nightmares*, 11. See also Berkowitz, *Something Happened*; Sandbrook, *Mad as Hell*; Schulman, *The Seventies*; Balmer, *Redeemer*; Kalman, *Right Star Rising*; Wilentz, *The Age of Reagan*; Lytle, *America's Uncivil Wars*; Self, *All in the Family*; and the essays in Schulman and Zelizer, *Rightward Bound*.

8 Perlstein, *Invisible Bridge*, preface.

9 Eric Bentley, "For the Right to Wear Our Hair Long," *New York Times*, 30 August 1970, 1.

10 Weiner and Stillman, *Woodstock Census*, quotation from p. 100.

11 Bayard Hooper, "The Real Change Has Just Begun," *Life*, 9 January 1970, 104, 102; "The Freedom to Be Idealistic," *Fortune*, January 1969, 60; "What They Believe," *Fortune*, January 1969, 70–71, 179–81, quotations from pp. 70, 179.

12 See Kelvin Pollard and Paola Scommegna, "Just How Many Baby Boomers Are There," Population Reference Bureau's website, http://www.prb.org/Publications/Articles/2002/JustHowManyBabyBoomersAreThere.aspx; and Brooks, *Last Season of Innocence*, 3.

13 Bellah et al., *Habits of the Heart*, 25; unnamed respondent cited in research compiled by the Dichter Institute for Motivational Research, "The Motivations of Consumerism," April 1973, Ernest Dichter Papers, box 113, Hagley Museum and Library, Wilmington, Del.

14 Bayard Hooper, "The Real Change Has Just Begun," *Life*, 9 January 1970, 102–5.

15 Dey, Astin, and Dorn, *American Freshman*, 92.

16 Cohen, *A Consumers' Republic*, 11; Herbert J. Gans, "The American Malaise," *New York Times*, 6 February 1972, M16.

17 Schlafly, *Power of the Positive Woman*, 11.

18 Hartman, *A War for the Soul of America*, 5. On market segmentation and niche marketing, see Cohen, *A Consumers' Republic*, chap. 7; and Schulman, *The Seventies*, 156.

19 Frank, *The Conquest of Cool*.

20 Steinbeck, as quoted in Perlstein, *Nixonland*, 94–95; Falwell, as quoted in Lassiter, "Inventing Family Values," 26.

21 Douglas, *Where the Girls Are*; Zaretsky, *No Direction Home*.

CHAPTER 1

1 The quotation is from Gerry Goffin, as cited in Adam Bernstein, "Gerry Goffin, Lyricist Who Co-Wrote Seminal '60s Hits, Dies at 75," *Washington Post*, 20 June 2014. For biographical details, see King's memoir, *A Natural Woman*; or Kutulas, "I Feel the Earth Move," 261–78.

2 See Bailey, *From Front Porch to Back Seat*; or Brooks, *Last Season of Innocence*, chaps. 1, 2.

3 Carmen Moore, "What If Joan Had Called Judy and Grace?," *Village Voice*, 23 September 1971, 55. King wrote both music and lyrics to the song.

4 Packard, *Sexual Wilderness*, 1.

5 Bailey, *Sex in the Heartland*, 4, 6; Solinger, *Wake Up Little Susie*.

6 The word "playthings" is Packard's, from his *Sexual Wilderness*, 133. The other quotation is from Nora Ephron, "If You're a Little Mouseburger, Come with Me. I Was a Mouseburger and I Will Help You," originally written in February 1970 and reprinted in Ephron's *Wallflower at the Orgy* (New York: Bantam Books, 1971), 24. On *Playboy*, see Fraterrigo, *Playboy*. On *Cosmopolitan*, see James Langer, *The Improbable First Century of Cosmopolitan Magazine* (Columbia: University of Missouri Press, 2010), 229–59.

7 The quotation is from Mead, *Culture and Commitment*, 28. The numbers come from King, Balswick, and Robinson, "The Continuing Premarital Sexual Revolution," 455–59; the discussion of "peer groups" is in Walsh, Ferrell, and Tolone, "Selection of Reference Group," 495–507. See also Packard, *Sexual Wilderness*.

8 Quotations are from Mead, *Culture and Commitment*, 28–29; and Yankelovich, *New Rules*, 88. See also Yankelovich, *New Morality*, 9–11; and Sorensen, *Adolescent Sexuality*, 59.

9 The quotations are from Packard, *Sexual Wilderness*, 73–74; Ericksen, *Kiss and Tell*, 80; Comfort, *Joy of Sex*, 4; and King, Balswick, and Robinson, "The Continuing Premarital Sexual Revolution," 458.

10 The quotations are from Ralph J. Gleason, "The Language of the Young," in Nobile, *The Con III Controversy*, 32; Robert Christgau, from a 2006 interview cited by Powers in *Writing the Record*, 128; Richard Goldstein, "Wiggy Words That Feed Your Mind," *Life*, 28 June 1968, 68; and Tracy Hotchner, "Stereotypical Sexism Still Seen, but Not Heard," *Los Angeles Times*, 26 May 1974, L18.

11 Quotations are from Altschuler, *All Shook Up*, 185; and Millard, *Beatlemania*, 188.

12 The quotations are from Goldstein, "Wiggy Words," 67. On the Beatles, see Frontani, *The Beatles*; or Millard, *Beatlemania*.

13 The early quotations are from Landau, as quoted in Anson, *Gone Crazy*, 81; Jann Wenner, *Rolling Stone*, 9 November 1967, 2; Samuel G. Freedman, "Liter-

ary 'Rolling Stone' Sells Out to Male Titillation," *USA Today*, 8 July 2002, A13; and Mary Harron, "McRock," in *Facing the Music: A Pantheon Guide to Popular Culture*, ed. Simon Firth (New York: Pantheon Books, 1988), 193. On the celebritization of musicians, see Shumway, *Rock Star*, preface. On *People*, see Curtis Prendergast and Geoffrey Colvin, *The World of Time Inc.: The Intimate History of a Changing Enterprise*, vol. 3 (New York: Atheneum, 1986), 433–40. On the *Village Voice*, see Powers, *Writing the Record*.

14 Quotations are from Ellen Willis, "Rock, Etc.," *New Yorker*, 26 February 1972, 79; Landau, "Performance: But I Was So Much Older Then," *Rolling Stone*, 30 September 1971, 42; Ken Barnes, "Top 40 Radio: A Fragment of the Imagination," in *Facing the Music: A Pantheon Guide to Popular Culture*, ed. Simon Firth (New York: Pantheon Books, 1988), 18 (quotations concerning audience and economics); and Pollock, *By the Time*, 147. On market segmentation and other aspects of the "consumers' republic," see Cohen, *A Consumers' Republic*.

15 The quotations are from Pollock, *By the Time*, 147; Susan Braudy, "James Taylor, a New Troubadour," *New York Times Magazine*, 21 February 1971, 28; Robert Palmer, "Taylor: After the Turmoil and the Wanderlust," *New York Times*, 8 April 1981, C24; and Robert Hilburn, "New Taylor Album a Step Back Up," *Los Angeles Times*, 18 June 1974, D8.

16 See Kutulas, "I Feel the Earth Move," 265, on female fans; and Thompson, *Hearts of Darkness*, chap. 15, on male rebellion and music.

17 The quotations are from Stephen Holden, "Singer-Songwriters Spin Their Tales," *New York Times*, 3 April 1988, 83; Ellen Willis, "Rock, Etc.," *New Yorker*, 26 February 1972, 79; "Talk of the Town: Taylor at Midnight," *New Yorker*, 25 November 1972, 37; Burt Korall, "James Taylor: Sunshine and . . . ," *Saturday Review* 53 (12 September 1970): 83; Grant S. McClellan, "Introduction: Youth and the Future Economy," in *American Youth in a Changing Culture* (New York: H. W. Wilson, 1972), 193; Simon, as quoted in Jon Pareles, "Ambition Never Gets Old," *New York Times*, 22 May 2016, AR27; Browne, quoted in Thompson, *Hearts of Darkness*, chap. 9; and Chuck Klosterman, "The Carly Simon Principle: Sincerity and Pop Greatness," in *This Is Pop: In Search of the Elusive at Experience Music Project*, ed. Eric Weisbard (Cambridge: Harvard University Press, 2004), 259, 261.

18 The Motion Picture Production Code of 1930 may be found at http://www.arts reformation.com/a001/hays-code.html. Shumway, *Modern Love*, 90–100. The studies are Donald Horton, "The Dialogue of Courtship in Popular Songs," *American Journal of Sociology* 62 (1957): 569–78; and James T. Carey, "Changing Courtship Patterns in the Popular Song," *American Journal of Sociology* 74 (1969): 720–31. Coontz, *Marriage*, 247.

19 The quotations are from Charles Michener, "The Pop and Op Sisters," *Newsweek*, 13 March 1972, 90; Simon, *Boys in the Trees*, chap. 12; and Robert Christgau, "Carly Simon as Mistress of Schlock," originally published in *Newsday* in January 1973 and reprinted in Christgau, *Any Old Way You Choose It*, 291.

20 Institute of Human Development survey respondent quoted in Weiss, *To Have*, 24. On the polls, see Jon C. Pennington, "It's Not a Revolution, but It

Sure Looks Like One: A Statistical Accounting of the Post-Sixties Sexual Revolution," *Radical Statistics* 83 (2003): 108–10.

21 On the sexualizing culture, see Allyn, *Make Love*, passim.

22 Quotations are from Pollock, *By the Time*, 126; *Rolling Stone* ad, in *New York Times*, 12 February 1969, 80; and Taylor, as cited in Stuart Werbin, "James Taylor and Carly Simon: The *Rolling Stone* Interview," *Rolling Stone*, 4 January 1973, 41.

23 King, *A Natural Woman*, 188; Packard, *Sexual Wilderness*, 121; Simon, *Boys in the Trees*, chap. 12. On the clash of new and old, see Lemke-Santangelo, *Daughters of Aquarius*, 62–63. On the groupie phenomenon, see Rhodes, *Electric Ladyland*, chap. 4.

24 Loraine Alterman, "Old Dan's Records," *New York Times*, 10 December 1972, D38; Wilson in Joanne Kaufman, "Life's Greatest Hits," *New York Times*, 13 March 2016.

25 Quotations are from Cohen, *Carole King*, 35; Karen Durbin, "Can a Feminist Love the World's Greatest Rock and Roll Band," *Ms.*, October 1974, 26; and Jon Landau, review of *Tapestry*, in *Rolling Stone*, 29 April 1971, 40.

26 The first quotation is from Robert Christgau, "The Joy of Joy," *Village Voice*, 15 April 1971, 45. The other quotations and information are from King, *A Natural Woman*, 172, 208–11, 217–24, quotation from p. 172.

27 The first quotation is "King as Queen?," *Time*, 12 July 1971, 52; the second is Robert Christgau, "Carole King: Five Million Friends," originally printed in *Newsday*, November 1972, and reprinted in *Any Old Way You Choose It*, 176; all the rest except the last come from Robert Hilburn, "Carole King's New Role as a Singer," *Los Angeles Times*, 22 May 1971, A6. The final quotation is from Cohen, *Carole King*, 35.

28 The quotations are from Barbara Rowes, "Women's Sound Knocks the Double Standard," *Los Angeles Times*, 15 July 1973, 48; and "Rock 'n' Roll's Leading Lady," *Time*, 16 December 1974, 66. The numbers come from Chapple and Garafalo, *Rock 'n' Roll Is Here to Pay*, 316.

29 Arlene Stein, "Rock against Romance: Gender, Rock 'n' Roll, and Resistance," in *Stars Don't Stand Still in the Sky*, ed. Karen Kelly and Evelyn McDonnell (New York: New York University Press, 1999)," 219. The ad appeared in *Rolling Stone*, 14 May 1970, 14. On the marketing plan for Simon's record, see Weller, *Girls Like Us*, 350.

30 Quotations are from Stephen Davis, "Simon's Second Album," *Rolling Stone*, 23 December, 1971, 66; and Stephen Holden, "Carly Simon's Emotion-Laden Self-Portrait," *New York Times*, 3 May 1987, H23.

31 The first quotation is Robert Draper's, as cited in Powers, *Writing the Record*, 16. See "It Happened in 1970," *Rolling Stone*, 4 February 1971, 44, for the title conferred upon Mitchell; and "Hollywood's Hot 100," *Rolling Stone*, 3 February 1972, 27, for the chart. Mitchell's response is cited in Mercer, *Will You Take Me as I Am*, 6; and Monk, *Joni*, 123. Simon, as quoted in Mark Rosin, "Carly Simon Letting Her Mind Flow," *Harper's Bazaar*, November 1972, 110; Simon, as quoted in Ben Fong-Torres, "A Session with 'Fired Up' Carly Simon: 'Oh

My Gosh, Here's This Body Again,'" *Rolling Stone*, 22 May 1975, 10. Charles M. Young envied her nursing son in his "Carly Simon: Life, Liberty, and the Pursuit of Roast Beef Hash," *Rolling Stone*, 1 June 1978, 42. Simon described her interviewer's claim to Stephen Davis, as quoted in Davis, *More Room*, 202. On *Rolling Stone*, see Robert Draper, *Rolling Stone Magazine: The Uncensored History* (New York: Doubleday Press, 1990), 217–20. The final Mitchell quotation comes from an interview conducted for the PBS American Masters documentary *Joni Mitchell: Woman of Heart and Mind*, 2003, included on DVD special features.

32 Quotations are from Dey, Astin, and Dorn, *American Freshman*, 21; Karen Durbin, "What Is the New Intimacy," *Ms.*, December 1978, 78; Rollins, as quoted in Nan Robertson, "Single Women over 30: 'Where Are the Men Worthy of Us?,'" *New York Times*, 14 July 1978, A12; Judy Klemesrud, "Women's Revolt: Harris Poll Detects 'Real Storm Signals,'" *New York Times*, 19 January 1971, 32; Giddens, *Transformation of Intimacy*, 1; and Nash, as cited in Weller, *Girls Like Us*, 294.

33 The *Oxford English Dictionary Online* dates the "affair [or] . . . sexual" use of the word "relationship" to 1974–75. The other quotations are from Joe Klein, "Growing Old Absurd," *Rolling Stone*, 30 June 1977, 61–62; Sorensen, *Adolescent Sexuality*, 113; M. E. Banachek, "The New Man/Woman Etiquette," *Mademoiselle*, July 1979, 103; and Paul Glick of the U.S. Census Bureau explaining the inclusion of cohabitation in the 1980 census to Jerry Cohen, for "Marriage Survives a Decade of the 'New Morality,'" *Los Angeles Times*, 14 January 1979, 20. The poll about living together comes from Dey, Astin, and Dorn, *American Freshman*, 21. The year 1974 was the first year the question was asked. The 1977 study is Donald W. Bower and Victor A. Christopherson, "University Student Cohabitation: A Regional Comparison of Selected Attitudes and Behavior," *Journal of Marriage and the Family* 39 (August 1977): 451.

34 Simon, as quoted in Werbin, "James Taylor and Carly Simon," 41; and by Davis, in *More Room*, 256. Mitchell, as cited in an interview by Echols in *Shaky Ground*, 210; Don Heckman, "Pop: Jim Morrison at the End, Joni at a Crossroads," *New York Times*, 8 August 1971, D15; Loraine Alterman, "Joni's Songs Are for Everyone," *New York Times*, 6 January 1974, A27.

35 The quotations are from Loraine Alterman, "Songs for the New Woman," *New York Times*, 11 February 1973, 156; and an unnamed *Village Voice* reviewer cited in Davis, *More Room*, 257. The poll is cited in Judy Klemesrud, "Women's Revolt: Harris Poll Detects 'Real Storm Signals,'" *New York Times*, 19 January 1971, 32.

36 Bailey, *Front Porch to Back Seat*, 75. The statistic comes from Sweet and Bumpass, *American Families and Households*, 83.

37 The quotations are from Davis, *More Room*, 216–17; Don Heckman, "Joni at a Crossroads," *New York Times*, 8 August 1971, D15; Falco, as cited by Monk, *Joni*, 82; and Ellen Willis, "Rock, Etc.," *New Yorker*, 3 March 1973, 104.

38 The quotations are from Young, "Carly Simon," 42; Joyce Haber, "The Wit and Wisdom of a Foxy Lady," *Los Angeles Times*, 4 May 1975, W25; Stephen E.

Rubin, "Carly Simon: Gin versus Begonias," *Saturday Review* 4 (16 October 1976): 39; and Carter, "The Language of Sisterhood," 229.

39 The quotation is from James T. Carey, "Changing Courtship Patterns in the Popular Song," *American Journal of Sociology* 74 (1969): 725. On "cock rock," see Whitely, "Little Red Rooster," 67–99. On Simon and Jagger, see Werbin, "James Taylor and Carly Simon," 36.

40 The quotations are from "Faces in the Crowd," *Time*, 24 June 1974; Simon, *Boys in the Trees*, chaps. 13, 16; and Cameron Crowe, "Joni Mitchell: The *Rolling Stone* Interview," *Rolling Stone*, 26 July 1979, 47, 15–16; Bangs, "James Taylor Marked for Death," 62; Bangs, review of Taylor's *One Man Dog*, originally published in *Creem's* February 1973 issue and reprinted in Bangs, "James Taylor Marked for Death," 114; and Christgau's 1972 *Newsday* review of Taylor's *Mudslide Slim* album, in Christgau, *Any Old Way You Choose It*, 212. On the new man, see Goldberg, *The New Male*. On Taylor's appeal to women and Lennon's opinion, see Thompson, *Hearts of Darkness*, chap. 12.

41 The quotations are from Simon, *Boys in the Trees*, chap. 19; Davis, *More Room*, 221–22; Paul Nelson, "Pinin' Simon: Still Slick after All These Years," *Rolling Stone*, 4 December 1975, 57; and Loraine Alterman, "James Taylor, the Quiet Superstar, Lives Happily Ever After," *New York Times*, 23 June 1974, 130.

42 Werbin, "James Taylor and Carly Simon," 41.

43 Browne, *Fire and Rain*, 23.

44 As quoted in Monk, *Joni*, 207.

45 Nelson, "Pinin' Simon," 57; Robert Hilburn, "Joni Mitchell's New: *For the Roses*," *Los Angeles Times*, 21 November 1972, D12.

46 The Fine quotation comes from Janice Mall, "About Women," *Los Angeles Times*, 2 November 1980, D24. The final one is from an unnamed source quoted in Laurie Johnson, "Men and Women Discuss the Issues at 2d Annual Feminist Parlay Here," *New York Times*, 14 October 1974, 37. The twenty-two types of men were in Susanna M. Hoffman's *The Classified Men*, described in Barbara Varro, "Anthropologist Types the Male Animal," *Los Angeles Times*, 12 October 1980, H10, H11. Fine and Carol Botwin both wrote books entitled *The Love Crisis*. On Botwin's book, see Beverly Stephen, "Good Man Still Hard to Find," *Los Angeles Times*, 9 December 1979, G21.

47 The Ellen Willis quotation is from her "Rock, Etc.," in *New Yorker*, 3 March 1973, 105. The quintessential book on assertiveness training is Manuel J. Smith's *When I Say No, I Feel Guilty: How to Cope—Using the Skills of Systematic Assertive Therapy* (New York: Dial Press, 1975).

48 Mitchell, as quoted in Mercer, *Will You Take Me as I Am*, 158. The description of Simon's album is Sheila Weller's in *Girls Like Us*, 446.

49 Anna Quindlen, "Relationships: Independence vs. Intimacy," *Los Angeles Times*, 28 November 1977, 36; Lindsey Van Gelder, "An Unmarried Man," *Ms.*, November 1979, 51–53, 73–75.

50 Quotation is from Johnson, "Men and Women," 37. Karin Durbin, "The Sexual Confusion," *Mademoiselle*, July 1972, 90, discusses the rising rates of impotence.

51 The quotations are from Jenkins, *Decade of Nightmares*, 30; and Emanuel Perlmutter, "'44-Caliber Killer' Wounds Two in Car Parked on Queens Street," *New York Times*, 27 June 1977, 39.

52 Landau, as cited in Anson, *Gone Crazy*, 231. The Springsteen quotation comes from Ed Ward, Geoffrey Stokes, and Ken Tucker, *Rock of Ages: The Rolling Stone History of Rock and Roll* (New York: Summit Books, 1986), 524. The other is from Gareth Palmer, "Bruce Springsteen and Masculinity," 103–4.

53 Yankelovich, *New Rules*, 5; Jerry Cohen, "Marriage Survives a Decade of the 'New Morality,'" *Los Angeles Times*, 14 January 1979, 20.

54 See the Gallup polls at http://www.gallup.com/poll/117328/marriage.aspx; and Peggy Orenstein, *Girls & Sex: Navigating the Complicated New Landscape* (New York: Harper Press, 2016), chap. 1.

CHAPTER 2

1 The quotations are from Clemente, *Dress Casual*, conclusion; and Peiss, *Cheap Amusements*, 56. On women as frivolous consumers, see Przybyszewski, *The Lost Art of Dress*, particularly 125–29, 153.

2 Echols, *Hot Stuff*, 186.

3 Alison Lurie, *The Language of Clothes* (New York: Random House, 1981).

4 Bailey, *From Front Porch to Back Seat*, 72; Przybyszewski, *The Lost Art of Dress*, introduction; "Down with the Barriers," December 1966, p. 13, box 88, Ernest Dichter Papers, Hagley Museum and Library, Wilmington, Del.

5 Wylie's article originally appeared in *Playboy* in 1958. See Kimmel, *Manhood in America*, 255–26. Report generated by W. R. Simmons and Associates and quoted in Handley, *Nylon*, 64.

6 See Cohen, *A Consumers' Republic*, 294–96; Cowie, *Stayin' Alive*, 9; or Rossinow, *Visions of Progress*, 195–98.

7 The first quotation is from the October 1955 issue, as quoted in Osgerby, *Playboys in Paradise*, 128. The second is Osgerby, *Playboys in Paradise*, 128. The statistic was cited in Gary Cross, *Men to Boys: The Making of Modern Immaturity* (New York: Columbia University Press, 2008), 34.

8 Osgerby, *Playboys in Paradise*, 129. On Cardin's suits, see Przybyszewski, *The Lost Art of Dress*, 238.

9 The quotation is from Frank, *The Conquest of Cool*, 189. On mod dressing, see Handley, *Nylon*, 105–6; or Przybyszewski, *The Lost Art of Dress*, 201–5.

10 The quotations are from Judy Klemesrud, "Athletes Today Are Turning in Blue Jeans for Peacock Feathers," *New York Times*, 7 December 1970, 58; an unnamed uniform manufacturer quoted in Cheryl Bentsen, "Athletes: Peacocks on Parade," *Los Angeles Times*, 21 May 1976, F1; "Down with the Barriers"; and G. C. Thelen Jr., "Peacock Revolt Arrives on Capitol Hill," *Los Angeles Times*, 11 May 1969, C6. Angela Taylor, "Men's Fashion in the 1960s: The Peacock's Glory Was Regained," *New York Times*, 15 December 1969, 62, talks about the best-dressed list.

11 The quotations are from "Down with the Barriers"; Erma Bombeck, "My Hubby Went Mod," *Good Housekeeping*, March 1972, 68; George Frazier, "Stop

the Peacock; I Want to Get Off," *Los Angeles Times*, 14 September 1969, 35; and Bill Cunningham, "A Climate of Seasonal Change," *Los Angeles Times*, 13 February 1976, F9. The statistic is from Frazier, "Stop the Peacock," 33.

12 The quotations are from "Male Vanity: Three Faces of Adam," *Newsweek*, 30 July 1973, 60; Leonard Sloane, "In Men's Wear, It's a 'Peacock Revolution,'" *New York Times*, 6 January 1969, 126; and Jason McCloskey, "Aquarius Rising: The Men's Fashion Revolt," *Gentlemen's Quarterly* (March 1970): 131.

13 Both quotations come from Al Martinez, "Men's Search for Beauty: A Big Business," *Los Angeles Times*, 5 June 1972, A1, the first from Martinez himself and the second from an unnamed source.

14 Quotations are from Jack Hyde, as cited in Julie Byrne, "Fashion Circle Looks at the Latest Ideas for Men, *Los Angeles Times*, 6 March 1969, D1; and Frank, *The Conquest of Cool*, 193. Art Buchwald, "Nehru Suits: The Edsels of the Clothing Industry," *Los Angeles Times*, 25 September 1969, section C. On "Youthscape" and accelerating fashion cycles, see Przybyszewski, *The Lost Art of Dress*, 229.

15 Mary Meehan, as quoted in Bill Ward, "The Anniversary of Everything," *Minneapolis Star Tribune*, 26 May 2014, E1; Bob Klein, as quoted in Martin Rossman, "Selling Youth Calls for New Approaches," *Los Angeles Times*, 20 May 1968, B11.

16 The quotations are from Sylvan Fox, "The Spirit Is Youth, the Style Is Money," *New York Times*, 6 January 1969, 97; Hugh Edwards of the Research Guild of Chicago, as quoted in Marylin Bender, "Youth Buyers: 'New Poor' Attitudes Govern Life Style," *New York Times*, 22 November 1970, 139; and Lee Adler, "Cashing In on the Cop-Out: Cultural Changes in Marketing Potential," *Business Horizons* 13 (February 1970): 21. The statistics are from McCloskey, "Aquarius Rising," 140. The assessment is Yankelovich's, in *New Morality*, 92–93.

17 The first quotation is from the lyrics of the 1966 song "Dedicated Follower of Fashion," written by Ray Davies. The others are from Wolfe's introduction to René König, *A La Mode: On the Social Psychology of Fashion*, translated by F. Bradley (New York: Seabury Press, 1971; English translation, 1973), 17; Reich, *Greening of America*, 234, 23; Merle Steir, "The Now People," *Madison Avenue*, June 1967, 23; and Lee Adler, "Cashing In on the Cop-Out: Cultural Changes in Marketing Potential," *Business Horizons* 13 (February 1970): 25. Clemente, *Dress Casual*, examines the rise of clothing informality coming from college campuses. Jundt, *Greening the Red, White, and Blue*, talks about "alternative consumption," 194–201.

18 The quotation is from Reich, *Greening of America*, 237. On Levis, the Gap, and Jefferson Airplane ads, see James Sullivan, *Jeans: A Cultural History of an American Icon* (New York: Gotham Books, 2006), 118–26.

19 The first quotation is from Gloria Emerson, "British 'His and Her' Hairdos Blur 'Him-Her' Line," *New York Times*, 23 July 1964, 29. The rest come from Art Seidenbaum, "Teen Hair Problem: Long and Short of It," *Los Angeles Times*, 24

April 1966, B3. On the "John-John" look, see Marylin Bender, "Sideburns Key to John-John Haircut," *New York Times*, 10 January 1967, 47.

20 See "Dress of Teen-Agers Upsets Adults Most," *New York Times*, 11 January 1967, 45. The statistic about high schools is from Przybyszewski, *The Lost Art of Dress*, 191. On court cases, see Paoletti, *Sex and Unisex*, chap. 5.

21 The quotations are from "The Bullet Biters," *Newsweek*, 7 February 1972, 65; Yankelovich, *New Morality*, 106; and Blair Sabol, "Dressing Up for Consciousness III," in Nobile, *The Con III Controversy*, 224.

22 The first two quotations are from Adler, "Cashing In on the Cop-Out," 24, 25. The next—from an unnamed source—and the information comes from Leonard Sloane, "Men's Sportswear," *New York Times*, 9 April 1972, F3. The last comes from Clemente, *Dress Casual*, introduction.

23 The first quotation is from "Didn't You Used to Be . . . Wait . . . Don't Tell Me," written by Allan Burns, original airdate, 10 October 1971. The descriptions of Nixon's look are John Brooks, "Beyond the Man in the Gray Flannel Suit," *New York Times*, 17 April 1977, 57; and Eli N. Evans, "All the Candidates' Clothes, *New York Times*, 19 September 1976, G23. On Ford, see Angela Taylor, "Men at Mid-Decade: Elegance Revival," *New York Times*, 1 January 1976, 36.

24 The first and third quotations are from Evans, "All the Candidates' Clothes." The second is from Marylin Bender, "The Male Head: Now Even Squares Are Going Long-Haired," *New York Times*, 22 September 1967, 42.

25 The quotations are from Joe Klein, "Campaign '75: Ford Plays It by the Book," *Rolling Stone*, 25 September 1975, 27; and John T. Molloy, *Dress for Success* (New York: Peter H. Wyden, 1975), 173. On the leisure suit's origins, see Blair Sabol, "Leisure Suits Offer Men a Fashion Breather," *Los Angeles Times*, 13 October 1974, 11.

26 The quotations are from "In Office, It's Suit Yourself," *Chicago Tribune*, 20 March 1976, 17; Genevieve Buck, "Leisure Suits Work a Full 9 to 5 Shift," *Chicago Tribune*, 14 September 1975, A3; Bill Cunningham, "Leisure Suit Rivals Tradition," *Los Angeles Times*, 1 July 1974, E1; Blair Sabol, "Leisure Suits Offer Men a Fashion Breather," *Los Angeles Times*, 13 October 1974, 11; and "'Leisure Look' Reflects Men's Lifestyle Change," *Burlington (Vermont) Daily Times News*, 9 March 1975, 5A. The statistics are from "In Office, It's Suit Yourself." See also Hillman, *Dressing for the Culture Wars*, chap. 6.

27 The first two quotations are from Yankelovich, *New Rules*, 82–84. The final one is cited in Nina S. Hyde, "Men's Fashion: Out of the Closet," *Washington Post*, 10 March 1974, H5. On REI, see Jundt, *Greening the Red, White, and Blue*, 221. The statistics come from John Robinson, "'Massification' and Democratization of the Leisure Class," *America in the Seventies: Some Social Indicators*, ed. Conrad Taeuber (Philadelphia: American Academy of Political and Social Science, 1978), 221. Thomas Frank talks about self-expression and conformity, in *The Conquest of Cool*, 12.

28 Peter Crowley, as cited in Craig Karpel, "Das Hip Kapital," *Esquire*, December 1970, 276.

29 The quotations are from Herbert Koshetz, "Dungarees of Denim: Worn-Out Look Has 'In' Appeal," *New York Times*, 7 February 1971, F7; and Ruth Robinson, "Giving Jeans That Lived-In Look," *New York Times*, 10 March 1975, 24. "Levi Strauss Rations Jeans in Cotton-Denim Shortage," *New York Times*, 6 August 1973, 43. The statistic is from Lawrence Levy, "Denim Rides Fashion's Wave Even Higher," *New York Times*, 29 June 1979, 121.

30 The quotations are from an unnamed interviewee in "The Motivations of Consumerism," April 1973, p. 67, box 113, Ernest Dichter Papers, Hagley Museum and Library, Wilmington, Del.; Joan Juliet Buck, as cited in Penelope Green, "Cheap Chic, Manifesto of a Fashion Revolution Is Back," *New York Times*, 16 September 2015; Blair Sabol, "Dressing for Consciousness III," in Nobile, *The Con III Controversy*, 222; Marylin Bender, "How to Be Profitably Hip," *New York Times*, 14 February 1971; McCloskey, "Aquarius Rising," 113; and Ron Hoff, as quoted in Jack O'Dwyer, "'New Morality' to Affect Advertising Techniques," *Chicago Tribune*, 23 June 1970, B6. The Harris poll results may be found in Norback, *The Complete Book of American Surveys*, 72. The descriptions of Berkeley are those of the author, who used to live near Cosmic Jeans.

31 The quotations are from Frank, *The Conquest of Cool*, 31; and the *New Haven Register*, as cited in Karpel, "Das Hip Kapital," 184.

32 The quotations are from Beth Ann Krier, "Kicking Up Heels over Earth Shoes," *Los Angeles Times*, 13 December 1973, E11; and Peter Gorner, "Ugly Shoe Bugaboo," *Chicago Tribune*, 14 October 974, B13. The rest of the information comes from Beth Ann Krier, "Earth Shoes—They're Uphill All the Way," *Los Angeles Times*, 3 January 1975, 18A; and Leonard Sloane, "A Down-to-Earth Shoe Drive," *New York Times*, 2 September 1976, 63.

33 The quotations are from Blahnik, as cited in Lina Lofaro and Kathleen Adams, "The Fate of the Earth Shoe," *Time*, 1 May 1995, 32; and Eleanor Jacobs, as quoted in "Down at the Heels," *Time*, 21 January 1974, 69.

34 Louis Botto, "If the Shoe Fits," *New York Times*, 25 August 1976, 234; George Gunset, "Shoe Firms Feeling Profit Margin Pinch," *Chicago Tribune*, 1 March 1973, C9.

35 Jerry Knight, "More Than Heel Was Negative," *Washington Post*, 8 September 1977, D17; Pete Cowan, "Earth Shoe's Last Stand," *Oakland Tribune*, 17 April 1977, 31. On knockoffs, see Carolyn Cole, "'Back to Earth' Shoes Popular," *Waterloo Courier*, 7 November 1974, 12.

36 Quotations are from Tom Zito, "In Earth Shoe's Footsteps," *Washington Post*, 21 April 1977, E1; and "Birkenstock Features Custom-Fit Shoes," *Los Angeles Times*, 3 December 1978, X18.

37 Herbert Gold, "All in the Non-Nuclear Family," *New York Times*, 5 June 1977, Sunday Book Review, 7. Padrino ad (1974) and Dexter ad (1971) are in *Fashion of the 70s: Vintage Fashion and Beauty Ads*, ed. Jim Heinmann (Cologne: Taschen, 2009).

38 The quotations are from "Ready, Set, Sweat," *Time*, 6 June 1977, 86; and Scott Miley, "Numerous Good Books Hit Christmas Market," in the *Anderson (Cali-*

fornia) Daily Bulletin, 14 December 1978, 6. On Carter's race, see Sandbrook, *Mad as Hell*, 307. On running more generally, see McKenzie, *Getting Physical*, chap. 4.

39 The quotations are from Steve Rushin, "From Barefoot to Fitbit," *Runner's World*, 29 March 2016, 77; Donald McIntyre, as cited in Rosemary Lopez, "Today's Joggers Keep Pace with Style," *New York Times*, 25 September 1977, 481; and Mark Jacobson, "The 'In' Sneakers Are Running Chic-to-Chic," *Chicago Tribune*, 5 January 1977, D1.

40 "The Jogging Shoe Race Heats Up," *Business Week*, 9 April 1979, 124. See Robinson, "'Massification' and Democratization of the Leisure Class," 217.

41 Rushin, "From Barefoot to Fitbit," 76; Phil Knight, "Pre and Me," *Runner's World*, June 2016, 76; Geoff Hollister, as quoted in Tom Jordan, *Pre: The Story of America's Greatest Running Legend, Steve Prefontaine* (Emmaus, Pa.: Rodale Press, 1977; this edition 1997), 160. On waffle trainers, see "Swift Profits," *Time*, 30 June 1980, 48. On Nikes more generally, see "The Jogging Shoe Race Heats Up," *Business Week*, 9 April 1979, 125.

42 Frank Brann, Levi Strauss vice president, as cited in Leonard Sloane, "Above and Beyond Levi's Jeans Image," *New York Times*, 30 August 1977, 57.

43 The first quotation is from Timothy Hawkins, "Q & A for Men," *Los Angeles Times*, 10 August 1979, G8. On Jordache, including quotation, see Barbara Ettore, "The Status Reapers," *New York Times*, 1 July 1979, F7.

44 Simon, *Boys in the Trees*, chap. 17.

45 The quotations are from Genevieve Buck, "'Turn-On' Togs Set Pace in Menswear," *Chicago Tribune*, 24 December 1975, 11; Roland Snyder and Kenneth Colman, both quoted in "Men's Stylish Shorts Are No Longer a Joke," *New York Times*, 17 May 1973, 50; Jim Gallagher, "Men's Fancy Pants: Colorful Shorts Go Top-Drawer," *Chicago Tribune*, 29 September 1976, B1–B2; Dick Kallman, as quoted in Buck, "'Turn-On' Togs," 11, 12; a May Company spokesperson, as quoted in Beth Ann Krier, "An Overview of Male Underwear," *Los Angeles Times*, 11 February 1973, F1; and Doug Boyle, as quoted in Michael Seiler, "Turnaround on the Runway for NOW," *Los Angeles Times*, 11 June 1975, 12.

46 The quotation is from Henry Allen, "The Male Narcissist: He Walks in Beauty . . . ," *Washington Post*, 11 June 1978, SM21.

47 The quotations are from Nina S. Hyde, "The Crush of Flash, Cash, and Fashion," *Washington Post*, 28 April 1977, D5; "Black Men's Flamboyant Fashions, *Ebony*, August 1972, 156–59; Echols, *Hot Stuff*, 186; and Cowie, *Stayin' Alive*, 317, 316.

48 The quotations are from Blair Sabol, "Jock Chic: Who Has the Form to Fit into All This Form Fit?," *Village Voice*, 16 July 1979, 33; Maupin, *Tales of the City*, 182; and Fran Lebowitz, as quoted in Echols, *Hot Stuff*, 122. "Macho Man" was written by Jacques Morali.

49 Echols, *Hot Stuff*, 123. On clones, see Martin Levine, *Gay Macho*, 59–61, quotation from p. 59; or Hillman, *Dressing for the Culture Wars*, 120. See also Sabol, "Jock Chic."

50 Simon, *Boys in the Trees*, chap. 19; Yankelovich, *New Morality*, 39.

51 See Kimmel, *Manhood in America*, 280–82.

52 On Calvin Klein underwear, see Ralph DiGennaro, "The New Appeal of Designer Underwear," *New York Times*, 12 September 1982, Style magazine, 137.
On Levi's Dockers, see http://www.marketplace.org/topics/business/workplace
-culture/dress-code-history-business-casual.

53 Przybyszewski, *The Lost Art of Dress*, 132; "Time Style and Design Poll," 5 March
2006, http://content.time.com/time/arts/article/0,8599,1169863,00.html.

CHAPTER 3

1 The quotations are from Armstrong, *Mary and Lou*, 51; and Reza Badiyi, as
cited in *She Turned the World On with Her Smile*.

2 Stephanie Coontz, *The Way We Never Were: American Families and the Nostalgia Trap* (New York: Basic Books, 1993), 23.

3 Caryn James, "Classic '70s Television, *New York Times*, 2 June 2013, Sunday
Book Review, 34; Leachman on *Mary Tyler Moore Show, a Celebration*. On the
ways fans identified with the program, see Neal Justin, "Turning the Mall On
with Her Smile," *Minneapolis Star Tribune*, 9 May 2002, B1; Neal Karlen, "The
House That's So, So . . . Mary," *New York Times*, 12 January 1995, C1; and Steve
Berg, "Minneapolis Keeps Hearth Warm for Mary," *Los Angeles Times*, 3 February 1977, G1.

4 Zaretsky, *No Direction Home*, 3, 4. See Schlafly, *Power of the Positive Woman*; or
Lasch, *The Culture of Narcissism*.

5 MacLean, *Freedom Is Not Enough*, 7; Cowie, *Stayin' Alive*, 12.

6 Weiss, *To Have*, chaps. 1, 2.

7 The quotation is from Paskin, "Mary Tyler Moore Rewind." See Maslin, "In
Prime Time," D1.

8 On the economy, see Berkowitz, *Something Happened*, 53–70; or Schulman,
The Seventies, 121–44. On workers' declining satisfaction, see Zaretsky, *No Direction Home*, 105–42; or Cowie, *Stayin' Alive*, passim.

9 Quotations are from the Port Huron Statement at http://www2.iath.virginia
.edu/sixties/HTML_docs/Resources/Primary/Manifestos/SDS_Port_Huron
.html; and Schulman, *The Seventies*, 135.

10 The quotations are from Weiner and Stillman, *Woodstock Census*, 191, 237;
Agis Salpukass, "Workers Increasingly Rebel against Boredom on Assembly
Line," *New York Times*, 2 April 1972, 34; Dey, Astin, and Dorn, *The American
Freshman*, 129 (p. 13 discusses trends regarding the business major); Daniel
Yankelovich, as cited in Fred M. Hechinger, "Youth's New Values," *New York
Times*, 28 May 1974, 39; and Sanders, "The Revolution Is Life versus Death,"
cited in Sarah Lyall, "Outsider Went Mainstream; but Message Changed
Little," *New York Times*, 4 July 2015, 1.

11 Rosen, *The World Split Open*.

12 Unemployment statistics are at http://data.bls.gov/timeseries/LNU04000000
?years_option=all_years&periods_option=specific_periods&periods
=Annual+Data. On the 1977 survey and youth's suspicion of big business, see
Norback, *The Complete Book of American Surveys*, 170, 10. On the corporate

13 The quotations are from Marc, *Comic Visions*, 139; and Yankelovich, *New Morality*, 104. On the idea of the workplace family, see Taylor, *Prime-Time Families*, 110–49.

14 Linder, "From Ozzie to Ozzy," 64.

15 Dalton, "Our Miss Brooks," 104.

16 Kohl, "Who's in Charge Here?," 231.

17 The quotations are from Orrick, "Successes and Failures of Working Women on Television," 66; and Treva Silverman, as quoted in Kohen, *We Killed*, 58. Cecil Smith, "Marlo Makes a Point for Womlib," *Los Angeles Times*, 17 March 1971, G17, focuses on the last episode.

18 George Gent, "TV Will Drip Social Significance," *New York Times*, 7 September 1970, 37; Richard Burgheim, "The New Season: Dripping with Relevance," *Time*, 28 September 1970, 66.

19 The quotation is from the subtitle of Trueth, "Breaking and Entering," 25. Kirsten Marthe Lentz, "Quality versus Relevance: Feminism, Race, and the Politics of Significance in 1970s Television," *Camera Obscura* 15 (2000): 45–93.

20 The quotations are from Dwight Whitney, "You've Come a Long Way, Baby," *TV Guide*, 19 September 1970, 38; CBS executive Mike Dann, paraphrased in Armstrong, *Mary and Lou*, 41; Cecil Smith, "Mary Tyler Moore: Her Charisma Makes the Comedy Show Go, *Los Angeles Times*, 13 December 1970, V2; and Whitney, "You've Come a Long Way, Baby," 38. "Truth" is Mary Tyler Moore's word, taken from *She Turned the World On with Her Smile*; and Smith, "Mary Tyler Moore."

21 Burns's quotation comes from *She Turned the World On with Her Smile*. Moore's is from Victoria A. Johnson, *Heartland TV: Prime Time and the Struggle for US Identity* (New York: New York University Press, 2008), 134.

22 The quotations are from Armstrong, *Mary and Lou*, 108; Jones, *Honey, I'm Home*, 198; and Paskin, "Mary Tyler Moore Rewind."

23 Chesebro, "Communications, Values, and Popular Television Series," 13; Kohen, *We Killed*, 248. On the character-driven nature of the program, see Feuer, "The MTM Style," 21, 55–57.

24 Silver, as quoted in Jennifer Armstrong, "Small Screen Queens," *Bust* 73 (February/March 2012): 55. "The wonderful thing that happens once a month" comes from "Rhoda's Sister Gets Married," written by Karyl Geld, original airdate, 29 September 1973.

25 On Mary's studio, see Anita Gates, "Room Enough to Stretch the Imagination," *New York Times*, 3 March 1996, H31. On her wardrobe, see Joyce Haber, "Mary Tyler Moore . . . Girl Who Takes Care of Herself," *Los Angeles Times*, 7 February 1971, C15; and Armstrong, *Mary and Lou*, 130.

26 On the Bechdel test, see http://bechdeltest.com/.

27 The quotations are from Schweitzer, *"The Mindy Project,"* 64; Harper, *I, Rhoda*, 94; and Harper on *The Mary Tyler Moore Show, A Celebration*.

28 "Phyllis Whips Inflation," written by Ed. Weinberger and Stan Daniels, original airdate, 18 January 1975.

29 "The Courtship of Mary's Father's Daughter," written by Elias Davis and David Pollack, original airdate, 23 December 1972.

30 The first quotation is from A.O. Scott, "Superhuman Resources," *New York Times*, 14 August 2016, AR-10. The descriptions of Ted's qualities are Knight's, from Charles Witbeck, "We All Got One Just Like Him," *Chicago Tribune*, 2 September 1973, 15. See Norback, *The Complete Book of American Surveys*, 163. On the Peter Principle, see http://money.howstuffworks.com/peter-principle .htm.

31 Jones, *Honey, I'm Home*, 4.

32 The quotations are from Taylor, *Prime-Time Families*, 14.

33 The quotations come from Burgheim, "The New Season"; and Grant Tinker and Bud Rukeyser, *Tinker in Television: From General Sarnoff to General Electric* (New York: Simon and Schuster, 1994), 93. See Moore's recollection of the first filming in *After All*, 162; or Bonderoff, *Mary Tyler Moore*, 70–71.

34 Burns, quoted in *She Turned the World On with Her Smile*; and "MTM and Her All-Star Team," *Newsweek*, 29 January 1973, 60.

35 Schweitzer, "*The Mindy Project*," 65.

36 Lynn Peril, in "Do Secretaries Have a Future?," *New York Times*, 27 April 2011, A27, talks about making coffee. U.S. Commission on Civil Rights, *Window Dressing*, 23; "Letters to the Editor," *Washington Post*, 22 August 1977, A20.

37 The undermining of collective bargaining and other aspects of labor militancy on television is discussed in Michael Parenti, *Make-Believe Media: The Politics of Entertainment* (New York: St. Martin's, 1992). Douglas, *Where the Girls Are*, 203.

38 The quotations are from Moore, as cited in Tom Shales, "Awaiting the 'Toughest Goodbye,'" *Washington Post*, 31 December 1976, C1; and Diane Rosen, "TV and the Single Girl," *TV Guide*, 9 November 1971, 16. On the Moore style, see "Exit 'Mary Tyler Moore,'" *Washington Post*, 22 March 1977, A16; or Carol Traynor Williams, "It's Not So Much, 'You've Come a Long Way, Baby' as 'You're Gonna Make It After All," *Journal of Popular Culture* 7 (1974): 982.

39 The quotations are from Stein, *View from Sunset Boulevard*, 20; and a 1977 ORC Public Opinion Poll, as cited in Norback, *The Complete Book of American Surveys*, 172. Maslin, "In Prime Time," D1. On worker satisfaction, see Angus Campbell, *The Sense of Well-Being in America: Recent Patterns and Trends* (New York: McGraw-Hill, 1981), 240.

40 "The Last Show," written by James L. Brooks, Allan Burns, Ed. Weinberger, Stan Daniels, David Lloyd, and Bob Ellison, original airdate, 19 March 1977. The other quotation is from Kohl, "Who's in Charge Here?," 234.

41 The quotations are from Karl E. Meyer, "A Farewell Bouquet for Mary Tyler Moore," *Saturday Review* 4 (19 March 1977): 49; Gloria Emerson, "Mary Richards, 1970–1977," *McCall's*, May 1976, 26; Amy Gross, "Woman Loves Work," *Mademoiselle*, March 1973, 206; the ideas of MTM executive producer Ed. Weinberger, as summarized in "'New Morality' on TV Debated," *Los Ange-*

les Times, 25 March 1976, E16; and Michael VerMeulen, "Mary Tyler Moore: America's Sweetheart Goes All the Way, but Will They Respect Her Tomorrow?," *Rolling Stone*, 13 November 1980, 48.

42 "The Lou and Edie Story," written by Treva Silverman, original airdate, 6 October 1973; Mary Murphy, "Breakthrough on Mary Tyler Moore," *Los Angeles Times*, 5 October 1973, D17.

43 The first quotations are from Jim McKairnes, "Recalling TV's Greatest Night of Programming, *Television Week*, 25 August 2008, 13; Lujack Super, as cited in Linda Lee Landis, "Is Saturday Night 'Whoopee' Gone?," *Chicago Tribune*, 25 August 1973, W11; and Nora Ephron, "A Fond Farewell to the Finest, Funniest Show on Television," *Esquire*, February 1977, 74. "Literate" was Grant Tinker's word, from Elaine Markoutsas, "Tinker's Toys: Sitcoms We Can Believe In," *Chicago Tribune*, 14 October 1974, B19. The final quotation is from Bette-Jane Raphael, "Whatever Happened to Mary Richards?," *McCall's*, September 1977, 20. Fey's comments were on the *Mary Tyler Moore Show, a Celebration*.

44 Frederic A. Birmingham, "$30 a Week and Lots of Credit Cards," *Saturday Evening Post*, October 1974, 33; Mary Tyler Moore, in Kathleen D. Fury, "Farewell, Mary Richards," *Ladies' Home Journal*, March 1977, 48. On the woman who moved to Minneapolis because Mary Richards lived there, see Gail Rosenblum, "She Walks Away from a Good Job toward a Leaner, Richer, Life," *Minneapolis Star Tribune*, 14 December 2010, B2. Winfrey's comments come from *Mary Tyler Moore Show, a Celebration*.

45 On the feminist bent of the show's writers, see Treva Silverman's comments in Kohen, *We Killed*, 70.

46 The quotations are from James Brooks, as cited in Dick Adler, "The Writer Wore Hot Pants," *TV Guide*, 15 July 1972, 36; and Cecil Smith, "Mary Tyler Moore to Be Host-Narrator of 'We the Women' Special," *Los Angeles Times*, 17 March 1974, M1.

47 The quotations are from Caroline Bird, "What's Television Doing for 50.9% of Americans?," *TV Guide*, 27 February 1971, 8; Gail Rock, "TV: Same Time, Same Station, Same Sexism," *Ms.*, December 1973, 24; Gloria Steinem in "A Fond Farewell," *Esquire*, February 1977, 79; and Perry Lafferty as quoted in Mary Murphy, "Can Females Become More Than Just Faces?," *Los Angeles Times*, 15 August 1973, E1.

48 The quotations are from Tom Cerones, as cited in Ellen Farley and William K. Knoedelseder Jr., "The Titillating Trend in TV: Sex Makes It to Prime Time," *Los Angeles Times*, 19 February 1978, Q1; and Robert Lindsey, "TV Tunes in Sex as Crime Fades," *New York Times*, 20 March 1978, C15, which also includes the female executive's opinion. The poll is in "This Is What You Thought about Sex on TV," *Glamour*, June 1979, 251.

49 The quotations are from Feuer, "MTM Enterprises," 18; "Ask Jennifer," written by Joyce Armor and Judie Neer," original airdate, 14 February 1981; Loni Anderson in Jean Cox Penn, "'I Really Am Snow White in My Fantasies,'" *Los Angeles Times*, 9 January 1981, K7; Kim Ode, "After All These Years, It's Hats Off to Mary," *Minneapolis Star-Tribune*, 5 February 2000, E1; and Ron Alridge,

"The Decline of Women on TV," *Chicago Tribune*, 17 May 1981, H3. On the posters and doll, see Penn, "'I Really Am Snow White in My Fantasies,'" K7.

50 See Dow, *Prime-Time Feminism*, 24–58.

51 Quotations are from Paskin, "Mary Tyler Moore Rewind"; "Exit 'Mary Tyler Moore,'" *Washington Post*, 22 March 1977, A16; and Oprah Winfrey on *Mary Tyler, a Celebration*; and Scott, "Superhuman Resources," AR-10.

52 Ode, "After All These Years," E1.

CHAPTER 4

1 Reprinted in G. B. Trudeau, *Stalking the Perfect Tan* (New York: Holt, Rinehart and Winston, 1977).

2 Haley, as quoted in Norrell, *Alex Haley*, chap. 6; "Everyday People," by Sylvester Stewart (aka Sly).

3 From Johnson's 15 March 1965 speech about the proposed Voting Rights bill, at http://www.historyplace.com/speeches/johnson.htm.

4 Melena Ryzik, "*Roots* for a New Era," *New York Times*, 22 May 2016, AR28; Marable, *Race, Reform, and Rebellion*, 89.

5 Marable, *From the Grassroots*, 6.

6 The quotations are from Wilson, *Declining Significance of Race*, 3; and Marable, *Race, Reform, and Rebellion*, 169.

7 Gilder, as quoted in Patterson, *Freedom Is Not Enough*, 138.

8 The report's full text may be found at http://www.blackpast.org/primary /moynihan-report-1965. On "social deviancies" of the 1970s, see Patterson, *Freedom Is Not Enough*, 138–39; and "The Broken Family: Divorce US Style," *Newsweek*, 12 March 1973, 47.

9 The Wallace and Reagan quotations come from Norrell, *The House I Live In*, 304. Both Phillips quotations are from Perlstein, *Nixonland*, 277. Porter, "Affirming and Disaffirming Actions," 64; Lewis, as quoted in Sandbrook, *Mad as Hell*, 244. For more on these aspects of 1970s racial ideology, see Norrell, *The House I Live In*, 269–302.

10 Norrell, *The House I Live In*, 272.

11 As cited in ibid., 274.

12 Marable, *Race, Reform, and Rebellion*, 172–73. On the changing economy's impact on African Americans, see Wilson, *Declining Significance of Race*, 88–121. On changing patterns of marriage and childbearing, see George A. Akerlof, Janet L. Yellen, and Michael L. Katz, "An Analysis of Out-of-Wedlock Childbearing in the United States," *Quarterly Journal of Economics* 111 (May 1996): 283.

13 The quotations are from Clifford Mason, "Why Does White America Love Sidney Poitier So?," *New York Times*, 10 September 1967, AR1, 21.

14 The quotations are from Eugenia Collier, "TV Still Evades the Nitty-Gritty Truth!," *TV Guide*, 12 January 1974, 6; Acham, *Revolution Televised*, 95; and "Farewell, Sherman Hemsley," *People*, 13 August 2012, 43.

15 Amos's and Rolle's quotations come from Acham, *Revolution Televised*, 138,

139; on the impact of the Moynihan Report on television images of black families, see ibid., 112. See also Bogle, *Prime Time Blues*, 200–205.

16 The quotations are from Van Peebles, as quoted in Guerrero, *Framing Blackness*, 91; George Gent, "Black Films Are In, So Are Profits," *New York Times*, 18 July 1972, 22; and Clayton Riley, "Shaft Can Do Everything—I Can Do Nothing," *New York Times*, 13 August 1972, D9. On the genre more broadly, see Guerrero, *Framing Blackness*, 68–111.

17 Quotations are from Guerrero, *Framing Blackness*, 96, 97, 100. Newton's response to *Sweet Sweetback* is in ibid., 86–87. On the degree to which Blaxploitation began to lose its collective edge and become more about urban hucksters, see ibid., 97.

18 The quotations are both from Dorothy Gilliam, "The Road to 'Overnight' Success," *Washington Post*, 20 October 1972, C1. One comparison to Blaxploitation films is Gary Arnold, "'Sounder': A 'New' Black Film," *Washington Post*, 20 October 1972, C1.

19 Quotations are from the American Revolution Bicentennial Administration, as cited in Zaretsky, *No Direction Home*, 149; and Hartman, *A War for the Soul of America*, 254. On the history of the concept of the "usable past," see Casey Nelson Blake, "The Usable Past, the Comfortable Past, and the Civic Past: Memory in Contemporary America," *Cultural Anthropology* 14 (August 1999): 423–35.

20 Richard Schickel, "Cold, Cold Ground," *Time*, 12 May 1975, 60; Guerrero, *Framing Blackness*, 33.

21 Lance Morrow, "Living with the 'Peculiar Institution,'" *Time*, 14 February 1977, 77.

22 The quotation comes from an unnamed woman, as cited in Patricia de Luna, "Amazing Reaction to *Roots*," *Long Beach Independent Press-Telegram*, 6 February 1977, L/S 6. On texts, see Glazer and Ueda, *Ethnic Groups in History Textbooks*, 17. On Black History Month, see "Black History Month," *Washington Post*, 19 February 1977, A12.

23 As quoted in Van Deburg, *Slavery and Race*, 84; and Eric Foner's foreword to *The Dunning School: Historians, Race, and the Meaning of Reconstruction*, ed. John David Smith and J. Vincent Lowery (Lexington: University Press of Kentucky, 2013), ix.

24 A good summary of this history and its pertinence for television is Van Deburg, "Historiography—Slavery on TV," 13–16.

25 See Van Deburg, *Slavery and Race*, 137–38. On Gutman's book, see Patterson, *Freedom Is Not Enough*, 133–36.

26 Jones, *Honey, I'm Home*, 54; Les Brown, "'Good Times' Will Drop Male Parent: Black Media Coalition Protests Move," *New York Times*, 7 June 1976, 49.

27 Paul D. Zimmerman, "In Search of a Heritage," *Newsweek*, 27 September 1976, 95.

28 Acham, *Revolution Televised*, 41–53.

29 Bogle, *Prime Time Blues*, 234–38.

30 Alex Haley, "My Search for Roots: A Black American's Story," *Reader's Digest*, May 1974, 73–78; quotations from pp. 73, 74. On some of the misrepresentations of his story, see Norrell, *Alex Haley*, chap. 7.

31 See http://www.officialkwanzaawebsite.org/index.shtml.

32 "Atypical" and "womanizer" come from Norrell, *Alex Haley*, chap. 2. The other quotation is from Walter Goodman, "Symbolic Truth Is Not a Synonym for History," *Los Angeles Times*, 24 April 1977, F1.

33 The quotations are from Larry L. King, "From the Seed of Kunta Kinte," *Saturday Review* 88 (18 September 1976): 20; Fiedler, as quoted in Norrell, *Alex Haley*, chap. 8; Willie Lee Rose, "An American Family," *New York Review of Books* 23 (11 November 1976): 3; King, "From the Seed of Kunta Kinte"; Christopher Lehmann-Haupt, "Corroborating Evidence," *New York Times*, 14 October 1976, 34 (two quotations); and Robert Kirsch, "Alex Haley Cultivates His Family Tree among the Griots," *Los Angeles Times*, 10 October 1976, T2. See also James Baldwin, "How One Black Man Came to Be an American," *New York Times*, 26 September 1976, BR1.

34 *Roots* producer Stan Margulies, as quoted in Gitlin, *Inside Prime Time*, 162; *Crossing Over*; Wolper and Troupe, *Inside Story of TV's Roots*, 27–28.

35 The quotations are from Fishbein, *"Roots,"* 288; Wolper and Troupe, *Inside Story of TV's Roots*, 73; Fishbein, *"Roots,"* 289; Wolper and Troupe, *Inside Story of TV's Roots*, 81; William Haley, as quoted in *Crossing Over*; and Blinn in *Crossing Over*. Lauren R. Tucker and Hemant Shah, "Race and the Transformation of Culture: The Making of the Television Miniseries *Roots*," *Critical Studies in Mass Communication* 9 (1992): 328–29.

36 The quotations are from Harry F. Waters, "The Black Experience," *Newsweek*, 24 January 1977, 59; and Zimmerman, "In Search of a Heritage," 94. See "Wolper Co Is Sued on Topless Scene," *New York Times*, 27 May 1976, 40; or Fishbein, *"Roots,"* 287.

37 ABC executive Brandon Stoddard, as quoted in *Crossing Over*. On Silverman's strategy, see Fishbein, *"Roots,"* 279–80.

38 The quotations are from "ABC's 'Roots' Garners a Top Nielsen Rating," *New York Times*, 26 January 1977, C20; and from a syndicated story with a Hollywood byline that appeared as "Alex 'Roots' Haley from Rags to Riches," in the *Connellsville (Pennsylvania) Daily Courier*, 16 February 1977, 20. The statistics come from J. Fred MacDonald, *Black and White TV: Afro-Americans in Television since 1948* (Chicago: Nelson-Hall, 1983), 215.

39 Quotations are from Les Brown, *"Roots'* Success in South Seen as Sign of Change," *New York Times*, 10 February 1977, 18; Morton S. Cohn, as quoted in "Southern Viewers Accept TV Show without Incident," *Chicago Tribune*, 13 February 1977, 14; Brown, *"Roots'* Success in South Seen as Sign of Change," 18; Duke, in "Southern Viewers Accept TV Show without Incident," 14; and Roger Wilkins, "The Black Ghosts of History," *New York Times*, 2 February 1977, 19. An analysis of the polls is C. Gerald Fraser, "Blacks and Whites Found to Have Misapprehensions on Impact of *Roots*," *New York Times*, 7 June 1977, 49.

40 Quotation is from Mary McGrory, "Will Success Spoil Alex Haley?," *Chicago*

Tribune, 2 March 1977, B4. Al Martinez, "*Roots*—The Burden of Instant Fame," *Los Angeles Times*, 17 December 1976, B1; "Senate Honors *Roots*' Author," *New York Times*, 15 March 1977, 20; Deirdre Carmody, "Haley Gets Special Pulitzer Prize," *New York Times*, 19 April 1977, 44.

41 Quotations are from Marable, *From the Grassroots*, 112; Keith Moore, "Haley's *Roots* Aren't for Exploitation," *Chicago Tribune*, 19 July 1977, A; and Mark Starr, "Haley's Star Shines for Chicago Youth," *Chicago Tribune*, 25 March 1977, B1. See also Mary McGrory, "Will Success Spoil Alex Haley?," *Chicago Tribune*, 2 March 1977, B4; and Van Deburg, *Slavery and Race*, 155.

42 Alex Haley, as quoted in Martinez, "*Roots*—The Burden of Instant Fame"; "Haley Forming *Roots* Foundation," *Chicago Tribune*, 3 April 1977. See also Herbert Mitgang, "Behind Haley's Suit against Doubleday," *New York Times*, 30 March 1977, 71; and Mark Ottaway, "Tangled Roots," *Sunday Times of London*, 10 April 1977, 16. Haley's response may be found in Alex Haley, "There Are Days When I Wished It Hadn't Happened," *Playboy*, March 1979, 216. On the suits, see "In the Wake of 'Roots,'" *Washington Post*, 26 April 1977, B5.

43 The quotations are from Zimmerman, "In Search of a Heritage," 96; Rose, "American Family," 3; and Anne S. Crowley, "Research Help Supplies Backbone for Haley's Book," *Chicago Tribune*, 24 October 1985, D10H. The Doubleday quotation comes from an ad in the *New York Times*, 24 February 1977, 33; this ad and Rose, "American Family," 3, describe Haley's plan to make research tools available.

44 Bailyn's quotation and the third one, by Oscar Handlin, are in Israel Shenker, "Some Historians Dismiss Report of Factual Mistakes in *Roots*," *New York Times*, 10 April 1977, 29. The Litwak quotation was cited in Harre W. DeMuro, "*Roots*," *Oakland Tribune*, 1 February 1977, 4. On the book's documentable elements, see Zimmerman, "In Search of a Heritage," 95; Gary B. Mills and Elizabeth Shown Mills, "'Roots' and the New 'Faction': A Legitimate Tool for Clio?," *Virginia Magazine of History and Biography* 89 (January 1981): 3–26; and Jesse T. Moore Jr., "Alex Haley's *Roots*: Ten Years Later," *Western Journal of Black Studies* 18 (1994): 75. Marable, *From the Grassroots*, 119.

45 Quotations are from Surlin, "*Roots*' Research," 318; unnamed woman quoted in Harry F. Waters, "After Haley's Comet," *Newsweek*, 14 February 1977, 97; and an unnamed woman quoted in Patricia de Luna, "Amazing Reaction to *Roots*," *Long Beach Independent Press-Telegram*, 6 February 1977, L/S6. On Bicentennial Minutes, see Sara Marshall, "The Grim American History of 'The Bicentennial Minute,'" *Awl*, 14 March 2013.

46 Quotation is from a *New York Times* ad for Doubleday, 24 September 1976, C19. The *TV Guide* ad is in the *New York Times*, 27 January 1977, C36. The ad for Israeli vacations is in the *Village Voice*, April 1977, 27. Alan M. Kriegsman, "America's Passage into the 'Then' Generation," *Washington Post*, 6 February 1977, F1, F12.

47 The quotations are from Zaretsky, *No Direction Home*, 148; Sugrue and Skrentny, "White Ethnic Strategy," 173; and Jacobson, *Roots Too*, 44. Both sets of authors argue for the importance of white ethnic development in the 1970s.

So too does the contemporary piece Hijiya, "*Roots*: Family and Ethnicity in the 1970s." "Megastar" is *Finding Your Roots'* host Henry Louis Gates's word; the others in the story about Affleck are Affleck's. All are cited in Sarah Kaplan, "After Omitting Details of Ben Affleck's Slave-Owning Ancestor, *Finding Your Roots* Is Suspended by PBS," *Washington Post*, 15 June 2015.

48 Eric Foner, "Why 130 Million Viewers Loved *Roots* in Black and White," *Seven Days* 1 (March 1977): 31.

49 Merrill Maguire Skaggs, "*Roots*: A New Black Myth," *Southern Quarterly* 17 (October 1978): the first two quotations are on p. 4, and the last is on p. 44.

50 Quotations are from Halford H. Fairchild, Russell Stockard, and Philip Bowman, "Impact of *Roots*," *Journal of Black Studies* 16 (March 1986): 311; Surlin, "*Roots* Research," 317; and Larry L. Carlin, "Letters to the *Times*," *Los Angeles Times*, 6 February 1977, F4.

51 Fairchild, Stockard, and Bowman, "Impact of *Roots*," 308.

52 Fishbein, "*Roots*," 284–85.

53 See http://www.blackpast.org/primary/national-advisory-commission-civil -disorders-kerner-report-1967.

54 The first quotation is from John Reid, as quoted in Thomas A. Johnson, "'Roots' Has Widespread and Inspiring Influence," *New York Times*, 19 March 1977, 30. The others come from Evelyn King, in Gloster B. Currant, "Cross-Country Survey on Roots—the Saga of Most Black Families in America," *Crisis* 84 (May 1977): 169; Charlayne Hunter-Gault, "'Roots' Getting a Grip on People Everywhere," *New York Times*, 28 January 1977, B5; Wilkins, "Black Ghosts of History," 19; Norrell, *Alex Haley*, preface; and Regé-Jean Page, as quoted in Melena Ryzik, "*Roots* for a New Era," *New York Times*, 22 May 2016, A28.

55 The quotation is from Joseph Moreau, *Schoolbook Nation: Conflicts over American History Textbooks from the Civil War to the Present* (Ann Arbor: University of Michigan Press, 2004), 276, 274. Ruth A. Protinsky and Terry M. Wildman, "*Roots*: Reflections from the Classroom," *Journal of Negro Education* 48 (Spring 1979): 171–81. The survey was of 10th, 11th, and 12th graders, 17 percent of whom were African American. The picture accompanied Waters, "After Haley's Comet."

56 Glazer and Ueda, *Ethnic Groups in History Textbooks*; quotations from pp. 15, 26, 58.

57 Daina Ramey Berry, as quoted in Neal Justin, "Roots for a New Generation," *Minneapolis Star Tribune*, 27 May 2016, E14: Wolper and Delmont, as cited in Ryzik, "*Roots* for a New Era," AR1; *Miniseries: Pioneers of Television*.

CHAPTER 5

1 All quotations are from a White House tape cited in James Warren, "Nixon on Tape Expounds on Welfare and Homosexuality," *Chicago Tribune*, 7 November 1999, 2, except the word "polarizing," which comes from Jack Gould, "Can Bigotry Be Laughed Away?," *New York Times*, 21 February 1971, D15.

2 "'New Morality' On TV Debated," *Los Angeles Times*, 25 March 1976, E16.

3 See Marc, *Comic Visions*.

4 The quotation is from Altman, *The Homosexualization of America*, viii. On the groups, see Rupp, *A Desired Past*, 162–63. A good history of gay advocacy is Faderman, *Gay Revolution*.

5 Quotations are from Reuben, *Everything You Always Wanted to Know about Sex*, 162; and Judy Klemesrud, "For Homosexuals, It's Getting Less Difficult to Tell Parents," *New York Times*, 1 September 1972, 32.

6 As cited in Foley, *Front Porch Politics*, 83.

7 Capsuto, *Alternate Channels*, 51–53.

8 All quotations but the last one are from "The Homosexual: Newly Visible, Newly Understood," *Time*, 31 October 1969, 56–57; the last is from Capsuto, *Alternate Channels*, 56.

9 "Judging Books by Covers," written by Norman Lear and Burt Styler, original airdate, 9 February 1971.

10 Laura Z. Hobson, "As I Listened to Archie Say 'Hebe,'" *New York Times*, 12 September 1971, D1.

11 Quotations are from Richard Levine, "How the Gay Lobby Has Changed Television," *TV Guide*, 30 May 1981, 6; Michael Kotis, "Homosexual Militance," *New York Times*, 19 February 1971, 37; and Lynn Hunt, *Inventing Human Rights: A History* (New York: W.W. Norton, 2007), 29. Hunt extended the theme to include sexual identity in her keynote address at the History and Law Society's San Francisco Rights Conference, September 2010.

12 Quotations are from Newton Dieter, "The Last Minority: Television and Gay People," *Television Quarterly* 13 (Fall 1976): 70; the GMTF's policy paper, cited in Capsuto, *Alternate Channels*, 99; and Vito Russo, "In Search of the New Culture," *Gay*, 30 October 1972, 6.

13 Quotations are from Levinson and Link, *Stay Tuned*, 111; and Charles Champlin, "Homosexuality Faced in *Certain Summer*," *Los Angeles Times*, 1 November 1972, F16.

14 Gilbert is quoted by Cecil Smith in two different articles: the first, "Finding, Filming American Family," *Los Angeles Times*, 11 January 1973, H22; and the second, "Super Home Movies? No, in Reality, It's *An American Family*," *Los Angeles Times*, 7 January 1973, N2.

15 Quotations are from Stephanie Harrington, "An American Family Lives Its Life on TV," *New York Times*, 7 January 1973; John O'Connor, "TV Arguments over *An American Family* Are Smothering Its Content," *New York Times*, 22 January 1973, 60, 141; ad, *New York Times*, 18 January 1973, 87; Anne Roiphe, "Things Are Keen but Could Be Keener," *New York Times*, 18 February 1973, Sunday magazine; and O'Connor, "TV Arguments," 60.

16 Jane Hoback of the National Organization for Women, testifying before the U.S. Congress, House of Representatives, Committee on Interstate and Foreign Commerce, *Hearings before the Subcommittee on Communications: The Issue of Televised Violence and Obscenity*, 25; Jenkins, *Decade of Nightmares*, 109.

17 Zaretsky, *No Direction Home*, 13.

18 "Some of My Best Friends Are . . . ," written by Patricia Jones and Donald Reiker, original airdate, 9 October 1976.

19 Quotations are from Joseph Turow, *Playing Doctor: Television, Story-Telling, and Medical Power* (New York: Oxford University Press, 1989), 112; "The Other Martin Loring," written by Dick Nelson and David Victor, original airdate, 20 February 1973; and the Gay Media Task Force platform, cited in Capsuto, *Alternate Channels*, 99.

20 Michael R. Real, *Mass-Mediated Culture* (Englewood Cliffs, N.J.: Prentice Hall, 1977), 125–30.

21 "The Outrage," written by David Price, original airdate, 8 October 1974.

22 The quotations are from Jeanne Cordova, "Community Plows Under 'Flowers of Evil,'" *Lesbian Tide*, January 1975, 16; "Flowers of Evil," story by Joshua Hanke and teleplay by John W. Bloch, original airdate, 8 November 1974; and Fay Spain, as quoted in Cecil Smith, "An Emasculated *Flowers of Evil*," *Los Angeles Times*, 8 November 1974, F27.

23 Falwell was cited in Barry D. Adam, *The Rise of a Gay and Lesbian Movement* (Boston: Twayne, 1987), 113. James Carlson, *Prime Time Law Enforcement: Crime Show Viewing and Attitudes toward the Criminal Justice System* (New York: Praeger, 1985), 195.

24 The quotation is from David Marc and Robert J. Thompson, *Prime Time, Prime Movers: From "I Love Lucy" to "L.A. Law"—America's Greatest TV Shows and the People Who Created Them* (Boston: Little, Brown, 1992), 153. On Ford's TV preferences, see Cowan, *See No Evil*, 124.

25 Lassiter, "Inventing Family Values," 23.

26 The first quotation is cited in Staiger, *Blockbuster TV*, 109. The second comes from U.S. Department of Health and Human Services, *Television and Behavior*, 38.

27 The first quotation is from "Too Candid Camera?," *Time*, 30 September 1974, 66. The rest are from John J. O'Connor, "TV: A Glimpse of Reality," *New York Times*, 18 September 1974, 81; Cecil Smith, "Don't Disturb the Kiddies, *Los Angeles Times*, 21 January 1975, G13; "The State: Suit Says TV Show Inspired Attack on Girl," *Los Angeles Times*, 11 October 1974, A2; and Montgomery, *Target Prime Time*, 103.

28 Joyce D. Brothers, "Needed: A Rating System to Guide Parents," *New York Times*, 12 January 1975, 127.

29 Dick Adler, "Jury Still Out on Family Hour," *Los Angeles Times*, 5 June 1975, G1.

30 The quotations are from the memoir of the censor who tangled with *Barney Miller* producer Danny Arnold, Alfred Schneider. See Alfred R. Schneider and Kay Pullen, *The Gatekeeper: My Thirty Years as a TV Censor* (Syracuse: Syracuse University Press, 2001), 111. For the rest of the story, see Cowan, *See No Evil*, 145–78.

31 The quotations are from Tom Shales, "Summing up a Season: Beyond the Malaise of the TV Viewer," *Washington Post*, 14 March 1976, 149; Harry F. Waters,

"Why Is TV So Bad?," *Newsweek*, 16 February 1976, 72–74; and John O'Connor, "Can Quality Programs Survive the Profit Squeeze?," *New York Times*, 15 December 1974, 183. Robert Rawitch and Lee Margulies, "TV's 'Family Hour' Ruled Unconstitutional," *Los Angeles Times*, 5 November 1976, A1.

32 The quotations are from Amir Hetsroni, "Three Decades of Sexual Content on Prime-Time Network Programming—a Longitudinal Meta-Analytic Review," *Journal of Communication* 57 (2007): 330; and Ellen Farley and William K. Knoedelseder Jr., "The Titillating Trend in TV: Sex Makes It to Prime Time," *Los Angeles Times*, 19 February 1978, Q1.

33 Paul L. Klein, as quoted in Les Brown, "New Sex-Oriented TV Shows Planned," *New York Times*, 23 February 1978, C20.

34 John J. O'Connor, "TV Is Getting Tough on Violence and Loose with Sex," *New York Times*, 11 September 1977, 65.

35 "The Gay Bar," written by Thad Mumford, Michael Endler, Bill Davenport, and Arthur Julian, original airdate, 3 December 1977.

36 "Angels in Chains," written by Barry Stern and Robert Earll, original airdate, 20 October 1976; Frank Swertlow, "'Porno Chic' on Increase," *Los Angeles Times*, 11 April 1977, E20.

37 "The 4th Sex," written by Rita Lakin, original airdates, 8 and 15 September 1975.

38 From the *WKRP* episode "Les on a Ledge," written by Hugh Wilson, original airdate, 2 October 1978.

39 Butler, "Performative Acts and Gender Constitution," 519–31. The *WKRP* episode is "Les on a Ledge." The *Taxi* episode is "Elaine's Strange Triangle," written by David Lloyd, original airdate, 10 December 1980.

40 Quotations are from Joan Hanauer, "Viewers' Opinions on TV Sex," *Los Angeles Times*, 20 January 1978, E26; John O'Connor, "Wait a Minute—Gay Gangsters? Gonorrhea?," *New York Times*, 15 October 1972, D19; and Elizabeth J. Roberts, of the Project on Human Sexuality, as cited in Lee Margulies, "Seminar Held on TV Sexuality," *Los Angeles Times*, 21 March 1977, E20.

41 "DDB Study Finds Public Wants Reins on Television Sex, but Shies from Total Censorship, Federal Control," *Broadcasting*, 23 January 1978, 46. See also Foley, *Front Porch Politics*, 80.

42 Echols, *Hot Stuff*, 46.

43 The quotations are from Jenkins, *Decade of Nightmares*, 11; and "Hiring of Homosexuals," poll date: June 1977, in Gallup, *The Gallup Poll*, 1143, specifically referring to teachers. "DDB Study Finds Public Wants Reins."

44 John Weisman, "He's Counting Every Jiggle and Cussword," *TV Guide*, 17 March 1979, 9.

45 The first two quotations are from Les Brown, "'Soap,' ABC's Explicit Comedy, Has Critics in Lather," *New York Times*, 27 June 1977, 40, the first quoting Everett C. Parker. The next three are from Les Brown, "Pressure against 'Soap' TV Ads Dismays Agency and ABC Aides," *New York Times*, 30 August 1977, G1. The conservative position is Foy Valentine of the Christian Life Commission, as quoted in "Advertisers Feel Pressure on 'Soap,'" *Broadcasting*, 29 August

1977, 22; and "Memo to Networks: 'Clean Up TV!,'" *Christianity Today* 22 (30 December 1977): 42.

46 Quotations are from Michael J. Robinson, "Prime Time Chic: Between Newsbreaks and Commercials, the Values Are L.A. Liberal," *Public Opinion* 2 (March/May 1979): 42; Mary Lewis Coakley, *Rated X: The Moral Case against TV* (New Rochelle, N.Y.: Arlington House, 1977), 13; and T. Lee Margulies, "Where Do We Draw the Line?," *Los Angeles Times*, 12 October 1979, E1. The resolutions are quoted in Reuben Herring, "Southern Baptist Convention Resolutions on the Family," *Baptist History and Heritage* 17 (1982): 39, 45.

47 Quotations are from Robinson, "Prime Time Chic," 47; Stein, *View from Sunset Boulevard*, 146; and Alfred A. Messer, as cited in Amy Larkin, "It's Time Television Learned about Overkill Says Psychiatrist," *Atlanta Constitution*, 18 September 1977, 26. The Wildmon comment comes from John Weisman, "He's Counting Every Jiggle and Cussword," *TV Guide*, 17 March 1979, 9.

48 Quotations are from Wildmon, as cited in Edwin McDowell, "TV Sex Upsetting Sponsors," *New York Times*, 30 May 1978 (two quotations), D6, D1; and Patrick J. Buchanan, "TV Shows a Double Image," *Chicago Tribune*, 21 June 1977, B4. On the Sears controversy and Ford, see Harry F. Waters, "Sex and TV," *Newsweek*, 20 February 1978, 58; and Weisman, "He's Counting Every Jiggle and Cussword," 9–19.

49 Quotations are from Waters, "Sex and TV," 61; and "'New Morality' On TV Debated," *Los Angeles Times*, 25 March 1976, E16.

50 Quotation and information on the groups comes from Lassiter, "Inventing Family Values," 13–28, quotation from p. 23.

51 All quotations but the last come from Berkowitz, *Something Happened*, 153. The last is from Harry F. Waters, "Sex and TV," 59. On Bryant and Briggs, see also Foley, *Front Porch Politics*, 85–89; or Faderman, *Gay Revolution*, 370–89.

52 Capsuto, *Alternate Channels*, 145; David Johnson, "SF Gay Pride Parade Draws 375,000," *Los Angeles Times*, 27 June 1977, C13; "Anita Bryant's Drive Cost Her a Show," *Los Angeles Times*, 25 February 1977, B2; "Teen Poll Ranks Anita Bryant with Hitler in Causing Harm," *Los Angeles Times*, 22 June 1978, 24; "Cherry Bombs, Catcalls Greet Anita Bryant," *Los Angeles Times*, 10 July 1977, A4; Russell Chandler, "Christians Have Strong Anti-Gay Bias, Poll Says," *Los Angeles Times*, 31 December 1977, A14.

53 "Homosexual Teachers" (no writer credited), original airdate, 31 October 1979.

54 Richard Levine, "Our Only Allies Now Are Our Worst Enemies," *TV Guide*, 6 June 1981, 52. On inoffensive programming, see Staiger, *Blockbuster TV*, 3.

55 Levine, "Our Only Allies Now Are Our Worst Enemies."

56 Quotations are from CBS censor Van Gordon Sauter, as quoted in James M. Wall, "Who Shapes TV Values?," *Christian Century* 94 (16 February 1977): 131; and Betty Friedan and Richard Gilbert, participating in the 1981 American Academy of Television Arts and Sciences conference on pressure groups, in Howard Rosenberg, "Pressure Groups and TV—the Shadow over Ojai," *Los*

Angeles Times, 13 May 1981, H9. See also Harry F. Waters, "TV: Do Minorities Rule?," *Newsweek*, 2 June 1975, 79.

57 The quotations are from the titles of two of Yankelovich's books, *New Rules* and *New Morality*; American Enterprise Institute spokesperson, cited in Michael J. Robinson, "Prime Time Chic: Between Newsbreaks and Commercials, the Values Are L.A. Liberal," *Public Opinion* 2 (March/May 1979): 43; and Wildmon, quoted in Jan R. Van Meter, "TV Must Brace for a Boycott," *Los Angeles Times*, 20 November 1981, E11. On Procter & Gamble, see Tony Schwartz, "50 TV Shows Rejected by Procter & Gamble," *New York Times*, 17 June 1981, C30. The word "nervous" comes from Lee Margulies, "Inside TV," *Los Angeles Times*, 21 May 1981, K1.

58 As quoted in Lee Margulies, "'Love, Sidney' Shuns Homosexuality Issue," *Los Angeles Times*, 9 May 1981, B8.

59 Gallup, *The Gallup Poll*, 1151.

60 The quotations are from Taylor Berman, "Joe Biden's *Will & Grace* Shout-Out Was 'One of the Proudest Moments' of Debra Messing's Life," *New York Magazine*, 10 May 2012; and Gallup polls at http://www.gallup.com/poll/1651/Gay-Lesbian-Rights.aspx.

61 See Susan Page, "Poll: Support for Gay Marriage Hits High After Ruling," *USA Today*, 1 July 2013.

62 Suzanne J. Kessler and Wendy McKenna, *Gender: An Ethnomethodological Approach* (Chicago: University of Chicago Press, 1978).

CHAPTER 6

1 Christian G. Appy, *American Reckoning: The Vietnam War and Our National Identity* (New York: Viking, 2015), introduction.

2 The quotations are from Margaret Singer at the 2001 memorial ceremony at Evergreen Cemetery in Oakland, California, as cited in Fondakowski, *Stories from Jonestown*, 3; and Jorgensen, "Social Construction and Interpretation of Deviance," 314.

3 The first quotation is from Jorgensen, "Social Construction and Interpretation of Deviance," 313. The others are from Reid, "At Home in the Abyss," 278; Graebner, "America's Poseidon Adventure," 158, 160, 162; and Dave Smith, "Skepticism as Our Saving Grace," *Los Angeles Times*, 10 December 1978, L4.

4 The quotations are from Jorgensen, "Social Construction and Interpretation of Deviance," 319; Jeanie Kasindorf, "Jim Jones: The Seduction of San Francisco," *New West*, 18 December 1978, 50; and Stephenson, *Dear People*, Introduction, xi.

5 Bill Drummond, "Ryan Press Strategy Backfired," *Los Angeles Times*, 20 December 1978, B20; Charles Krause, "Ryan Sensed Cultists Would Attack," *Los Angeles Times*, 20 November 1978, 19.

6 Kilduff and Tracy, "Inside People's Temple," 34, 38. The other Kilduff quotation is from David Shaw, "The 'Missed' News Story: Why and How," *Los Angeles Times*, 27 July 1979, B1. The Krause quotation comes from Layton, *Seductive*

Poison, xv–xvi. The final quotations are from Shaw, "'Missed' News Story," B1, B22.

7 The quotations are from Theodore H. White, "Reporters for the Public—Not for the Politicians," *San Francisco Chronicle*, 26 November 1978, Sunday Punch, 6; and W. Joseph Campbell, *Getting It Wrong: Ten of the Greatest Misreported Stories in American Journalism* (Berkeley: University of California Press, 2010), 116. The polls are Harris Poll, cited in Jon Nordheimer, "Americans Finding New Course Is Vital," *New York Times*, 5 July 1976, 18; and Weiner and Stillman, *Woodstock Census*, 93. On TV news breaking with the Establishment, see Charles L. Ponce de Leon, *That's the Way It Is: A History of Television News in America* (Chicago: University of Chicago Press, 2015), 125.

8 The quotations are from Martha Angle and Robert Walters, "*New Times* Magazine May Be Dead, but Its Jogging Successor Is Thriving," syndicated article appearing in the *Ukiah (Calif.) Daily Journal*, 19 December 1978, 2; Clay Felker, founding editor of *New York Magazine*, as quoted in Leonard Downie Jr., *The New Muckrakers* (New York: New American Library, 1976), 240; Jorgensen, "Social Construction and Interpretation of Deviance," 314; and Jean Clancey, as quoted in Fondakowski, *Stories from Jonestown*, 281.

9 Krause, *Guyana Massacre*, 85, 83, 84; "The 'Quickly' Phenomenon," *Time*, 18 December 1978, 88.

10 The second and last quotations come from Bill Drummond, "Ryan Press Strategy Backfired," *Los Angeles Times*, 20 December 1978, B20. The others are from Reiterman with Jacobs, *Raven*, 481; Jim Schermerhorn of the *San Francisco Examiner*, as quoted in Jerry Burns, "How Jim Jones Tried to Manipulate the Press," *San Francisco Chronicle*, 24 November 1978, 4; and Krause, *Guyana Massacre*, 16, 85.

11 The quotations are from James S. Gordon, "Jim Jones and His People," *New York Times*, 7 January 1979, Sunday Book Review, 1; Lee Margulies, "The Making of 'Mad Messiah,'" *Los Angeles Times*, 19 May 1979, E22; Howard Rosenberg, "Networks Put 'Guyana' on Hold," *Los Angeles Times*, 1 December 1978, I32; and Jonestown tape excerpt cited in "Hurry My Children, Hurry," *Time*, 26 March 1979, 28. The cartoon appeared in the *Chicago Tribune* on 4 December 1978, B2.

12 Editorial note attached to Tim Reiterman, "What Jones Said to Reiterman," *San Francisco Examiner*, 20 November 1978, 18; Terry Schmitt, as quoted in "Greg Robinson: From the First It Was 'Magic,'" *San Francisco Examiner*, 20 November 1978, C; Michael Douglas, as quoted in "Fonda Tilts Forces of Nuclear Energy in *China Syndrome*," *New York Times*, 16 March 1979, C6; Anthony Katsaris, as quoted in Klineman and Butler, *The Cult That Died*, 351. The Sung interview appeared on 20 November 1978.

13 The TV news stories are from *NBC Nightly News*, 20 and 23 November 1978. "Sect Lined Up to Get Poison," *Los Angeles Times*, 20 November 1978, 1; "Day by Day, a New Stunning Horror," *Chicago Tribune*, 26 November 1978, 18. The phrase "grisly mathematical puzzle" was NBC newsman John Chancellor's from *NBC Nightly News*, 23 November 1978.

14 Roger Mudd, *CBS Evening News*, 20 November 1978. *CBS Evening News*, 21 November 1978, and *ABC News*, 23 November 1978, talk about body doubles.

15 The quotations except the second are from Cahill, "In the Valley of the Shadow of Death." The second is from James Reston, "Jonestown: A Virulent Madness That Still Awaits Exorcism," *Los Angeles Times*, 18 November 1979, F5.

16 The first and last quotations are from Jim Willse, "On the Scene at Jonestown; A Nightmare," *San Francisco Examiner*, 22 November 1978, 5. The rest are from captions to pictures that appeared in the *San Francisco Examiner*, 21 November 1978, 4.

17 The quotations are from Charles B. Seib, "What the Media Did," *Washington Post*, 1 December 1978, A19; and Colman McCarthy, "The Jonestown Massacre: Don't Try to Explain It," *Los Angeles Times*, 29 November 1978, SD9.

18 Quotations are from Kondracke, "My Heart Belongs to Daddy," *New Republic*, 9 December 1978, 9; "Reverend Jim Jones," *People*, 25 December 1978; Lance Morrow, "The Lure of Doomsday," *Time*, 4 December 1978, 30; Kenneth A. Briggs, "Fringe Religions Find Fertile Soil in United States," *New York Times*, 28 November 1978, A14; and Ellen Goodman, "The Spookiness of Cults," *Los Angeles Times*, 24 November 1978, D11. *Newsweek*, "The World of Cults," 4 December 1978, 78, provides the number.

19 The quotations are from Carter's 15 July 1979 "Crisis of Confidence" speech at http://www.pbs.org/wgbh/americanexperience/features/primary-resources /carter-crisis/; Eleanor Blau, "ACLU Aide Warns on Seizing Cultists," *New York Times*, 6 February 1977, L27; and Jim Siegelman and Flo Conway, "Still Jonestownism Runs On," *New York Times*, 15 November 1979, A31. On political correctness, see Ruth Perry, "A Short History of the Term *Politically Correct*," in *Beyond PC: Toward a Politics of Understanding*, ed. Patricia Aufderheide (Minneapolis: Gray Wolf Press, 1992).

20 The quotations are from Sue Jenson, "Letters to the Editor," *San Francisco Chronicle*, 28 November 1978, 44; Mike Lavelle, "Letter to the Editor," *Chicago Tribune*, 13 December 1980, N8; Carl Rowan, "In the Name of Religion," *San Francisco Examiner*, 24 November 1978; Annie Nakao, "Lawyer Aims to Keep Holdings of Peoples Temple from State," *San Francisco Examiner*, 27 November 1978, 8; and Jimmy Carter, at a 30 November 1978 press conference, The American Presidency Project website, http://www.presidency.ucsb.edu/ws /index.php?pid=30222. The polls are from Russell Chandler, "Survivors of Peoples Temple Can't Forget," *Los Angeles Times*, 18 November 1979, 22.

21 Quotations are from Tom Goldstein, "Survey Finds Public Critical of Lawyers," *New York Times*, 11 February 1978, 26; and Marc Galanter, "The Great American Lawyer Joke Explosion," *Humor—International Journal of Humor Research* 21 (2008): 390. On the 1960s and 1970s, see Thomas F. Burke, *Lawyers, Lawsuits, and Legal Rights: The Battle over Litigation in American Society* (Berkeley: University of California Press, 2002), 9–12. The numbers come from Warren Weaver Jr., "Lawyers Criticized in ABA's Survey," *New York Times*, 13 September 1974, 18.

22 The first two quotations are from Charles McCabe, "What Did Lawyers

Know?," *San Francisco Chronicle*, 30 November 1978, 55; followed by Diane Johnson, "Heart of Darkness," *New York Review of Books* 26 (19 April 1979): 4; and Dianna Waggoner, "Attorney Charles Garry Is Still a Believer—If Not in Jim Jones, Then in His 'Utopia,'" *People*, 11 December 1978, 42. Garry, as quoted in Ivan Sharpe, "I Guess I'm Responsible," *San Francisco Examiner*, 22 November 1978, 1. On the lawsuits, see Nora Gallagher, "Jonestown: The Survivors' Story," *New York Times*, 18 November 1979, 139. On the impact of his actions on government employees and his version of the story, see U.S. Congress, House of Representatives, Committee on Foreign Relations, *Assassination of Representative Leo J. Ryan*, 27–29, 328.

23 The first quotation is from Kondracke, "My Heart Belongs to Daddy," 9. The last is from Nick Thimmesch, "A Vulture Named Mark Lane Circles over Guyana's Dead," *Chicago Tribune*, 29 November 1978, D2. On the "hit squads," see Narda Zacchino, "Cult Has Plan to Kill Defectors, Attorney Says," *Los Angeles Times*, 26 November 1978, A3, A31.

24 The quotations are Graham Hovey, "Ryan Aide Cites Lack of Warning on Guyana Danger," *New York Times*, 4 December 1978, B17; Ryan's aide Joe Holsinger, as quoted in Robert Barkdoll, "Ryan Aide Raps Probe of Cult," *Los Angeles Time*, 21 November 1978, A9; "U.S. State Department Ignored Defector's Warning on Jonestown," *Ukiah (California) Daily Journal*, 22 November 1978, 2; and Tom Reston, as quoted in "Had No Proof of Cult Danger, US Insists," *Chicago Tribune*, 3 December 1978, B31.

25 Quotations are from John Peer Nugent, *White Night: The Untold Story of What Happened Before—and Beyond—Jonestown* (New York: Rawson, Wade, 1979), 103; Keith Powers, "The Strange Deal between Guyana and Peoples Temple," *San Francisco Chronicle*, 27 November 1978, 1; Layton, *Seductive Poison*, 140–41, 154; and Krause, *Guyana Massacre*, 15.

26 Quotations are from an unsigned note left behind in Jonestown, probably Carolyn Moore, 18 November 1978, in Stephenson, *Dear People*, xv, xvi; "Life in Jonestown," *Newsweek*, 4 December 1978, 65; David Johnston, "Jones—the Dark, Private Side Emerges," *Los Angeles Times*, 24 November 1978, B1; and Charles Garry, as quoted in Wallace Turner, "Sect Lawyer Explains Role in Custody Fight over Boy," *New York Times*, 27 November 1978, 14.

27 Quotations are from Feinsod, *Awake in a Nightmare*, 134, 160; and "Paranoia and Delusions," *Time*, 11 December 1978, 35. On the drugs, see "Why Leo Ryan and Jim Jones Met on That Day of Death in the Jungles of Guyana," *People*, 4 December 1978, 31, 32. Pete Carey, "Toward the End, Jones Slipped from Reality into Fantasy World," *San Jose Mercury News*, 29 November 1978.

28 Jenkins, *Decade of Nightmares*, 11, 12; Anthony Lewis, "The Making of an Assassin," *New York Times*, 31 October 1976, Sunday Book Review, 6.

29 The quotations are from Lowell D. Streiker, who served as a psychologist for the group, in "Reflections of the Human Freedom Center," in *The Need for a Second Look at Jonestown*, ed. Rebecca Moore and Fielding M. McGeehee III (Wales: Edwin Mellin Press, 1989), 158. The third is from an unidentified Cen-

ter member; the fourth is from Center member Joyce Shaw. Both are cited in Bella Stumbo, "Cult Conclave Still Incredulous," *Los Angeles Times*, 17 December 1978, C6. On Gregory and Beter, see Rebecca Moore, "Reconstructing Reality: Conspiracy Theories about Jonestown," *Journal of Popular Culture* 36 (Fall 2002): 205.

30 Quotations are from "Grisly Guyana Discovery," *Ukiah (California) Daily Journal*, 24 November 1978, 1; Keith Power, "Tests Ordered to Prove It's Jones' Body," *San Francisco Chronicle*, 23 November 1978, 1; Tamburello in Fondakowski, *Stories from Jonestown*, 303; House Foreign Affairs Committee staff investigator George Berdes, as quoted in "Jonestown Death Squad Can't Be Ruled Out, Hearing Told," *Los Angeles Times*, 16 May 1979, B12 (two quotations); and Neva Sly on *NBC Nightly News*, 16 November 1979.

31 The first and last quotations are from Dan Sullivan and Phil Zimbardo, "Jonestown Survivors Tell Their Story," *Los Angeles Times*, 9 March 1979, E10, E11, E1. The rest are from Dale Parks, as quoted in Ethan Feinsod, *Awake in a Nightmare*, 178; and Charles Krause and Leonard Downie Jr., "Survivor Tells of 'Concentration Camp,'" *San Francisco Chronicle*, 23 November 1978, 2 (two quotations).

32 Krause, *Guyana Massacre*, 20.

33 The quotations are from Rebecca Moore, as quoted in Fondakowski, *Stories from Jonestown*, 25; "Sect Lined Up to Get Poison," *Los Angeles Times*, 20 November 1978, A1; "A Final Ritual: Cyanide," *Chicago Tribune*, 21 November 1978, 1; J. Brown to President Carter, 5 December 1978, in Stephenson, *Dear People*, xix; Charles Krause, "Jones Ordered Cultists to Drink Cyanide Potion, *Los Angeles Times*, 21 November 1978, B1; and exchange between Christine Miller and Jim Jones, as quoted in Fondakowski, *Stories from Jonestown*, 248.

34 Willard Gaylen, as quoted in Carey Winfrey, "Why 900 Died in Guyana," *New York Times*, 25 February 1979, Sunday magazine, 10; "Life in Jonestown," *Newsweek*, 4 December 1978, 62, 63, 64.

35 Quotations are from mother of victim, quoted in Kenneth A. Briggs, "Religious 'Brainwashing' Dispute," *New York Times*, 9 April 1977, 8; Krause, *Guyana Massacre*, 45; Layton, quoted in Stephen Hall, "Ryan Murder Suspect Became a 'Robot,'" *San Francisco Chronicle*, 28 November 1978, 6; and Katsaris, quoted in George Hunter, "Temple 'Mind-Programmed' Maria!—Father," *Ukiah (California) Daily Journal*, 12 April 1978, 1. On brainwashing, see Graebner, *Patty's Got a Gun*, 69–75.

36 The quotations are from Graebner, *Patty's Got a Gun*, 122; and Laurence Layton, as quoted in Stephan Hall, "How the Temple Shattered a Family," *San Francisco Chronicle*, 27 November 1978, 4.

37 Quotations are from *NBC Nightly News*, 1 December 1978; and "Who Must Pay the Costs?," *Chicago Tribune*, 25 November 1978, W10.

38 Quotations are from Delaware senator William Roth, as cited in "2 US Senators Question Temple Airlift Costs," *Los Angeles Times*, 1 December 1978, 22; North Carolina senator Jesse Helms, as cited in ibid.; "Dispute Lingers on

Cemetery for Jonestown Bodies," *New York Times*, 22 April 1979, 27; and two unnamed callers to a Dover radio show, in Gregory Jaynes, "Handling the Guyana Bodies Has Delaware City on Edge," *New York Times*, 30 November 1978, A16.

39 The quotations are from John Peer Nugent, *White Night: The Untold Story of What Happened Before—and Beyond—Jonestown* (New York: Rawson, Wade, 1979), 243; Francis Russell, "The Kingdoms of Death," *National Review* 31 (16 February 1979): 220; and "Another Day of Death," *Time*, 11 December 1978, 24.

40 The quotation is from the unnamed mayor of Madison, Wisconsin, as cited in Tom Eastham, "S.F.'s Name Takes a Beating," *San Francisco Examiner*, 28 November 1978, 5. On the political assassinations, see Talbot, *Season of the Witch*, 322–36.

41 Quotations are from Pete Carey, "Toward the End, Jones Slipped from Reality into Fantasy World," *San Jose Mercury News*, 29 November 1978; Carll Tucker, "A Monster's Bill of Rights," *Saturday Review* 6 (17 February 1979): 64; Smith, "Skepticism as Our Saving Grace" (3 quotations); Deborah Layton, as quoted in Stanley Nelson's 2006 documentary, "Jonestown: The Life and Death of Peoples Temple," transcript at http://www.pbs.org/wgbh/american experience/features/transcript/jonestown-transcript/; and Smith, "Skepticism as Our Saving Grace."

42 The congressional investigation is U.S. Congress, House of Representatives, Committee on Foreign Relations, *Assassination of Representative Leo J. Ryan*, quotations from pp. 80, 24. The FBI's file is dated 12 January 1979, quotation from p. 22. On the State Department study, see "Study Faults US in 913 Sect Deaths," *Chicago Tribune*, 4 May 1979, 2; and William (Bill) Raspberry, "What Government Mustn't Do," *Chicago Tribune*, 5 December 1978, B4.

43 Quotations are from Johnson, "Heart of Darkness," 3; Rebecca Moore in Fondakowski, *Stories from Jonestown*, 24; Gregory Jaynes, "Handling the Guyana Bodies Has Delaware City on Edge," *New York Times*, 30 November 1978, A16; and Kondracke, "My Heart Belongs to Daddy," 10.

44 The quotations are from Moore's diary, as quoted in Stephenson, *Dear People*, 147; Lee Siegel, "Welcome to the Age of the Unfunny Joke," *New York Times*, 20 September 2015, SR2; and Cahill, "In the Valley of the Shadow of Death"; except the one on "stylized ritual," which comes from Smith, "Skepticism as Our Saving Grace."

45 The quotations are from Michael Carter, "Drinking the Kool-Aid," November 2003, in Stephenson, *Dear People*, 153; Barbara Saltzman, "Contender for Bad Taste Award," *Los Angeles Times*, 8 December 1978, 36; cartoon dated 1979 from the John R. Hall Papers, California Historical Society, San Francisco; and Brian Britt, "Revisiting 'Drinking Kool-Aid,'" *Chicago Tribune*, 24 November 2008, 1.

46 The quotations are from Cahill, "In the Valley of the Shadow of Death." On seventies humor, see Zoglin, *Comedy at the Edge*. The *Saturday Night* skit occurred on 2 December 1978.

47 Diane Johnson, "After Jonestown," *New York Review of Books* 28 (8 October 1981): 3.
48 Tim Cahill, "In the Valley of the Shadow of Death."

CONCLUSION

1 Yankelovich, *New Rules*, xvii–xviii.
2 "Mockingbird," written by Inez and Charlie Fox.
3 Cherlin, as quoted in Tamas Lewin, "Millennials' No. 1 Roommates Are Their Parents," *New York Times*, 25 May 2016, A3.

Bibliography

PAPERS AND ONLINE ARCHIVES
Berkeley, California
    University of California at Berkeley, Bancroft Library
        San Francisco Examiner Photographic Archives
        Social Protest Collection
Los Angeles, California
    University of California at Los Angeles
        UCLA Television and Film Archives
San Diego, California
    San Diego State University
        Alternative Considerations of Jonestown and Peoples Temple,
            Primary Documents, http://jonestown.sdsu.edu/?page_id=13052
San Francisco, California
    California Historical Society
        John R. Hall Papers
        Peoples Temple Collection
Wilmington, Delaware
    Hagley Museum and Library
        Ernest Dichter Papers

NEWSPAPERS
Chicago Tribune
Los Angeles Times
New York Times
Washington Post

GOVERNMENT DOCUMENTS
U.S. Commission on Civil Rights. *Window Dressing: Women and Minorities in Television.* Washington, D.C.: Government Printing Office, 1977.
U.S. Congress. House of Representatives. Committee on Foreign Relations. *The Assassination of Representative Leo J. Ryan and the Jonestown Guyana Tragedy.* Washington, D.C.: Government Printing Office, 1979.
———. Committee on Interstate and Foreign Commerce. *Hearings before the Subcommittee on Communications: The Issue of Televised Violence and Obscenity.* Washington, D.C.: Government Printing Office, 1977.
U.S. Department of Commerce. *Social Indicators, 1973: Selected Statistics on Social Conditions and Trends in the United States.* Washington, D.C.: Government Printing Office, 1973.
U.S. Department of Health and Human Services. Public Health Service.

Television and Behavior: Ten Years of Scientific Progress and Implications for the Eighties. Rockville, Md.: National Institute of Mental Health, 1982.

U.S. Department of Justice. Federal Bureau of Investigation. *Documents Pertaining to the Murder of Congressman Leo Ryan (Freedom of Information Act).* Washington, D.C.: Government Printing Office, 1979.

MEMOIRS, COMPILATIONS, AND ORAL HISTORIES

Bangs, Lester. "James Taylor Marked for Death" (originally written in 1971). Reprinted in Lester Bangs, *Psychotic Reactions and Carburetor Dung*, edited by Greil Marcus, 53–81. New York: Alfred A. Knopf, 1987.

Cahill, Tim. "In the Valley of the Shadow: Guyana after Jonestown." *Rolling Stone*, 25 January 1979.

Christgau, Robert. *Any Old Way You Choose It: Rock and Other Pop Music, 1967–1973.* Baltimore: Penguin Books, 1973.

Fondakowski, Leigh. *Stories from Jonestown.* Minneapolis: University of Minnesota Press, 2013.

Harper, Valerie. *I, Rhoda: A Memoir.* New York: Gallery Books, 2014.

King, Carole. *A Natural Woman: A Memoir.* New York: Grand Central Publishing, 2012.

Kohen, Yael. *We Killed: The Rise of Women in American Comedy.* New York: Sarah Crichton Books, 2012.

Layton, Deborah. *Seductive Poison: A Jonestown Survivor's Story of Life and Death in the Peoples Temple.* New York: Doubleday, Anchor, 1998.

Lear, Norman. *Even This I Get to Experience.* New York: Penguin Press, 2014.

Levinson, Richard, and William Link. *Stay Tuned: An Inside Look at the Making of Prime-Time Television.* New York: St. Martin's Press, 1981.

Moore, Mary Tyler. *After All.* New York: Dell, 1996.

Simon, Carly. *Boys in the Trees: A Memoir.* New York: Flatiron Books, 2015.

Stein, Ben. *The View from Sunset Boulevard.* New York: Basic Books, 1979.

Stephenson, Denice, ed. *Dear People: Remembering Jonestown.* Berkeley: Heyday Books, 2005.

Wolper, David L., and Quincy Troupe. *The Inside Story of TV's Roots.* New York: Warner Books, 1978.

OTHER PRIMARY SOURCES

Altman, Dennis. *The Homosexualization of America, the Americanization of the Homosexual.* New York: St. Martin's Press, 1982.

Carter, Angela. "The Language of Sisterhood." In *The State of Language*, edited by Leonard Michaels and Christopher Rocks, 226–34. Berkeley: University of California Press, 1980.

Chapple, Steve, and ReeBee Garafalo. *Rock 'n' Roll Is Here to Pay.* Chicago: Nelson Hall, 1977.

Chesebro, James W. "Communications, Values, and Popular Television Series." In *Television: The Critical View*, 4th ed., edited by Horace Newcomb, 17–51. New York: Oxford University Press, 1982.

Comfort, Alex. *The Joy of Sex: A Gourmet Guide to Love Making.* New York: Simon and Schuster, 1972.

Cowan, Geoffrey. *See No Evil: The Backstage Battle over Sex and Violence on Television.* New York: Simon and Schuster, 1979.

Dey, Eric, Alexander Astin, and William Dorn. *The American Freshman: Twenty-Five Year Trends, 1966–1990.* Los Angeles: UCLA Higher Education Research Institute, 1991.

Friedman, Norman L. "Responses of Blacks and Other Minorities to Television Shows of the 1970s about Their Groups." *Journal of Popular Film* 7 (1978): 85–102.

Gallup, George, ed. *The Gallup Poll: Public Opinion, 1972–1977.* Wilmington, Del.: Scholarly Resources, 1978.

Goldberg, Herb. *The New Male: From Macho to Sensitive but Still All Male.* New York: Signet, 1979.

Hijiya, James A. "*Roots*: Family and Ethnicity in the 1970s." *American Quarterly* 30 (Autumn 1978): 548–56.

Horowitz, Susan. "Sitcom Domesticus: A Species Endangered by Social Change." In *Television: The Critical View,* 4th ed., edited by Horace Newcomb, 106–11. New York: Oxford University Press, 1987.

Jorgensen, Danny L. "The Social Construction and Interpretation of Deviance: Jonestown and the Mass Media." *Deviant Behavior* 1 (1980): 309–32.

Kilduff, Marshall, and Ron Javers. *The Suicide Cult: The Inside Story of the People's Temple Sect and the Massacre in Guyana.* New York: Bantam, Doubleday, Dell Publishing Group, 1978.

Kilduff, Marshall, and Phil Tracy. "Inside People's Temple." *New West* 1 (August 1977): 30–38.

King, Karl, Jack O. Balswick, and Ira E. Robinson. "The Continuing Premarital Sexual Revolution among Female College Students." *Journal of Marriage and the Family* 39 (August 1977): 455–59.

Klineman, George, and Sherman Butler. *The Cult That Died.* New York: G. P. Putnam's Sons, 1980.

Krause, Charles A. *Guyana Massacre: The Eyewitness Account.* New York: Berkeley Books, 1978.

Lasch, Christopher. *The Culture of Narcissism: American Life in an Age of Diminishing Expectations.* W.W. Norton, 1978.

Marable, Manning. *From the Grassroots: Essays toward Afro-American Liberation.* Boston: South End Press, 1980.

Maslin, Janet. "In Prime Time, the Workplace Is Where the Heart Is." *New York Times,* 10 February 1980, D1.

Maupin, Armistead. *Tales of the City.* New York: Harper Perennial, 1978; this edition 1996.

Mead, Margaret. *Culture and Commitment: A Study of the Generation Gap.* Garden City, N.Y.: Natural History Press, 1970.

Nobile, Philip, ed. *The Con III Controversy: The Critics Look at the Greening of America.* New York: Pocket Books, 1971.

Norback, Craig, ed. *The Complete Book of American Surveys*. New York: New American Library, 1980.

Packard, Vance. *The Sexual Wilderness: The Contemporary Upheaval in Male-Female Relationships*. New York: David McKay, 1968.

Reich, Charles A. *The Greening of America: How the Youth Revolt Is Trying to Make America Livable*. New York: Random House, 1970.

Reid, David. "At Home in the Abyss: Jonestown and the Language of Enormity." In *The State of Language*, edited by Leonard Michaels and Christopher Ricks, 277–88. Berkeley: University of California Press, 1980.

Reiterman, Tim, with John Jacobs. *Raven: The Untold Story of the Rev. Jim Jones and His People*. New York: Dutton, 1982.

Reuben, David. *Everything You Always Wanted to Know about Sex, but Were Afraid to Ask*. New York: Bantam, 1969.

Roszak, Theodore. *The Making of the Counter Culture*. Garden City, N.Y.: Anchor Books, 1969.

Schlafly, Phyllis. *The Power of the Positive Woman*. New York: Jove, 1977; this edition 1983.

Sorensen, Robert. *Adolescent Sexuality in Contemporary America: Personal Values and Sexual Behavior, Ages Thirteen to Nineteen*. New York: World, 1973.

Staines, Graham L., and Robert O. Quinn. "American Workers Evaluate the Quality of Their Jobs." *Monthly Labor Review* 102 (January 1979): 3–12.

Surlin, Stuart H. "'Roots' Research: A Summary of Findings." *Journal of Broadcasting* 22 (1978): 309–20.

Sweet, James, and Larry Bumpass. *American Families and Households*. New York: Russell Sage, 1980.

Walsh, Robert H., Mary Z. Ferrell, and William Tolone. "Selection of Reference Group, Perceived Reference Group Permissiveness, and Personal Permissiveness Attitudes and Behavior: A Study of Two Consecutive Panels (1967–1971; 1970–1974)." *Journal of Marriage and the Family* 38 (August 1976): 495–507.

Weiner, Rex, and Deanne Stillman, eds. *Woodstock Census: The Nationwide Survey of the Sixties Generation*. New York: Viking, 1979.

Wilson, William Julius. *The Declining Significance of Race: Blacks and Changing American Institutions*. Chicago: University of Chicago Press, 1978.

Wolfe, Tom. "The 'Me' Decade and the Third Great Awakening." *New York Magazine* 23 (August 1976), at http://nymag.com/news/features/45938/.

Yankelovich, Daniel. *New Rules: Searching for Self-fulfillment in a World Turned Upside Down*. New York: Bantam Books, 1981.

———. *The New Morality: A Profile of American Youth in the 70s*. New York: McGraw-Hill, 1974.

SECONDARY SOURCES

Acham, Christine. *Revolution Televised: Prime Time and the Struggle for Black Power*. Minneapolis: University of Minnesota Press, 2004.

Allyn, David. *Make Love, Not War: The Sexual Revolution: An Unfettered History.* New York: Routledge, 2000.

Altschuler, Glenn C. *All Shook Up: How Rock and Roll Changed America.* New York: Oxford University Press, 2003.

Anson, Robert Sam. *Gone Crazy and Back Again: The Rise and Fall of the Rolling Stone Generation.* Garden City, N.Y.: Doubleday, 1981.

Armstrong, Jennifer Keishin. *Mary and Lou and Rhoda and Ted and the Brilliant Minds Who Made the Mary Tyler Moore Show a Classic.* New York: Simon and Schuster, 2013.

Bailey, Beth. *From Front Porch to Back Seat: Courtship in Twentieth-Century America.* Baltimore: Johns Hopkins University Press, 1988; this edition 1989.

———. *Sex in the Heartland.* Cambridge: Harvard University Press, 1999.

Balmer, Randall. *Redeemer: The Life of Jimmy Carter.* New York: Basic Books, 2014.

Bellah, Robert N., Richard Madsen, William M. Sullivan, Ann Swidler, and Steven M. Tipton. *Habits of the Heart: Individualism and Commitment in American Life.* Berkeley: University of California Press, 1985.

Berkowitz, Edward D. *Something Happened: A Political and Cultural Overview of the Seventies.* New York: Columbia University Press, 2006.

Bogle, Donald. *Prime Time Blues: African Americans on Network Television.* New York: Farrar, Straus and Giroux, 2001.

Bonderoff, Jason. *Mary Tyler Moore.* New York: St. Martin's, 1986.

Brooks, Victor. *Last Season of Innocence: The Teen Experience in the 1960s.* New York: Rowman & Littlefield, 2012.

Browne, David. *Fire and Rain: The Beatles, Simon and Garfunkel, James Taylor, CSNY, and the Lost Story of 1970.* Cambridge: DeCapo Press, 2011.

Butler, Judith. "Performative Acts and Gender Constitution: An Essay in Phenomenology and Feminist Theory." *Theatre Journal* 40 (December 1988): 519–31.

Capsuto, Steven. *Alternate Channels: The Uncensored Story of Gay and Lesbian Images on Radio and Television, 1930s to the Present.* New York: Ballantine, 2000.

Carroll, Peter N. *It Seemed Like Nothing Happened: America in the 1970s.* New Brunswick, N.J.: Rutgers University Press, 1982, 1990.

Clemente, Deirdre. *Dress Casual: How College Students Redefined American Style.* Chapel Hill: University of North Carolina Press, 2014.

Cohen, Lizabeth. *A Consumers' Republic: The Politics of Mass Consumption in Postwar America.* New York: Alfred A. Knopf, 2003.

Cohen, Mitchell S. *Carole King: A Biography.* Burbank: Sire Books, 1976.

Coontz, Stephanie. *Marriage: A History.* New York: Viking, 2005.

Cowie, Jefferson. *Stayin' Alive: The 1970s and the Last Days of the Working Class.* New York: New Press, 2010.

Crossing Over: How Roots Captivated an Entire Nation. Documentary included on the *Roots* DVD, 2007.

Davis, Stephen. *More Room in a Broken Heart: The True Adventures of Carly Simon*. New York: Gotham Books, 2012.

D'Emilio, John, and Estelle B. Freedman. *Intimate Matters: A History of Sexuality in America*. New York: Harper and Row, 1988.

Douglas, Susan J. *Where the Girls Are: Growing Up Female with the Mass Media*. New York: Random House, 1994.

Dow, Bonnie. *Prime-Time Feminism: Television, Media Culture, and the Women's Movement since 1970*. Philadelphia: University of Pennsylvania Press, 1996.

Echols, Alice. *Hot Stuff: Disco and the Remaking of American Culture*. New York: Norton, 2010.

———. *Shaky Ground: The Sixties and Its Aftershocks*. New York: Columbia University Press, 2002.

Ehrenreich, Barbara, Elizabeth Hess, and Gloria Jacobs. *Remaking Love: The Feminization of Sex*. Garden City, N.Y.: Anchor/Doubleday, 1986.

Epstein, Barbara. *Political Protest and Cultural Revolution: Nonviolent Direct Action in the 1970s and 1980s*. Berkeley: University of California Press, 1991.

Ericksen, Julia A., with Sally A. Steffan. *Kiss and Tell: Surveying Sex in the Twentieth Century*. Cambridge: Harvard University Press, 1999.

Faderman, Lillian. *The Gay Revolution: The Story of the Struggle*. New York: Simon and Schuster, 2015.

Feinsod, Ethan. *Awake in a Nightmare: Jonestown, the Only Eyewitness Account*. New York: W.W. Norton, 1981.

Feuer, Jane. "MTM Enterprises: An Overview." In *MTM: "Quality Television,"* edited by Jane Feuer, Paul Kerr, and Tise Vahimagi, 1–31. London: British Film Institute, 1984.

———. "The MTM Style." In *Television: The Critical View*, 4th ed., edited by Horace Newcomb, 52–84. New York: Oxford University Press, 1987.

Fishbein, Leslie. "*Roots*: Docudrama and the Interpretation of History." In *American History/American Television: Interpretations of the Video Past*, edited by John E. O'Connor. New York: Frederick Ungar, 1992.

Foley, Michael Stewart. *Front Porch Politics: The Forgotten Heyday of American Activism in the 1970s and 1980s*. New York: Hill and Wang, 2013.

Frank, Thomas. *The Conquest of Cool: Business Culture, Counterculture, and the Rise of Hip Consumerism*. Chicago: University of Chicago Press, 1997.

Fraterrigo, Elizabeth. *Playboy and the Making of the Good Life in Modern America*. New York: Oxford University Press, 2009.

Frontani, Michael. *The Beatles: Image and the Media*. Jackson: University Press of Mississippi, 2007.

Giddens, Anthony. *The Transformation of Intimacy: Sexuality, Love and Eroticism in Modern Societies*. Palo Alto: Stanford University Press, 1992.

Gitlin, Todd. *Inside Prime Time*. New York: Pantheon Books, 1983; this edition 1985.

Glazer, Nathan, and Reed Ueda. *Ethnic Groups in History Textbooks*. Washington, D.C.: Ethics and Public Policy Center, 1983.

Graebner, William. "America's Poseidon Adventure: A Nation in Existential

Despair." In *America in the Seventies*, edited by Beth Bailey and David Farber, 157–80. Lawrence: University Press of Kansas, 2004.

———. *Patty's Got a Gun: Patricia Hearst in 1970s America*. Chicago: University of Chicago Press, 2008.

Guerrero, Ed. *Framing Blackness: The African American Image in Film*. Philadelphia: Temple University Press, 1993.

Handley, Susannah. *Nylon: The Story of a Fashion Revolution*. Baltimore: Johns Hopkins University Press, 1999.

Hartman, Andrew. *A War for the Soul of America: A History of the Culture Wars*. Chicago: University of Chicago Press, 2015.

Hillman, Betty Luther. *Dressing for the Culture Wars: Style and the Politics of Self-presentation in the 1960s and 1970s*. Lincoln: University of Nebraska Press, 2015.

Hine, Thomas. *The Great Funk: Falling Apart and Coming Together (on a Shag Rug) in the Seventies*. New York: Farrar, Straus and Giroux, 2007.

Jacobson, Matthew Frye. *Roots Too: White Ethnic Revival in Post–Civil Rights America*. Cambridge: Harvard University Press, 2006.

Jenkins, Philip. *Decade of Nightmares: The End of the Sixties and the Making of Eighties America*. New York: Oxford University Press, 2006.

———. *Mystics and Messiahs: Cults and New Religions in American History*. New York: Oxford University Press, 2000.

Jones, Gerard. *Honey, I'm Home: Sitcoms: Selling the American Dream*. New York: St. Martin's, 1992.

Jundt, Thomas. *Greening the Red, White, and Blue: The Bomb, Big Business, and Consumer Resistance in Postwar America*. New York: Oxford University Press, 2014.

Kalman, Laura. *Right Star Rising: A New Politics, 1974–1980*. New York: W.W. Norton, 2010.

Kimmel, Michael. *Manhood in America: A Cultural History*. New York: Free Press, 1996.

Kohl, Paul R. "Who's in Charge Here? Views of Media Ownership in Situation Comedies." In *The Sitcom Reader: America Viewed and Skewed*, 1st ed., edited by Mary M. Dalton and Laura R. Linder, 227–38. Albany: State University of New York Press, 2005.

Kutulas, Judy. "'Dedicated Followers of Fashion': Peacock Fashion and the Roots of the New American Man, 1960–1970." *Sixties* 5 (December 2012): 167–84.

———. "'I Feel the Earth Move': Carole King, Tapestry, and the Liberated Woman." In *Impossible to Hold: Woman and Culture in the 1960s*, edited by Avital H. Bloch and Lauri Umansky, 261–77. New York: New York University Press, 2005.

———. "Liberated Women and New Sensitive Men: Reconstructing Gender in 1970s Workplace Comedies." In *The Sitcom Reader: America Viewed and Skewed*, 1st ed., edited by Mary M. Dalton and Laura R. Linder, 217–25. Albany: State University of New York Press, 2005.

Lassiter, Matthew D. "Inventing Family Values." In *Rightward Bound: Making America Conservative in the 1970s*, edited by Bruce J. Schulman and Julian E. Zelizer. Cambridge: Harvard University Press, 2008.

Lehman, Katherine J. *Those Girls: Single Women in Sixties and Seventies Popular Culture*. Lawrence: University Press of Kansas, 2011.

Lemke-Santangelo, Gretchen. *Daughters of Aquarius: Women of the Sixties Counterculture*. Lawrence: University Press of Kansas, 2009.

Levine, Elana. *Wallowing in Sex: The New Sexual Culture of 1970s American Television*. Durham, N.C.: Duke University Press, 2007.

Levine, Martin P. *Gay Macho: The Life and Death of the Homosexual Clone*. New York: New York University Press, 1998.

Linder, Laura R. "From Ozzie to Ozzy: The Reassuring Nonevolution of the Sitcom Family." In *The Sitcom Reader: America Viewed and Skewed*, 1st ed., edited by Mary M. Dalton and Laura R. Linder, 61–71. Albany: State University of New York Press, 2005.

Lytle, Mark Hamilton. *America's Uncivil Wars: The Sixties Era from Elvis to the Fall of Richard Nixon*. New York: Oxford University Press, 2006.

MacLean, Nancy. *Freedom Is Not Enough: The Opening of the American Workplace*. Cambridge: Harvard University Press, 2006.

Marable, Manning. *Race, Reform, and Rebellion: The Second Reconstruction in Black America, 1945–1982*. Jackson: University Press of Mississippi, 1984; this edition 1986.

Marc, David. *Comic Visions: Television Comedy and American Culture*. Malden, Mass.: Blackwell, 1989; this edition 1997.

Mary Tyler Moore, a Celebration: Pioneers of Television. Produced by Boettcher/Trinklein, 2015.

McKenzie, Shelly. *Getting Physical: The Rise of Fitness Culture in America*. Lawrence: University Press of Kansas, 2013.

Mercer, Michelle. *Will You Take Me As I Am: Joni Mitchell's Blue Period*. New York: Free Press, 2009.

Millard, André. *Beatlemania: Technology, Business, and Teen Culture in Cold War America*. Baltimore: Johns Hopkins University Press, 2012.

Miniseries: Pioneers of Television. Produced by Boettcher/Trinklein, 2013.

Monk, Katherine. *Joni: The Creative Odyssey of Joni Mitchell*. Vancouver, B.C.: Greystone Books, 2012.

Montgomery, Kathryn C. *Target Prime Time: Advocacy Groups and the Struggle over Entertainment Television*. New York: Oxford University Press, 1989.

Norrell, Robert J. *Alex Haley and the Books That Changed a Nation*. New York: St. Martin's, 2015.

———. *The House I Live In: Race in the American Century*. New York: Oxford University Press, 2005.

Orrick, Amy. "Successes and Failures of Working Women on Television." *Working Woman* 5 (November 1980): 64–68.

Osgerby, Bill. *Playboys in Paradise: Masculinity, Youth, and Leisure-Style in Modern America*. New York: Oxford University Press, 2001.

Ozersky, Josh. *Archie Bunker's America: TV in an Era of Change, 1968–1978.* Carbondale: Southern Illinois University Press, 2003.

Palmer, Gareth. "Bruce Springsteen and Masculinity." In *Sexing the Groove: Popular Music and Gender*, edited by Sheila Whitely, 100–117. London: Routledge, 1997.

Paoletti, Jo B. *Sex and Unisex: Fashion, Feminism, and the Sexual Revolution.* Bloomington: Indiana University Press, 2015.

Paskin, Willa. "Mary Tyler Moore Rewind: It's Wonderful, Current, Not Funny. "Blog post, 26 April 2013, at http://www.salon.com/2013/04/26/mary_tyler _moore_rewind_its_wonderful_current_not_funny/.

Patterson, James T. *Freedom Is Not Enough: The Moynihan Report and America's Struggle over Black Family Life.* New York: Basic Books, 2010.

Pattison, Robert. *The Triumph of Vulgarity: Rock Music in the Mirror of Romanticism.* New York: Oxford University Press, 1987.

Peiss, Kathy. *Cheap Amusements: Working Women and Leisure in Turn-of-the-Century New York.* Philadelphia: Temple University Press, 1986.

Perlstein, Rick. *The Invisible Bridge: The Fall of Nixon and the Rise of Reagan.* New York: Simon and Schuster, 2014.

———. *Nixonland: The Rise of a President and the Fracturing of America.* New York: Scribner, 2008.

———. "That Seventies Show." *Nation* 291 (8 November 2010): 25–34.

Pleck, Elizabeth H. *Not Just Roommates: Cohabitation after the Sexual Revolution.* Chicago: University of Chicago Press, 2012.

Pollock, Bruce. *By the Time We Got to Woodstock: The Great Rock 'n' Roll Revolution of 1969.* New York: Backbeat Books, 2009.

Porter, Eric. "Affirming and Disaffirming Actions: Remaking Race in the 1970s." In *America in the 70s*, edited by Beth Bailey and David Farber, 50–74. Lawrence: University Press of Kansas, 2004.

Powers, Devon. *Writing the Record: The Village Voice and the Birth of Rock Criticism.* Amherst: University of Massachusetts Press, 2013.

Przybyszewski, Linda. *The Lost Art of Dress: The Women Who Once Made America Stylish.* New York: Basic Books, 2014.

Rhodes, Lisa L. *Electric Ladyland: Women and Rock Culture.* Philadelphia: University of Pennsylvania Press, 2005.

Rosen, Ruth. *The World Split Open: How the Modern Women's Movement Changed America.* New York: Viking Press, 2000.

Rossinow, Doug. *Visions of Progress: The Left-Liberal Tradition in America.* Philadelphia: University of Pennsylvania Press, 2008.

Ruoff, Jeffery. *An American Family: A Televised Life.* Minneapolis: University of Minnesota Press, 2002.

Rupp, Leila. *A Desired Past: A Short History of Same-Sex Love in America.* Chicago: University of Chicago Press, 1999.

Sandbrook, Dominic. *Mad as Hell: The Crisis of the 1970s and the Rise of the Populist Right.* New York: Alfred A. Knopf, 2011.

Schulman, Bruce J. *The Seventies: The Great Shift in American Culture, Society, and Politics*. New York: Free Press, 2001.

Schulman, Bruce J., and Julian E. Zelizer, eds. *Rightward Bound: Making America Conservative in the 1970s*. Cambridge: Harvard University Press, 2008.

Schweitzer, Dahlia. "*The Mindy Project*: Or Why 'I'm the Mary, You're the Rhoda' Is the RomComSitCom's Most Revealing Accusation." *Journal of Popular Film and Television* 43 (2015): 63–69.

Self, Robert O. *All in the Family: The Realignment of American Democracy since the 1960s*. New York: Hill and Wang, 2012.

She Turned the World On with Her Smile: The Making of The Mary Tyler Moore Show. Documentary included on *The Mary Tyler Moore Show*, first season, DVD set.

Shumway, David R. *Modern Love: Romance, Intimacy, and the Marriage Crisis*. New York: New York University Press, 2003.

———. *Rock Star: The Making of Musical Icons from Elvis to Springsteen*. Baltimore: Johns Hopkins University Press, 2014.

Solinger, Rickie. *Wake Up Little Susie: Single Pregnancy before Roe v. Wade*. New York: Routledge, 1992.

Staiger, Janet. *Blockbuster TV: Must-See Sitcoms in the Network Era*. New York: New York University Press, 2000.

Sugrue, Thomas J., and John D. Skrentny. "The White Ethnic Strategy." In *Rightward Bound: Making America Conservative in the 1970s*, edited by Bruce J. Schulman and Julian E. Zelizer, 171–92. Cambridge: Harvard University Press, 2008.

Talbot, David. *Season of the Witch: Enchantment, Terror, and Deliverance in the City of Love*. New York: Free Press, 2012.

Taylor, Ella. *Prime-Time Families: Television Culture in Postwar America*. Berkeley: University of California Press, 1989.

Thompson, David. *Hearts of Darkness: James Taylor, Jackson Browne, Cat Stevens, and the Unlikely Rise of the Singer-Songwriter*. Milwaukee: Backbeat Books, 2012.

Tropiano, Stephen. *The Prime Time Closet: A History of Gays and Lesbians on TV*. New York: Applause Theatre and Cinema Books, 2002.

Trueth, Michael V. "Breaking and Entering: Transgressive Comedy on Television." In *The Sitcom Reader: America Viewed and Skewed*, 1st ed., edited by Mary M. Dalton and Laura R. Linder, 25–34. Albany: State University of New York Press, 2005.

Van Deburg, William L. "Historiography—Slavery on TV: A True Picture?" *OAH Magazine of History* 1 (Fall 1985): 13–16.

———. *Slavery and Race in American Popular Culture*. Madison: University of Wisconsin Press, 1984.

Weiss, Jessica. *To Have and to Hold: Marriage, the Baby Boom, and Social Change*. Chicago: University of Chicago Press, 2000.

Weller, Sheila. *Girls Like Us: Carole King, Joni Mitchell, Carly Simon—and the Journey of a Generation*. New York: Attria Books, 2008.

Whitely, Sheila. "Little Red Rooster v. the Honky Tonk Woman: Mick Jagger, Sexuality, Style and Image." In *Sexing the Groove: Popular Music and Gender*, edited by Sheila Whitely, 67–99. London: Routledge, 1997.

Wilentz, Sean. *The Age of Reagan: A History, 1974–2008*. New York: HarperCollins, 2008.

Zaretsky, Natasha. *No Direction Home: The American Family and the Fear of National Decline, 1968–1980*. Chapel Hill: University of North Carolina Press, 2007.

Zoglin, Richard. *Comedy at the Edge: How Stand-Up in the 1970s Changed America*. New York: Bloomsbury, 2008; this edition 2009.

Index

ABC (American Broadcasting Company), 85, 86, 94, 123–26, 129, 139, 143, 144, 151–54, 158–59, 162–63, 174, 176–77

Adidas shoes, 64, 66

Advertising, 21, 52, 53, 59–63, 67, 73, 78, 202

Affirmative action, 32, 80, 108, 110, 111, 181

African, The (Courlander), 128

African Americans, 7, 17, 69, 106–36; depicted as servants, 117; exemplary and inoffensive characters, 142; family challenges for, 109; gaining from knowledge about Africa, 121; given agency through *Roots*, 129; history of, 116–17; images of male, 112–13, 130–31; Nixon exploiting prejudice against, 110; perception of *Roots* by, 127; strong culture of enslaved, 118–19; successfully presented in *Sounder*, 114; traditional gender roles of, 108–9; unmarried birthrate of, 111; writers, directors, producers, and actors, 119–20

Afros, 55, 121

Albums. *See individual titles*

All in the Family (TV show), 98, 137–38, 140

Alterman, Loraine, 26, 31

American Bandstand (TV show), 20

American Bar Association, 181

American Civil Liberties Union, 159, 180

American Christian Cause, 163

American Family, An (TV series), 144–45

American Family Association, 158

American Psychiatric Association, 139

Amos, John, 113, 119

Anderson, Loni, 68

Angelou, Maya, 123–25

Annie Hall (movie), 37

Anti-Establishment stance: cast and crew of *The Mary Tyler Moore Show* and, 100; coexisting with marketplace, 72; costuming and, 55, 65, 67; credibility gap and, 10; dark humor and, 195; fostering and fighting change, 201–2; free speech, Jim Jones, and, 171–72, 197; history of, 134; media reflecting, 7; TV sponsors and, 160. *See also* Establishment, the

Antiwar movement, 1, 55, 81, 195

Arnold, Danny, 153

Asner, Ed, 91–92, 94, 124

Assertiveness, 35, 39, 40, 153, 200–201

Autobiography of Malcolm X, The, 110, 117

Autobiography of Miss Jane Pittman, The (movie), 120, 133

Baby boomers: breakup songs and, 37; Carly Simon prototypical of, 28; clothing and, 68, 73; dark humor and, 195; *The Mary Tyler Moore Show* showing changes affecting, 78–86; singer-songwriters selling to, 48–49; spreading sixties' ideas, 8–23; wishing to legalize same-sex relations, 165

Badiyi, Reza, 75

Bailey, Beth, 17, 32, 46, 102

Bailyn, Bernard, 128

Bangs, Lester, 34

Barney Miller (TV show), 151–52, 163

Baxters, The (TV show), 162

Beatles, 14, 20–21, 25, 49, 52, 54

Bechdel Test, 89

Bellah, Robert, 8

Berkeley, 59, 167, 170, 185–86, 195

Beverly Hillbillies, The (TV show), 84

Bicentennial, 114, 117

Biden, Joe, 165

Big Bang Theory, The (TV show), 99

Billboard charts, 26, 27

Birkenstocks, 63, 195

Birth control pill, 18, 24–25, 77

Birth of a Nation (movie), 118–19

Black Culture, Black Consciousness
  (Levine), 119

Black Family in Slavery and Freedom,
  The (Gutman), 119

Black History: Lost, Stolen or Strayed
  (TV show), 120

Black history month, 117

Black Panthers, 55, 181

Blaxploitation films, 113–14

Blazing Saddles (movie), 115

Blood on the Tracks (music album), 40

Blue (music album), 32–33

Blue Ribbon Sports, 65–66

Bob Newhart Show, The (TV show), 146

Boomers. *See* Baby boomers

Born Innocent (movie), 150–51

Boycotts, 74, 147, 151, 158, 160, 162,
  164

Brady Bunch, The (TV show), 155

Brainwashing, 180, 189

Briggs, John, 161

Briggs Initiative, The, 162

Brill Music, 14, 20

Brinkley, David, 176

Brooks, James L., 86–87, 96–97, 101–2

Brooks, Mel, 115

Brothers, Dr. Joyce, 151

Brown, Bob, 175–76

Brown, Helen Gurley, 17

Brown, James, 71

Browne, Jackson, 14, 22, 26, 34–36, 41

Buchanan, Pat, 160

Buchwald, Art, 51

Bunker, Archie (*All in the Family*),
  141–42

Burns, Allan, 86–87, 94, 96–97, 101–2

Burton, LeVar, 116

Butch Cassidy and the Sundance Kid
  (movie), 114

Butler, Judith, 156

Cabaret (movie), 114

Cable television, 124, 133, 160, 162

Cahill, Tim, 177, 194

Capsuto, Steven, 161

"Carly Simon Principle" (Chuck
  Klosterman), 22–23

Carmichael, Stokely, 121

Carnaby Street, 49, 52

Carson, Johnny, 49

Carter, Jimmy, 4, 5, 64, 66, 126, 160,
  179, 180, 183, 190

CBS (Columbia Broadcasting System),
  86–87, 98, 100, 101, 119, 124, 129,
  139, 151–53, 173, 174, 176

CBS Bicentennial Minutes, 129

Censorship, 7, 10, 23, 25, 150–52, 159,
  172

Charlie's Angels (TV show), 160, 165

Cheap Chic (Milinaire and Troy), 59

Cheers (TV show), 99, 103

Chesebro, James W., 88

Chicago Tribune, 64

Children, effect of TV on, 77, 85, 113,
  125, 138, 142, 146, 150–52, 157–58,
  165, 179

Christgau, Robert, 23–24, 34

CIA (Central Intelligence Agency), 182,
  184, 190

Civil rights movement, 1, 2, 17, 107–8,
  110, 117–20, 126, 133–34, 139, 151

Clemente, Deirdre, 52

Clone dressing, 70–71

Clothing, 32, 44–74, 140, 157, 201

Cohabitation, 31, 43

Cohen, Lizabeth, 9, 10, 21

Comfort, Alex, 19

Concerned Relatives, 170, 187–88

Consciousness-raising, 28, 82, 86, 90

Conservatives: activism model serving, 3–5; disturbed by gender role and sexuality changes, 41, 96, 130, 148–51, 153, 157–66; panicking over sixties, 11–12, 77, 106, 108–10, 201; Schlafly speaking for, 10; Southern white, 4, 134

Coontz, Stephanie, 23, 76

Cosby, Bill, 113, 120

Cosby Show, The (TV show), 132–33

Cosmopolitan magazine, 17, 85

Counterculture: changing what manhood means, 71; cults and, 181; described by singer-songwriters, 29, 38; Harvey Milk and, 69; men's new styles and, 49–56; rapidly unseating norms, 1, 9; recasting meaning of intercourse, 24; shoes reflecting, 63–64; slogan of, 18

Courlander, Harold, 127–28

Cowie, Jefferson, 6, 69

Croce, Jim, 34, 36

Cronkite, Walter, 77

Crouse, Timothy, 31

Cults, 179–81, 188–89, 192–94, 197–98

Crystal, Billy, 158

Dance, 20, 26, 44–46, 53, 58, 68, 70, 74, 153, 156

Dashikis, 121

Dates and dating, 15, 25, 91, 94, 99, 102, 155

Daughters of Bilitis, 139

Davis, Ossie, 123

Davis, Stephen, 32

Declining Significance of Race, The (Wilson), 108

"Dedicated Follower of Fashion" (The Kinks), 52

Dee, Ruby, 123

Denim, 26, 53, 54, 57–59, 66

Deprogrammers, 180

Diana Ross and the Supremes, 39

Dick Van Dyke Show, The (TV show), 84

Dieter, Newton, 143

Diff'rent Strokes (TV show), 132

Disaster genre, 168–69, 172, 184

Disco, 41, 42, 44, 46, 64, 67–70, 74, 153, 156

Divorce, 37, 76, 86–87, 104, 109, 143–49

Docudramas, 123, 144–45, 174

Documentaries, 120, 123, 134, 138, 140, 143, 165–66

Doonesbury (comic strip), 106–10, 112, 129, 133

Doubleday and Company, 127

Douglas, Michael, 175

Douglas, Susan, 12, 95

Dover, Delaware: Jonestown bodies brought to, 191–92

Dow, Bonnie, 103

Drugs, 14, 19, 41, 109, 145–46, 148, 158–59, 183, 185

Du Bois, W. E. B., 118

Dunning, William A., 118

Du Pont, E. I., 46

Du Pont Chemical Company, 47

Dwyer, Richard, 169

Dylan, Bob, 40, 200

Earthquake (movie), 168

Earth shoes, 60–63

Echols, Alice, 69, 70–71

Ehrlichman, John, 137

Emmy Awards, 94, 100, 120, 144, 174

Engel, Georgia, 90

Environment, 3, 59, 81, 181

Ephron, Nora, 17, 99

Equal Employment Opportunity Commission, 95

Equality: assuming value of in day-to-day life, 1; boomers caring about, 2, 15, 200, 202; driving reshaped sexual norms, 17, 35, 39, 41, 43; Jonestown survivors striving for, 186; mass consumption and, 9; racial, 107–11, 120, 133; school curricula hiding failures at, 117; sixties' justice movements and, 10; unavailable economically, 80; workplace, 95

Equal Pay Act of 1963, 80, 95

Establishment, 10, 52, 59, 81, 96, 97, 104–5, 130, 132, 136, 149, 172, 180, 202

Evangelicals, 5, 11, 55, 149, 158, 162, 180

Evergreen Cemetery in Oakland, 192

Everything You Always Wanted to Know about Sex, but Were Afraid to Ask (Reuben), 139

Falwell, Jerry, 11, 149

Families: affected by enslavement, 106–36; redefined, 1, 4, 9, 12, 75–105, 140; stereotyped by majority culture, 107

Family (TV show), 162

"Family values," 72, 130, 137–66

Family viewing hour, 151–52

Father Knows Best (TV show), 88, 101, 146–47

Fawcett, Farrah, 68, 155

FBI, 184–85

Fear of Flying (Jong), 32

Federal Communications Commission, 151, 163

Feminine Mystique, The (Friedan), 90

Feminism, 5, 28, 30–33, 36, 39–41, 72, 82, 94–96, 100–103, 112, 130, 157

Fey, Tina, 77, 98–99

"Fire and Rain" (Taylor), 36

Folk music, 14, 20, 22

Foner, Eric, 118, 130

Ford, Gerald, 126, 149, 189

"Forever My Love" (Carly Simon and Taylor), 37

"Fountain of Sorrow" (Browne), 26

Frank, Thomas, 11, 51, 59

Franklin, John Hope, 118

Free love, 25, 28, 30, 31, 36

Free speech, 152, 171, 203

"Free to Be, You and Me" (Thomas), 199–200

Freedom of Information Act, 181

Freedom Summer, 114

Friedan, Betty, 90

Fromme, Lynette "Squeaky," 189

Further Tales of the City (Maupin), 186

Gaines, Ernest, 120

Gans, Herbert, 9

Garry, Charles, 170, 181

Gay bars, 153, 156

Gay liberation movement, 69–71, 140, 143

Gay Media Task Force, 143, 147

Gender roles, 38–45, 51, 61, 68, 70, 74–76, 88, 92, 96–101, 107–10, 130, 138, 143, 154–56, 165–66, 190, 199

Generation gap, 8, 15, 51, 54–55, 75, 149

Gilbert, Craig, 144–45

Gilder, George, 108–9

Gloria Vanderbilt brand, 67

Goffin, Gerry, 14–20, 24

Goldstein, Richard, 19, 20

Gone with the Wind (movie), 115, 118, 125, 128

Good Times (TV show), 86, 112, 119, 132

Goodman, Ellen, 179

Graebner, William, 185, 190

Grammy Awards, 14, 27

Gray flannel suit, 46–49, 55, 71, 111

Greatest Generation, 2, 199–201

Great Society, 80

Greening of America, The (Reich), 53

Greenwich Village, 139

Guess Who's Coming to Dinner (movie), 111

Guest, Christopher, 34

Gutman, Herbert, 119

Guyana, 167, 170, 174–77, 180–89, 193–96

Hair (movie), 1

Haldeman, H. R., 137

Haley, Alex, 106–8, 119–32, 134–36, 186

Haley, William, 124
Handlin, Oscar, 128
Happy Days (TV show), 124, 129
Hare Krishnas, 179–80, 189
Harper, Valerie, 89–90, 94, 100
Harris Poll, 30, 140
Hartman, Andrew, 114
"Have a Good Time" (Paul Simon), 41
HBO (Home Box Office), 151
Hearst, Patricia, 190
Hefner, Hugh, 17, 48
Hemsley, Sherman, 112
Hersh, Seymour, 171–72
Hippies, 14, 22, 25, 33, 40, 53–54, 57,
    62, 67–68, 81, 146, 148–49
Historical revisionism, 117–18, 128,
    134
Hite, Shere, 40
Hobson, Laura Z., 142
Holbrook, Hal, 144
Hollis, Harry N., Jr., 159
Hollywood Reporter, 195
Homosexuality, psychiatric "cure" for,
    139, 147
Honeymooners, The (TV show), 47
Hot L Baltimore (TV show), 154
Human Freedom Center, 185
Hunt, Lynn, 143
Hyde, Jack, 41

"I Do It for Your Love" (Paul Simon),
    37
"I Feel the Earth Move" (King), 26
I Love Lucy (TV show), 83, 88
Immigrants, 177, 135
Inflation, 10, 80–81
Investigative journalism, 171–72
"It's Too Late" (King), 37
"I Will Survive" (Gaynor), 201

Jackson, Jesse, 113–14
Jacoby, Scott, 144
Jagger, Mick, 33–35
Jeans, 19, 26, 27, 35, 36, 48, 53–54,
    58–59, 67–74, 176

Jefferson Airplane, 53
Jeffersons, The (TV show), 112, 155
Jenkins, Philip, 4–6, 40, 146, 157, 185
Johnson, Diane, 194, 196
Johnson, Lyndon, 4, 10, 80, 107, 194
Jones, Gerard, 87–88
Jones, Jim, 167–98
Jonestown tragedy, 167–98; survivors
    of, 168, 180, 184, 186, 189–97
Jordache brand, 67
Joy of Sex, The (Comfort), 19
Juffure, Gambia, 121
"Jungle juice," 167, 196

Kalsø, Anne, 60
Karenga, Marlana, 121
Katsaris, Maria, 187–88
Katsaris, Steven, 186
Kennedy, John F., 168, 182
Kennedy, John F., Jr., 54
Kerner Report of 1968, 133
Kessie, Jack, 48
Khaisa, Gurusher Singh, 63
Kilduff, Marshall, 171
King, Carole, 14, 16, 21, 24, 26, 31–32,
    37, 78, 81, 86
King, Martin Luther, Jr., 117, 182
Kinks, the, 42
Kinsey, Alfred, 139
Kinsolver, Lester, 171
Kinte, Kunta, 116, 121, 123–27, 131–34
Klosterman, Chuck, 22–23
Kojak (TV show), 148–49
Kool-Aid, 167, 169, 188, 192–97
Krause, Charles, 171, 174, 187–90, 194
Ku Klux Klan, 126, 162
Kwanzaa, 121

Ladies of the Canyon (music album),
    28, 37
Lafferty, Perry, 101–2
Landau, Jon, 42
Lane, Mark, 182, 195
Lasch, Christopher, 3, 77
Lassiter, Matthew D., 150

"Late for the Sky" (Brown), 36

Latinos, 42, 69

Laverne and Shirley (TV show), 124

Layton, Deborah, 184, 193

Layton, Larry, 190

Leachman, Cloris, 77, 79

Lear, Norman, 86–87, 95, 112, 132, 141, 143, 162–63

Leisure suits, 56–58, 64

Levine, Lawrence, 119

Levine, Martin P., 71

Levinson, Richard, 143–44

Levi Strauss, 53, 58–60

Lewis, Anthony, 185

Liberation movements: African American, 112–21; GLBT, 137–66; new man's, 50–71; seventies and, 1–11, 199; singer-songwriters and, 18–43; women's, 75–104

Life magazine, 7–9, 19, 20

Lightfoot, Gordon, 36

Linder, Laura R., 83

Link, William, 143–44

Little Big Man (movie), 114

Litwak, Leon, 128

Looking for Mr. Goodbar (movie), 41

Los Angeles Times, 27, 67, 98, 99, 101, 144, 150–52, 174, 176, 188

Love Actually (movie), 15, 32

MacLean, Nancy, 78

Made-for-television movies, 143–44, 150, 154

Mademoiselle magazine, 30

Malcolm X, 110, 117, 121

Malden, Karl, 149

Man in the Gray Flannel Suit, The (movie), 47

Mandingo (movie), 115, 124

Manson, Charles, 148, 185, 189

Marable, Manning, 108, 111, 128

Marc, David, 82–83

Marcus Welby (TV show), 146, 148–49

Marketing: Dockers and, 73; to families of one, 78; Haley and, 120, 127; market segmentation, 21; new styles for men and, 49–53; Nike's style of, 66; promoting "normative America," 10; of *Roots*, by ABC executives, 124; spurning, 59; on TV to hold boomers, 85; to women, 27; young people falling for, 60

Marriage: birth control pill and, 77; Carole King groomed for, 14; economic inequality and, 32; enhancement movements, 41; gay, 165; interracial, 132; not allowed to enslaved, 109; at older age, 8, 17, 21, 76; relationships versus, 30–39; rewriting happiness in, 23–24; sex outside of, 17–18, 24, 43, 111, 202; traditions of, 15

Mary Richards (*The Mary Tyler Moore Show*), 75–79, 81–82, 88–90, 95–98, 101

Mary Tyler Moore Show, The (TV show), 32, 56, 75–105, 138, 142, 161, 195

M*A*S*H (TV show), 98, 142, 151, 154

Mattachine Society, 139

Maude (TV show), 95–96, 153–54

Maupin, Armistead, 70, 71, 186

McCartney, Paul, 21, 25

McLeod, Gavin, 100

Mead, Margaret, 18

"Me decade," 5, 7, 10

Middle Passage, 124, 135

Milk, Harvey, 69, 192, 196

Millennials, 105

Mimetic characters, 88, 90, 143, 146

Mindy Project, The (TV show), 99, 103

Minneapolis, 75, 77, 82, 85, 100

Mitchell, Andrea, 174

Mitchell, Joni, 1, 3, 14, 26–28, 31, 37–38

Molloy, John T., 57

Montgomery, Kathryn, 150

Moore, Mary Tyler, 75–105

Moore, Rebecca, 194

Moral Majority, 163–64

Moscone, George, 192, 196
Moynihan, Daniel Patrick, 109, 112
Ms. Foundation, 199–200
Ms. magazine, 30, 31, 101
MTM Enterprises, 86, 102, 146

Nash, Graham, 30
National Archives, 127
National Association for the Advancement of Colored People (NAACP), 119, 126
National Black Media Coalition, 119
National Book Award, 126
National Federation for Decency, 158
National Organization for Women, 38, 68
National Talk to Your TV Day, 160
Native Americans, 55, 130, 135
NBC (National Broadcasting Company), 86, 94, 139, 150–53, 164, 169, 175–76, 186, 191–92
NBC Nightly News, 186
Nehru jackets, 49, 51, 55, 62
New Journalism, 172
New man, 34, 36, 44–74, 141
News media, 41, 172, 174
Newsweek magazine, 55, 91, 109, 124, 135, 150, 162, 178, 179, 189
Newton, Huey, 113
New West magazine, 171
New York Review of Books, 196
New York Times, 9, 21, 28, 30, 32, 49, 50, 56, 104, 113, 126, 139, 145, 171
Nielsen ratings, 85, 149
Nike shoes, 66
Nixon, Richard, 4, 10, 55, 56, 110, 137, 138, 141, 148, 162
Norrell, Robert J., 110, 134
"No Secrets" (Carly Simon), 39

Occupational Safety and Health Administration, 80
O'Connor, Carroll, 141
O'Connor, John, 145, 156
Orenstein, Peggy, 43

Packard, Vance, 18, 25
Parks, Patricia, 187
Parks, Rosa, 201
PBS (Public Broadcasting System), 120, 130, 144–45
Peacock revolution, 49, 51, 70
Peculiar Institution, The (Stampp), 118
People magazine, 21, 179, 181, 185
Peoples Temple, 168–94, 197
Perlstein, Rick, 4, 6
Peter Principle: Why Things Always Go Wrong (Peter), 93
Phillips, Kevin, 110
Phillips, Ulrich, 118
Pill, the. *See* Birth control pill
Playboy magazine, 17, 19, 25, 48–49
Playing Possum (music album), 29–30, 40
Poitier, Sidney, 111, 113, 127
Police dramas, 147–49, 151, 154–55
Policewoman (TV show), 148–49
Political correctness, 179–81
Polyester, 58, 69
Pornography, 41, 43, 154, 160, 184
Porter, Eric, 110
Port Kaituma, 175
Poseidon Adventure, The (movie), 168
Premarital sex. *See* Sex: premarital or outside of marriage
Pryor, Richard, 195
Przybysewski, Linda, 46

Radio, 19, 21, 38, 53, 83, 102, 112, 119, 160, 191
Randall, Tony, 164
Rape, 41, 124, 131, 150, 151
Raskind, Richard, 155
Raspberry, William, 194
Reader's Digest, 110
"Ready or Not" (Browne), 35
Reagan, Ronald, 4, 6, 13, 72, 163, 202
Real Men Don't Eat Quiche (Feirstein), 41
Reconstruction, 118, 133
Reed, Robert, 124, 155

REI (Recreational Equipment Inc.), 58

Reich, Charles A., 53

Reiterman, Tim, 175

Relationships, 9, 24, 26, 29, 30, 38, 157

Resistance: at center of Jonestown narratives, 197; by enslaved, 118–19, 195; to Establishment by families, 136; to family norms by boomers, 76; as focus of songs, 201; at heart of *Roots*, 131, 135; men's, as need to stand out, 71; Quixotic attempts at, 188; rock's advocacy of, 19; by survivors of Jonestown, 186; TV viewers fantasizing about, 83; whites discomfited by, 132

Reuben, David, 139

Revisionism, 117–18

"Revolution Will Not Be Televised, The" (Scott-Heron), 120

Rhoda (TV show), 86, 101, 151

Richards, Renee, 155

Rich Man, Poor Man (movie), 124

"River, The" (Springsteen), 42

Rivera, Geraldo, 172

Robinson, Greg, 175–76

Rock 'n' roll, 1, 14, 19–27, 33–35, 38, 42, 49, 53, 57, 77, 86

Roll, Jordan, Roll (Genovese), 119

Rolle, Esther, 112–13

Rolling Stone magazine, 20, 25, 28, 29, 30–34, 36, 177, 184, 196

Rolling Stones, 33

Romance, 14–19, 22–25, 28–33, 35, 37–38, 41, 43, 59, 87, 104, 123–24, 128, 201, 203

Roots (Haley/movie), 106–36; black writers, directors, producers and actors in, 119–20; challenging stereotypes, 136; college credit for watching, 125; creating a new kind of textbook, 136; featuring well-known TV stars, 124; offering agency, 129; peaking interest in Africa, 121; place of in American cultural history, 107; and plagiarism accusations by Harold Courlander, 127–28; reflecting ABC's success with big TV events, 124–25; remake of, 135–36; showing strong culture of enslaved, 118–19; using Haley's grandmother's tales of "the African," 120–21; white characters included in, 120, 124–26

Rosen, Ruth, 82

Rosie the Riveter, 46, 100

Runner's World magazine, 66

Running and running shoes, 63–70, 74

Russia, 184, 188, 202

Ryan, Leo, 169, 170, 173–74, 176, 181–84, 186–87, 190, 192

Sandbrook, Dominic, 4, 6

Sanders, Bernie, 81

Sanford and Son (TV show), 112, 132, 142

San Francisco, 53, 69, 150, 161, 167, 172, 174, 183, 191, 192, 197

San Francisco Chronicle, 171, 183, 190

San Francisco Examiner, 170, 171, 175, 178

Saturday Night Fever (movie), 44, 45, 69

Saturday Night Live (TV show), 195–96

Save Our Children, 161

Schickel, Richard, 115

Schlafly, Phyllis, 10, 161

Scientology, 179–80

Sears and Roebuck, 40, 53, 64, 160

Secretaries, 28, 81–84, 88, 95, 96

Sergeant Pepper's Lonely Hearts Club Band (music album), 20

Seventies, the: conservatives' counteroffensives during, 201–2; diversity during, 138, 140, 157, 198; James Taylor representing new man of, 21, 36; norms rewritten in, 200–201; pessimism during, 185, 201; racial politics of, 132; and redefined family and gender roles, 15, 136; resilience as important goal during, 168, 201;

as state of mind, 13; workers during, 78; work for change during, 3, 6; work versus family during, 79

Sex: premarital or outside of marriage, 8, 18, 19, 23, 24, 43, 111, 157; "sex, drugs, and rock 'n' roll," 77

Sex and the Single Girl (Brown), 17

Sexuality: defined by clothes, 45; dynamics of in workplace, 95; heteronormative on TV, 139, 157; identity and, 137–66; patterns and practices of, 14, 15, 17, 157, 160, 164; repression of, 25, 147

Sexual revolution: challenge to gender norms and traditional sexual standards, 17, 45, 72, 166; conservatives fearful of, 149; hipper wardrobes spurred by, 51, 68; less marriage and fewer kids result of, 77; men still scoring better during, 25; serial monogamy and, 30; tasteless TV about, 154; young women empowered by, 24–26, 31–33

Shaft (movie), 113, 114

Sideburns, 49, 50, 56, 200

Silent Generation, 2

Silver, Susan, 88

Silverman, Fred, 124, 152

Simon, Carly, 14, 20, 22, 23, 25, 26, 29, 67, 71, 85, 98, 202

Simon, Paul, 14, 22, 37, 40, 41

Singer-songwriters, 22–43, 68, 137, 152, 165

Singletons, 17, 19, 24, 30, 32, 41, 42, 65, 75–92, 98–103, 157

Sitcoms: commenting on masculinity, 155; few positive black males on, 113, 119; Fred Silverman and, 152; gays not shown on in eighties, 162; gays shown in positive light on by late seventies, 142–43; high hopes versus real life on, 79, 87–90; inoffensive, positive gays on, 100, 142, 145, 148, 165; Nixon's view of gays on, 137; Norman Lear and, 86; on

Saturday night, 98–99; relatable heroes on, 146; relevancy of, 143; *The Mary Tyler Moore Show* inspiring other, 99, 103; women of color rarely on, 83; women seeking liberation on, 32, 82, 100; workplace families on, 82–84, 91, 94, 100–102; written by women, 149

Sixties, the: boomers still longing for, 23, 203; California seen as Eden during, 192; changing views of sex and gender during, 24, 91, 98, 138, 166; constructed self of, 130, 190; cults seen as brought on by, 179, 198; diversity's value introduced during, 107, 114; dress rebellion during, 55, 57, 67, 74; middle-aged men's loss of status during, 51; relevancy TV programming and ideals of, 150; responsible protest during, 108, 131; as undermining established truths, 11; values of colliding with seventies' realities, 78; values of in workplace, 104

Sixty Minutes (TV show), 171

Skrentny, John D., 129

Slave Community, The (Blassingame), 119

Slave Religion (Raboteau), 119

Sly and the Family Stone, 107, 132

Soap (TV show), 154, 158, 165

Solinger, Rickie, 17

Songs. *See individual titles*

Songwriters. *See individual artists*

Sounder (movie), 114

Spain, Fay, 148

Spann, William B., Jr., 181

Sponsors of TV programs. *See* Television: sponsors of

Stampp, Kenneth, 118

Standards and Practices offices, 139, 163

State Department, 173–74, 180, 182, 193

Steinem, Gloria, 77, 79

Still Crazy after All These Years (music album), 40, 41

Stockholm Syndrome, 190

Stoddard, Brandon, 123

Stoen, John Victor, 184

Stoen, Tim, 183, 187

Stonewall incident, 139, 140

Strongest Poison, The (Lane), 182

Sweet Baby James (music album), 21

Sweet Sweetback's Baadasssss Song (movie), 113

Swinging singles, 17, 30

Symbionese Liberation Army, 190

Synanon, 179

Tales of the City (Maupin), 70

Talk shows, 126, 143

Tapestry (music album), 14, 26–27, 40, 78

Taxi (TV show), 156

Taylor, James, 14, 21–22, 25–26, 34–41, 45, 67, 71, 93, 202

Teenagers. *See* Youth

Television, 75–166; ABC's success with big TV events, 124–25; African Americans depicted on, 106–36; cable, 102, 124, 160; congressional subcommittee (1977) investigating, 146; conservative definition of family on, 76, 83, 85, 140, 149; conservative protests of, 159–161; cultural lens provided by, 6; dark humor on, 195; definitions of family and gender roles in, 7, 82–83, 98–99, 136, 140, 165; Family Viewing Hour on, 152; GLBTs get chance to try new identities on, 137–66; graphic depiction of tragedy on, 177; heteronormative, 139, 152; nostalgic, 114, 147; real gay characters on, 141, 153, 162; sex and violence on, 146, 150–51, 156, 158–59, 172; singletons shown on, 78, 84, 93, 99; socially significant, 7, 86, 95, 100–102, 107–8, 137–39, 143, 149–50,

155–59, 162, 165–66; sponsors of, 138–39, 147, 160–62; TV sidekicks on, 89, 103; workplace depicted by, 82–84, 100, 104; youth's influence on, 165. *See also* ABC; Cable television; CBS; NBC; PBS; *individual program titles*; *names of actors, producers, and executives*

That Certain Summer (movie), 143–44

That Girl (TV show), 85, 88

"That's the Way I Always Heard It Should Be" (Carly Simon), 23, 28

Thom McAn shoes, 62, 64

Thomas, Marlo, 85

Thompson, Emma, 15, 32

Three's Company (TV show), 102, 152–53, 160, 164

Time magazine, 27, 178, 179, 185, 192

Tinker, Grant, 86

Today Show (TV show), 169

Tolerance: conservatives limiting, 108; toward gays, 140, 142–43, 147, 164–66; toward new man, 74; political correctness and, 7–8, 18, 182–83; pursuit of happiness and, 9; as strong value shown on TV, 5, 13, 138, 200

Tonight Show (TV show), 49, 126

Tracy, Phil, 171

Transgender persons, 137, 155, 165, 166

Travolta, John, 44–45, 69

Trudeau, G. B., 106, 108, 110

Turn Off Your TV Week, 160

TV. *See* Television

TV Guide, 111, 129

Tyson, Cicely, 114, 125, 120

Ukiah, California, 182

Underwear, 55, 68, 73

Unemployment, 80, 82, 111, 138

Unification Church, 189

Unions, 4, 42, 47, 80, 95, 111

Unisex styling, 63, 67–68

U.S. embassy in Guyana, 193

U.S. history textbooks, 117, 119, 135–36, 178

Valium, 177, 185
Victor, David, 146–47
Vietnam War, 3, 4, 7, 10, 54, 80, 171, 177, 178, 199
Village People, the, 70
Violence: blaxploitation films and, 113; commercial value of, 172; and Jonestown tragedy, 168–69; on *Roots*, 124, 134–35; in San Francisco, 192; on TV, 124, 134, 145–46, 149–51, 158

Walker, Jimmie, 112
Waltons, The (TV show), 114, 133
Washington Post, 62
Watergate, 3, 7, 10, 56, 172
Way We Were, The (movie), 37, 114
Webster (TV show), 132
Weinberger, Ed., 138
Wenner, Jann, 25
White, Betty, 92
White, Dan, 192–93
Whites: as audience for shows featuring African Americans, 106–7, 111–12; Caucasian sense of superiority, 107; as crafting *Roots* miniseries, 123; depicted in *Gone with the Wind*, 115; disassociating themselves from slave owners, 130; "good white people," 124; knowledge of about Africa, 121; largesse of depicted on TV, 132; in *Roots*, 120; sensibilities of considered by producer of *Roots*, 123; as watching whites oppress blacks, 124–26; white males only heroes in U.S. textbooks, 117; whites-only drinking fountain, 120; writing Southern history before World War II, 118

Wildmon, Donald, 158, 164
Will & Grace (TV show), 165
Willis, Ellen, 21, 22, 33, 39
Wilson, William Julius, 108–9
Winant, Ethel, 100–101
Winfrey, Oprah, 100, 104
WJM (*The Mary Tyler Moore Show*), 82, 91, 93, 95–97, 172
WKRP in Cincinnati (TV show), 86, 101, 102, 155
Wolfe, Tom, 8, 53, 172
Wolper, David, 123–24, 135–36
Wolper, Mark, 135–36
Women's movement, 3, 15, 17, 27, 28, 31, 32, 51, 77, 78, 90, 93, 102, 166
Woodstock, 7, 34, 55
Workplace families, 75–105
World War II, 118, 139
Writers Guild of America, 100, 152

X, Malcolm. *See* Malcolm X

Yankelovich, Daniel, 2, 7, 8, 15, 18, 43, 44, 55, 57, 60, 86, 99, 163
"You Keep Me Hanging On" (Supremes), 39
"You Make It Easy" (Taylor), 36
Young, Robert, 149
"You're So Vain" (Carly Simon), 20, 33, 38
Youth, 2, 7, 10, 14–24, 30–31, 42–55, 58–59, 62–63, 79, 81, 85–86, 93, 127, 150, 162, 164–65, 172, 203
"You Turn Me On, I'm a Radio" (Mitchell), 38
"You've Got a Friend" (King), 15
Yuppies, 72–73

Zaretsky, Natasha, 77–78, 129, 146
Zevon, Warren, 181
Zimbardo, Phil, 185